Sayyid Abu'l A'la Mawdūdī

ISLAM'S POLITICAL ORDER

THE MODEL, DEVIATIONS AND MUSLIM RESPONSE

---

al- Khilāfah wa al-Mulūkīyah

Translated by Tarik Jan

Edited by Anis Ahmad

IPS Press is the publishing arm of Institute of Policy Studies, Islamabad – an independent think tank dedicated to promoting policy-oriented research. Pakistan Affairs, International Relations and Faith and Society are some of the major study areas at IPS.

Islam's Political Order
The Model, Deviations and Muslim Response
Sayyid Abu'l A'la Mawdudi

Translated by Tarik Jan
Edited by Anis Ahmad

Published by

IPS Press
Institute of Policy Studies
Nasr Chambers, 1, MPCHS Commercial Centre, E-11/3, Islamabad, Pakistan
Tel: +92 51 8438391-3 Fax: +92 51 8438390
Email: publications@ips.net.pk URL: www.ips.org.pk

With permission of Islamic Foundation, UK

ISBN 978-969-448-167-8

Printed in Pakistan by
AZ Printers, Rawalpindi

Contents

Chapter – 3: Al-Khilāfah al-Rāshidah and its Characteristics

Chapter – 4: From the Rightly Guided Caliphate to Monarchial Absolutism

Chapter – 5: The Difference between the Caliphate and Monarchial Absolutism

Chapter – 6: The Rise of Religious Differences and their Causes

Chapter – 7: Abu Ḥanīfah's Accomplishment

Acknowledgments

I am grateful to Professor Khurshid Ahmad, Chairman Institute of Policy Studies, and Dr Anis Ahmad, General Editor of the Mawdudi Essentials Project, for their assistance in making this controversial but important book available to English readers. Their cooperation was more than on one count. They discussed the manuscript, argued on my approach, differed on my insistence to have an abridged edition, and came up with constructive ideas to facilitate the project.

Second, the support staff in the Institute of Policy Studies, people in the IT and composition sections who helped as much as they could without dragging their feet on it.

Tarik Jan

Editor's note

As a normal practice, foreign words and expressions, which are often few, receive italicization in the text with a glossary at the end or in the beginning of a book. In such cases, italicized words may even look nice and do not detract from the uniformity of the text. Their excessive use, however, as in the present case, would have marred the visual landscape of the text, mutilating its uniformity.

Still another practice followed is to italicize foreign expressions and then highlight them by their meanings placed in the parenthesis. In our view, the latter form is overdone and makes no sense. It is enough if we give parenthetical expression to a foreign word without its italicization, for when it is parenthesized we succeed in expressing its foreignness. At the same time, it averts the need for a glossary at the end saving the reader the inconvenience of flipping pages over to the glossary. The transliteration key used is traditional.

This remarkable work of Mawlānā Sayyid Abul A'la Mawdūdī (1930-1970), when published, for the first time, initiated an intellectual discourse in the region. His view-point on policy measures taken by the third khalīfah al-rāshid invited strong criticism from the traditional 'ulamā. The Mawlānā's purpose was not to criticize the third caliph, as such, but to trace logical and historical roots of the ultimate tragedy the Ummah faced in the form of transition from Khilāfah to a hereditary succession which was totally a foreign phenomenon to Islam.

We have abridged the original *Khilafat wa Mulukiyat*, especially chapters 4 and 5, without blunting its edge or impairing its thesis. We have taken out its appendix for we thought there was no need to defend the sources when the text spoke for itself. We hope this will augment its usefulness without detracting from the fervor and taste of the original.

Today when an ongoing debate is taking place on the nature of Islamic state, "political Islam" and relation between state and "religion" this research work of the Mawlana provides a resume of how the Qur'an and the Sunnah of the Prophet (pbuh), visualize modern Islamic state.

This translation, with minor abridgment, was made possible with the devotion professional excellence and cooperation of my very dear colleague, for over past forty years, Tarik Jan who not only kept the real spirit and vigor of the original work alive in his beautiful translation but also helped in making the text more elaborate for the reader.

Prof. Anis Ahmad Ph.D
May 20, 2017

Preface

The central theme of this book relates to the nature of the Islamic caliphate and its makeup. How did it actualize itself in the first century of Islam? What were the causes that led to its shift to monarchy? And finally when the change did take place, what was the Ummah's reaction to this change?

To explain it, I have compiled all those pertinent Āyat (verses) of the Qur'ān that have relevance to the primary political issues enabling the readers to have a glimpse of the Islamic state that the Qur'ān wants to have.

The second chapter deals with the principles of Islamic governance in the light of the Qur'ān, the Sunnah, and the precepts and sayings of the prominent Ṣaḥābah (raḍi Allahu 'anhu).

The third chapter speaks of the distinguishing characteristics of the pious caliphate as known in the history.

The fourth chapter delineates the causes that led to the shift from the caliphate to monarchy. While the following two chapters discuss the difference between the caliphate and monarchy, the change that the monarchy caused and the way the caliphal fall led to schismatic polarization and conflicts among the Muslims, followed by the 'ulamā's effort to bridge the cleavages wrought by the change in the system of governance as typified by Imām Abū Ḥanīfah's and Abū Yūsuf's works.

Some contents of this book invited adverse criticism from different segments of society which I have tried to answer in the appendix at the end [now dropped in the English version]. The readers can arrive at their own conclusion by comparing the two.

Abu'l A'lā
Lahore
27 Ṣafar 1386 A.H./1965

Introduction

From Caliphate to Monarchy

Anis Ahmad

The contemporary discourse on Islam in general addresses issues relating to Islamic governance, role of "religion" and religious scholars ('ulamā and mujtahidīn), the status and role of women in power-sharing and non-Muslim minorities in the Islamic political order. Historical analyses of such issues undertaken by both Western Orientalists and Muslim scholars carry an obvious cultural baggage. Some of the classical Western studies still influence the intellectual pursuits of later writers. William Muir's *The Caliphate, its Rise, Decline and Fall* (1915), betraying the nineteenth century Christian bias, remains a source for many of their misgivings. They avoid considering Thomas Arnold's *The Caliphate* (1924) because it negates the notion that the caliphate (Khilāfah) was a Muslim counterpart to papacy. Julius Wellhausen's *The Arab Kingdom and its Fall* (1927) is still a source of inspiration for many Western students of early Islamic history. Most of the research work follows the traditional Orientalist approach, looking into the emergence of Islamic culture and civilization as the Arab thirst for power and empire building. Some like Sha'bān's *Islamic History a New Interpretation* (1999) pursue a tribal and ethnic interpretation of the rise of Islam. Philip K. Hitti's *History of the Arabs* (1937), though a comprehensive effort to look into the total impact of Islam in space-time, failed to rise above the basic misconception of interpreting Islam as Arab history and culture. Consequently, the Islam's ascendance in most of the Orientalist works is viewed as the rise of the Arab power. Arabization or 'urubah is projected as the dominant character of Islamic civilization[1].

---

1 For an excellent treatment of the concept of 'Urubah, see Ismā'il Rāji al-Fārūqi, *On Arabism Urubah and Religion* (Amsterdam: Djambatan, 1962).

The fact is that Islam did not emerge as a movement for Arabization. On the contrary, the revolutionary message of the Qur'ān and the Sunnah challenged, contested, and Islamized the traditional tribal culture. The Qur'ān substituted tribalism and nationalism with a moral base. "We created you all from a male and a female, and made you into nations and tribes so that you may know one another. Verily the noblest of you in the sight of Allah is the most Allah-fearing of you".
(*al-Ḥujurāt 49:13*)

The Prophet ('alayhi as-salām) reaffirmed the same in his last sermon. While referring to the above Qur'ānic Āyah (verse), he condemned ethnic, racial, linguistic, and geographic nationalisms.

Transcending the inherent Arab ideology of tribal nationalism, the new principle, introduced by him was the unity of humans based on ethical values and behavior, that is, taqwā (Allah-consciousness). Consequently, whoever excels in ethical behaviour was superior to others irrespective of colour, race or ethnicity. This transformation of the Arabs into a color blind, classless, and internationalist Muslim community (Ummah) or a globalized humanity is often overlooked by Western writers when they talk about Islam as an Arab phenomenon, and the Prophet (upon him be peace) as an Arabian prophet and statesman.

The Prophetic model (uswah) of governance was part of his revelatory role in restructuring a morality-based civilization, which the Muslims took as the ideal for its later institutional development. The concept of the realm of the sacred and the secular, a dualism in space-time, has been a foreign idea in the Islamic vision of life. The term secular in its modern political sense, first used in the English language towards the middle of the sixteenth century, denoted the doctrine that God or divine guidance and providence, has no role in public policy and management of the people's affair.[2]

The separation between "religion" and state has been essentially a Christian concept and not necessarily a fruit of

---

2 Bernard Lewis, *What Went Wrong, Western Impact and Middle Eastern Response* (Oxford: Oxford University Press, 2002), p. 96.

modernity. Lewis' view on this aspect of Christianity is right when he says: "The founder of Christianity lead his followers to render unto Caesar the things which are Caesar's; and unto God the things, which are God's, and for centuries Christianity grew and developed as a religion of downtrodden until Caesar himself became a Christian and inaugurated a series of changes by which the new faith captured the Roman Empire and some would add was captured by it. The founder of Islam was his own Constantine and founded his own empire. He did not therefore create - or need to create - a church. The dichotomy of *regnum* and *sacrerdoium* so critical in the history of western Christendom had no equivalent in Islam."[3]

In the same continuation, Lewis refers to a comment made by Imām Khomeini "Islam is politics or it is nothing".[4] He further elaborates the de jure and de facto position of integration of these two aspects in the Islamic history. "In the Islamic state, as ideally conceived and as it is indeed exerted from medieval through to Ottoman times almost into the nineteenth century, there could be no conflict between Pope and Emperor; in classical Middle Eastern Islam, the two mighty powers which these two represented were one and same, and the caliph was the embodiment of both".[5]

The role of 'ulamā or scholars throughout the Islamic history has not been like that of the Christian clerics but of knowledgeable persons who with their rational and scientific approach interpret the Qur'ān and the Sunnah and offer their views based on these two sources. They do not share in divinity nor are supposed to be innocent or immune from error. There is no possibility of their role as mediators between a common follower of Islam and his Allah. They do not carry any ecclesiastical authority. The 'ulamā are not clergy in the strict sense of the term.

Nevertheless, governance is a core issue addressed by Islam in its Scripture as well as in the Prophet's noble example. "The first

3 Bernard Lewis, *Islam in History, Ideas, People, and Events in the Middle East* (New Delhi: Arya Books, 1998), p. 261.

4 Ibid. p. 262.

5 Ibid. p. 263.

question that arose on Muhammad's death was whether any state should survive it at all."[6] The later history and the ongoing discourse on Khilāfah and monarchy show how crucial this question has been.

Contrary to the tradition in Arabian and in other contemporary civilizations, like the Roman Christian world, Muslim India, and Persia, Islam came forward for the first time in the history of humanity, with a social re-organization realized on the "religion" basis rather than on lineage. "Allah was the personification of state supremacy. His Prophet, as long as he lived, was His legitimate vicegerent and supreme ruler on earth. As such, Muḥammad, in addition to his spiritual function, exercised the same temporal authority that any chief of a state might exercise".[7]

Thus, not only at the historic but also at the conceptual level consensus exists on the integration of "spiritual religious" and the temporal functions of the Prophet. This consensus comes from classical Muslim scholars as well as modern-day Muslim thinkers of all shades and by implication of the leadership, Khalīfah, amīr, mas'ūl or imām of the Muslim community, after the Prophet ('alayhi as-salām).

Realization of state, and integration and unification of otherwise two separate institutions enjoys therefore a consensual (ijmā'i) position in the past fifteen centuries of Islam. The twentieth-century Shi'i scholar Imām Khomeini in his doctrine of *Vilāyat al-Faqīh*, the famous 1969 lecturers in Najaf, makes this point clear. Later in his book *al-Hukūmat al-lslāmiyah* (Islamic Government),[8] he confirmed that Islam as a "religion" must include a governmental

---

6 Marshall G.S. Hodgson, *The Venture of Islam: Conscience and History in a World Civilization* (Chicago: The University of Chicago Press, 1974) vol. 1, p. 187.

7 Philip K. Hitti, *History of the Arabs* (London: Macmillan, 1970), p. 120; also see chapter four. "Politics and War' in Joseph Schacht and C.E. Bosmorth, *The Legacy of Islam* (Oxford: Oxford University Press, 1974) p. 165.

8 Ayatullah Khomeini, *Islamic Government* (New York: Manor Books Inc. 1979).

system. "The separation of religion from government and its relegation to a system of worship and ritual is completely alien to the spirit and teachings of Islam, a perversion perpetuated and reinforced by imperialism and U.S. agents in order to subjugate and exploit the lands of Islam."[9]

The translation of Imām Khomeini's concept of an Islamic state into the Iranian model, in terms of its impact, is no less important than the creation of Pakistan in 1947 as a de jure Islamic state. Iqbāl, Jinnāh and Mawdūdī shared together in their dream and vision of Pakistan as a "premier Islamic state,"[10] as declared specifically by the founder of the country Mohammad Ali Jinnah. The founder was clear about the nature of this new state. He repeatedly mentioned that the state would be directed by the principles of Islamic social justice, fair play and consultation or *shūrā*,[11] the divine guidance of the Sharī'ah[12] and the Prophetic model. He invited experts to help the state in realization of this goal. While inaugurating the State Bank of Pakistan, he specifically asked the bank officials to work out

---

9 Sami Zubaida, *Islam the People and the State: Political Ideas and Movements in the Middle East* (London: I.B. Tawris & Co. Ltd., 2001), p.16.

10 "This Dominion which represents the fulfillment in a certain measure, of the cherished goal of 100-million Muslims of this sub-continent came into existence on August 14, 1947. Pakistan is the premier Islamic state and the fifth largest in the world." See, *Quaid-i-Azam Mohammad Ali Jinnah: Speeches and Statements* (Islamabad: Government of Pakistan, 1993) p. 155.

11 "It is my belief that our salvation lies in following the golden rules of conduct set for us by our great law-giver the Prophet of Islam. Let us lay the foundation of our democracy on the basis of truly Islamic ideals and principles. Our Almighty has taught us that "our decisions in the affairs of the state shall be guided by discussion and consultation" (*al-Shūrā* 42:38). Speech at Sibi Darbar, Feb 14, 1948, Quaid-i-Azam Mohammad Ali Jinnah*: Speeches and Statements*, 1993, p.142.

12 "Quaid-i-Azam Mohammad Ali Jinnah, Governor General of Pakistan speaking at a reception given to him on the holy Prophet's birthday by the Bar Association of Karachi said that he would not understand a section of the people who deliberately wanted to create mischief and made propaganda that the Constitution of Pakistan would not be made on the basis of Sharī'ah. The Quaid-i-Azam said the Islamic principles today are as applicable to life as they were thirteen hundred years ago". Address to the Bar Association Karachi Jan 25, 1948 *Speech, Statement and Messages* of the Quaid-i-Azam, edited by K.A. Yusufi, (Lahore, Bazm-i-Iqbal, 1996) vol. IV, p. 2669.

an economic model based on Islamic social justice so that we free ourselves of Western capitalism, which is known for its exploitation and inequity causing a widening gap between the poor and the rich.[13]

To bring Pakistan on the world map was indeed a gigantic task accomplished by the father of the nation Muhammad Ali Jinnah. But to develop a blue-print of an Islamic political system and spell out a scheme for transformation of the new state into an Islamic republic was a task of a different kind that only Iqbāl or Mawdūdi could have taken up. Wilfred Smith realizing the enormity of the task makes a very perceptive comment: "Pakistan came into being as already an Islamic state not because its form was ideal but because, in so far as, its dynamic was idealist.... To set up an Islamic state therefore was the beginning not the end of an adventure. To achieve an Islamic state was to attain not a form but a process."[14]

For the Westernized intellectuals steeped in a secular-liberal tradition, Islam as the ideology of state was a utopia. Utopian goals, in their view, reflect nostalgia for re-establishing a "once existing" but no more relevant golden age of the past. They reject existence of an Islamic polity in the Qur'ān.[15]

Ideology, in their understanding, has rhetoric of its own, which is simultaneously rational and emotive. It is assumed that

---

13 "I shall watch with keenness the work of your research organization in evolving practices comparable with ***Islamic ideals*** of social and economic life. The economic system of the west has created almost insolvable problems for humanity and to many of us it appears that only a miracle can save it from disaster that is now facing the world.... The adoption of Western economic theory and practice will not help us in achieving our goal of creating a happy and contented people. *We must workout our destiny in our own way and present to the world an economic system based on true Islamic concept of equality of mankind and social justice.*

We will thereby be fulfilling our mission as Muslims and giving to humanity the message of peace which alone can save it and secure the welfare, happiness and prosperity of mankind." Emphasis added.

The *Civil and Military Gazette* July 2, 1948, Khurshid A.K. Yusufi, ed. *Speech, Statement and Messages of the Quaid-i-Azam* (Lahore, Bazm-i-Iqbal, 1996) vol. IV, p. 2787

14 Wilfred Cantwell Smith, *Islam in Modern History* (New York: Mentor Books, 1957) p. 218-219.

15 John L. Esposito, *Islam and Politics* (New York: Syracuse University Press, 1984), p.68.

ideology, as it is defined, tries to motivate people, mobilize and forge them into one single force and as such generates an authoritarian tendency, which they say is self-evident truth. To them, Pakistan as an ideal Islamic state is just a slogan, a utopia and an unachievable goal.

A major confusion, perhaps, of the Westernized secular mindset is that it regards Islam, like other world religions, a set of certain rituals, ceremonies, festivals and dogmas. In the backdrop of the decline of Christianity as a political force in the West and subsequent rise of rationalism, scientism, logical positivism, modernism, liberalism and post-modernism, they feel uncomfortable in accepting Islam as state ideology. Their belief in dualism of sacred and profane makes it difficult for them to accept the unified approach of Islam in which state and "religion" are not two separate entities but two sides of the same coin representing an organic unity.

The newly created society and state in Pakistan necessitated loud thinking to crystallize its own understanding of the basic issues yet to be defined in its constitution as objectives of state and society. The founding father could only provide in his over a dozen post-August 11, 1947 statements, policy guidelines, and directives on the Islamic character of the future political order in the country. Development of specific details was a task for the academicians, scholars, legislators, and intellectuals of the country. Sayyid Mawdūdi responded to these issues with the vigour of a scholar and the vision of a strategist and a futurist.

Mawdūdī (1903-1979) was a prolific writer. But it is because of his very candid exposition, systematic approach, and structural discussion that he has been considered as the most influential twentieth-century revivalist thinker of Islam.[16] His works cover a vast area of Islamic disciplines like exegesis of the Qur'ān (tafsīr), socioeconomic thought, history, education, law, politics, and world affairs. Besides, he was an ideologue *par excellence*, social reformer,

16 Wilfred Cantwell Smith, *Islam in Modern History* (Princeton University Press, 1957), p.236.

statesman, and the founder and leader of one of the leading revivalist movement of the Islamic world: the Jamā'at-i-Islāmi with its independent organizational set ups in Pakistan, India, Bangladesh, Kashmir, and Sri Lanka. His works have been translated and published in over twenty-four languages during his lifetime, playing a key role in creating a global Islamic resurgence. He also pioneered a movement for Islamization of knowledge, questioning the epistemic foundations of social and applied sciences.[17] The impact of his revolutionary writings still needs assessment. His emphasis on Islam as a complete way of life transformed the common vision of Islam from a traditional "religion" into a dynamic, spiritual, moral, social, economic and political movement and a major agent for change. His monumental work *Tafhīm al-Qur'ān*, a unique exposition of the meaning and message of the Qur'ān has a simple non-polemical and non-theological format, yet its logical and scientific language has made impact on the minds of millions of Muslims as well as non-Muslims the world over. His contributions in the area of contemporary Islamic political thought remain seminal and path breaking.

The three Abrahamic faiths share the role of "religion" in state. Judaism feels proud of the political role played by the Old Testament prophets David and Solomon, who symbolize the integration of the so-called secular and religious functions and authority. Later, Judaism as a minority faith and culture also learnt how to survive, interact and influence the majority faith, culture and political power. Zionism consequently played a decisive role in the formulation of policies in Europe, the United States, and a major player in the state of Israel. The strategic role of the Jews as a minority pressure group in the United States and in Europe does not call for elaboration. It is quite at home in developing a working relationship with the centers of power, may those be religious or secular at the global level.

Christianity in its different phases in history has suffered from an inherent dilemma of church and state. At times, the Church was an embodiment of the Divine as much as the Civil Authority. Itself a victim of persecutions, prior to Christianization of Roman Empire,

17 Malik Badri, "A Tribute to Maulana Mawdudi', *The Muslim World,* (Oct, 2003) vol. 93, No. 3 & 4, p. 501.

soon it claimed validity of its faith, and was unwilling to accommodate other deities or the public rites associated with the Roman culture. With the extension of support of Emperor Constantine (280-337 C.E.), Christian Church became an institutionalized wing of Roman government. The emperor enjoyed broad responsibility of ensuring the unity of faith and directing imperial resources toward essentially religious ends. Among the early ideologues, Saint Augustine of Hippo (354-430) encountered the ever-increasing role of state. The dilemma of Christianity, however, mirrors in the compromise of Saint Augustine's principled position that state should strictly confine itself to protection of peaceful persons from religiously motivated attacks along with his own opinion that armies of the Roman state should suppress and persecute heresy.[18]

The collapse of Roman Empire in the West exposed Christianity to new challenges. Christian Church as the major source for trans-European political, cultural and spiritual unity, without a political authority had to evolve its own institutional role. Thomas Aquinas (1224-1274) viewed secular political power responsible for promotion of virtue and justice among its subjects irrespective of their religious commitment. At the same time, he also considered secular government responsible for promotion and diffusion of the true religion of Rome, a goal, which only a true Christian ruler could achieve.

The sixteenth-century reformation heralded by Martin Luther (1483-1546) also highlighted the role of state as an agent of confessional enforcement, in a state of affairs where Catholicism and Protestantism were having perpetual clash and conflict. It was in this age of religious intolerance and persecution that Baruch Spinoza (1632-1677) and John Locke (1632-1704) advocated for tolerance, freedom of views and religion neutral role vis-à-vis state. In North America, George Washington (1732-1799) and John Adams (1735-1826) recognized the role of religion in dissemination of morality and virtue yet their emphasis remained on freedom of the individual and

18 Gary J. Nederman, "Religion and State" in Maryanne Cline Horowitz, ed., *New Dictionary of the History of Ideas* (New York: Charles Scribner and Sons, 2005), vol.5, p. 2079.

freedom for established churches. First amendment (1789) stated: "Congress shall make no law respecting an establishment of religion, or prohibiting the free exercise thereof."

Thomas Jefferson used the phrase "separation of church and state" for the first time in his letter to Connecticut Baptists in 1802.[19] The ground reality, however, remains that every dollar bill printed by the so-called secular United States carries a creedal statement "in God we believe." With its pride in secularism, the secular U.S. has exempted religious institutions from taxation, and legislature pays chaplains from tax money, which very much circumscribes the dictum of separation between state and religion.

As a continuation of the Abrahamic tradition, Islam scripturally, historically, and conceptually defined itself as a natural middle path for humanity. The Qur'ān repeatedly talks about Islam as *din al-fitrah* and the final messenger of Allah Sayyidnā Muḥammad ('alahyi as-salām) as one sent to humanity (*kāffatan lin-nās*). Nevertheless, it recognizes the right of others to live by their own doctrines, creeds and faith (*lakum dīnukum wa liya dīn*) and principle of tolerance and abstaining use of force in matters related to choice of religion *(lā ikrāha fi al-dīn).*

Referring to Allah's Power, Authority and Guidance the Qur'ān uses a comprehensive, term hukm (authority, sovereignty, legal and political power) for Allah the Exalted. "All authority to govern, hukm, belongs to Allah, He has commanded that you serve none but Him, this is the manifest *din* (the right way of life)." (*Yūsuf* 12:40). The term sovereignty here connotes more than its political and legal dimensions. It complements the basic and seminal principle of tawhīd, Oneness, Uniqueness and Transcendence of Allah. By implication Allah's authority and power is not in the masjid (mosque), a "sacred" place alone. In fact, Islam does not recognize separation between sacred or holy space and time and an unholy or secular and profane space and time.

---

19 Martin R. Marty, "Religion & State" in *New Dictionary of history of ideas,* Vol. 5 p. 2086.

When the Qur'ān declares: "This day I have perfected your dīn for you and have given you My bounty in full measure and has been pleased to assign for you Islam as your dīn (way of life)," (*al-Mā'idah* 5:3). The completion of dīn does not stand for the rituals alone. It refers to the din's relevance with state, society, individual as well as the whole of humanity.

Historically the Messenger of Allah combined the functions of a prophet, a statesman, a judge, and a military commander. His successors, al-Khulāfā al-Rāshidīn, also combined in their conduct the political, "religious," civil and legal roles. However, after around forty years of the Prophet's death, a significant shift in the political arena exposed the Muslim community to apparently an aberration, and a deviance in the form of the introduction of hereditary succession. This began with the first Umayyad ruler Mu'āwiyah, when he nominated his son Yazīd as his successor.

This issue has attracted attention of the Muslim political thinkers, jurists and theologians throughout the past fifteen centuries. In the recent history of the Muslim Ummah, particularly with the decline and disintegration of the symbolic Khilāfah al-Uthmāniyah (1924) Muslim intellectuals vigorously deliberated on the concept of Khilāfah, its need, viability and legitimacy in the context of the dynamics of an Islamic state.

Egyptian scholar 'Ali 'Abdul Rāziq (1888-1966)[20] questioned the scriptural foundations of not only Khilāfah but also of an Islamic political system. Rashid Ridā (1865-1935) came up with a historic approach, calling for the revival of Khilāfah. Indian scholar Abu'l Kalām Azād (1888-1958) also addressed the issue at a historical level. The fall of Khilāfah and the systematic secularization of state in Turkey was not a normal event. Muhammad Rashid Rida considered realization of an Arab Khilāfah or dawlah indispensable for maintaining temporal and spiritual authority, thus given the title caliphate or Grand Imamate (Imāmah al-'Uzmā). During this period, other Muslim scholars came with notions such as "*al-Islam din wa dawlahaa*" a combination of

20 'Ali Abdul Raziq, *al-Islam wa Usul al-Hukm,* (Cairo, 1922).

din with state, attributed to 'Abdul Razzāq al Sanhūri (1895-1971). In this intellectual climate, perhaps the most comprehensive and persuasive discussion on Islamic political order, conceptual and historical, was offered by Mawdūdī (1903-1979) in his several academic treaties.

The political response of the Muslim Ummah in South Asia against the British imperialism was diverse. Territorial nationalism, conceptualizing Muslims and Hindus as one nation, came from none but the Rector of Deoband Hussain Ahmad Madani (1879-1957). It was contested by Allama Iqbal (1872-1938), Quaid-i-Azam Muhammad Ali Jinnah (1876-1948), and Sayyid Mawdūdi. Allama Iqbal, who once praised the Himalayas and traced his Brahmin origin, publicly rejected the Madani's views, and advocated two-nation theory. Jinnah emerged as the key champion of the two-nation theory and this vision was supported by renowned Islamic scholars, specifically Shabbīr Ahmad 'Uthmāni (1887-1949), Sayyid Sulaymān Nadvi (1884-1953) and Abu'l A'lā Mawdūdī (1903-1979). In order to articulate the concept of Muslims and Hindus as two nations, Mawdūdi's book *Mas'alah-i Qawmiyat* (1938) was widely circulated by the Muslim League leadership in order to support and validate its political and ideological stand of two-nation theory, from an academic and Islamic legal viewpoint.

A logical corollary of the emergent situation was to address afresh the concept of Islamic society and state in a futuristic context. Mawdūdi wrote a series of articles later published in a book entitled *Musalmān aur mawjuda siyasi kashmakash* (Muslims and the current political struggle) in order to help Muslims understand the issues involved, affecting their identity and political destiny. The complexity of the issue called for more than one person to address it. Nevertheless, if we look critically, perhaps, most of the academic works of Sayyid Mawdūdī were in one way or another a systematic response to this socio-political challenge that the Muslim Ummah encountered after the fall of the Uthmāni Khilāfah and struggle for freedom from British rule in India.

Mawdūdī's concept of the Islamic state has two equally important dimensions. A powerful and lucid academic discourse based on solid objective and scientific research spelling out the contours of an Islamic political order. Second, a systematic effort to look into the history of the Muslim Ummah, discussing the arrangement needed so as to develop a deep understanding of the ground realities of the Ummah's intellectual, ethical, social and political crisis. His interpretation of Islam as a complete way of life leads him to draw from the Qur'ān and the Sunnah the principles of polity and society. His outstanding work *Four Key Concepts of the Qur'ān* (*Qur'ān ki char bunyādi istalāhen*) sets the direction for his future elaborations and comprehensive treatises on the Islamic political order. His other writings such as *Mas'ala-i khilāfat*, Delhi, 1922, *Islam ka siyāsi nizām*, Lahore, 1939; *Islami hukumat kis tarah qa'im hoti hay*, Lahore 1941; *Islami hukumat mayn dhimiyun kay huqūq*, Lahore 1948; *Islami dastūr ki tadwin* and *Islami dastūr ki bunyādain*, Lahore 1952 led to the crystallization of his views, reflected in his later works such as *Islami riyāsat*, Lahore 1962 and *Khilāfat wa mulūkīyat*, Lahore, 1965.

While addressing the issue of the caliphate and kingship, its historical development and impact on the Muslim society, he did not confine his discourse to a historical résumé. His treatment of the issue cannot be separated from the intellectual crisis in which he found the Muslim Ummah in the twentieth century. The Muslim world particularly countries like Pakistan, Turkey, Egypt, Syria, Iraq, Sudan, Malaysia, Indonesia, Yemen and Iran in the second half of the twentieth century were struggling to discover their Islamic roots. Army dictatorships substituted the overseas colonizers in several Muslim countries. People contested their legitimacy in most of these countries. The yearning of the Muslim masses for the revival of the caliphate and for building their political system on the pattern of al-Khilāfah al-Rāshidah called for a fresh look on the issue.

Should state be religion-neutral?

Sayyid Mawdūdī's major contribution lies in addressing invariably some of the most challenging questions on Islamic political order. Secular Western mind finds it very difficult to reconcile with the political role of "religion". They define religion in its classical Western and Eastern understanding as personal faith, a set of rituals, ceremonies, offerings, devotions and festivals while they take society and state as separate entities. State, they assume, must remain religion neutral, if not anti-religion.

The secularists' argument against religion's role in state, politics and society is that if a state has a religion it becomes partisan interfering with people's faith. Second, such a state would not be able to ensure religious equality to all its citizens when it may succumb to bias and unfairness towards its non-Muslim citizens. They further claim that if the Pakistani state has Islam as its "religion," it may create problems of interpretation. In other words, which interpretation of the Qur'ānic text or of Ḥadīth will it follow? Therefore, summing up the issue, the secularists plead that state should have nothing to do with religion.

Before we respond to these questions, it will be in the fitness of things to point out that the historical process of transition from Khilāfah to Mālikiyah (kingship) when reflected through the mirror of Islamic history should not be interpreted as a total distancing or separation of "religion" from state. State even when annexed by istila' (naked force) by the mulūk (kings and monarchs) continued to define itself as an Islamic state. It remained committed to the supremacy of the Sharī'ah, presence of independent Islamic judiciary, promotion of Islamic social norms, independent Islamic educational and social institutions.

This continued to be the official policy, even under monarchy whose Islamic legitimacy people often publicly questioned. Relevance of religion to state and society was not the issue; the cause of contention was how to check transfer of power through succession and revive shūrā's decision-making system.

Having said so, it has to be acknowledged that the shift from caliphate to monarchial absolutism did represent a serious deviation from the qualitative, merit-based, consultative (shūrāwi) political order of Islam, which believed in public accountability of the rulers before Allah and the people. That is why most of the treatments on the subject assign first priority to Sovereignty of Allah in an Islamic political order. This does not mean elected representatives in a parliament or legislature shall have no role to play. Indeed lawmaking is an ongoing process in any developing and growing society. However, the principles that go into lawmaking, and which define the purpose and objective of law, human life, society and state, are provided in the case of Muslim community, by the Sharī'ah (divine command). For example, the Sharī'ah declares that killing of one person unjustly is like killing the whole of humanity while saving one single soul is like saving the life of all humanity (*al-Mā'idah* 5:32). In the light of this universal Qur'ānic principle a legislature shall have to develop laws and regulations in order to promote and protect life of its citizens irrespective of their religious affiliation, colour or racial origin.

It is a historical reality that Islamic law based on principles of Sharī'ah (usūl al-fiqh) in economic, social and legal matters did remain operative even when political deviance resulted into kingship and monarchy under the Umayyad, 'Abbāsid, Mamlūk, Fātimīd, and 'Uthmāni or even Mughal rulers. Therefore, historically "religion" and state dichotomy has not been a central issue for Islam in its history prior to the advent of European colonial rule in Muslim lands.

Islam "dīn" or religion

A more basic question raised by Mawdūdi, in this respect is - can Islam be regarded a religion like Hinduism, Judaism or Christianity? Referring directly to the Qur'ān, in his seminal work *Four key concepts of the Qur'ān* (2006), he holds the view that the Arabic term madhhab, synonymous with the English word "religion", is not used even once in the Qur'ān or in the Prophetic Sunnah. The Qur'ān, invariably, in about ninety-eight places uses the term *dīn* in its comprehensive connotation of commands, directives and teachings dealing with personal and family life, worship, social relations, economy, political system, law and financial accountability. This leaves no ambiguity in the mind of a perceptive reader of the Qur'ān and Sunnah about the supremacy of the Sharī'ah or sovereignty of Allah the Exalted.

The term "religion" in its traditional Eastern and Western connotation bears little relevance to Islam. Islam is a complete way of life, with its own cultural, ethical, legal social, political and economic system as it has its own distinct form and expression for prayer, worship and devotion. All are parts of an integrated whole.

State and religion dichotomy

The suggestion that the advent of mulūkiyah (kingship) was a de-facto separation between "religion" and state, or a form of secularization of state is out of tune with the reality of the Muslim experience and based on a total misunderstanding of the notion. To begin with, Islamic state is an ideological state and as such, it cannot be religion-neutral. It is responsible for making it convenient for its citizens to live by the Islamic principles and teachings. The Qur'ān explicitly states that "(Allah will certainly help) those who when We bestow upon them authority in land (tamkīn fi al ard) shall establish (system of) prayers, (system of) Zakāh, enjoin good (ma'rūf) and forbid evil (munkar)". (*al-Ḥajj* 22:41). Here the Qur'ān has specified four basic obligations and responsibility of an Islamic state namely establishment of a system of public piety through prayer (Ṣalāh), a system of just and sharing economy through Zakāh; realization of ma'rūf (good and ethical behaviour) in public policy and eradication and frustration of unethical practices or nahi 'an al-munkar. Operationalization of these four state obligations is called by the Qur'ān as establishing Allah's rule (ḥākimiyah) and of 'adl al ijtimā'i (social justice).

In the realm of law, the Qur'ān makes the political authority responsible for implementation of justice in civil as well as criminal matters. The Qur'ānic political system makes no plea for any privileged class based on divine right to rule. There is no place for any "clergy" to execute anyone in the name of Islamic Sharī'ah. It is no more than a myth that the so-called theocratic 'ulamā are allowed to take law in their hands. In Islam, it is state alone, which can implement criminal penalties and civil punishments. The political teachings of the Qur'ān include how to dispense justice within the framework of the Sharī'ah. Islamic laws relating to inheritance, family, economic transactions, crime and punishment are integral part of the directives and commands of the Qur'ān and the Sunnah or along with processes for dispensation of justice (adab al-Qāḍī). With explicit commands in all these above areas of law, the Qur'ān makes state and society equally responsible for implementation of total Islamic system of life. *Amr bi al-ma'rūf* is both public and private responsibility. It is in this sense that Islam has no separation between the so-called secular and the religious. Iqbal correctly remarks, "The essence of tawhīd as a working idea is equality, solidarity and freedom." The state from Islamic standpoint is an endeavour to transform these principles into space and time forces, an aspiration to realize them in definite human organization. It is in this sense alone that the state in Islam is a theocracy, not in the sense it is headed by a representative of God on earth who can always screen his despotic will behind his supposed infallibility. All that is secular is therefore sacred in the roots of its being. There is no such thing as a profane world. All this immensity of matter constitutes a scope for the self-realization of spirit. All is holy ground. As the prophet so beautifully puts it, "The whole of this earth is a masjid." The state according to Islam is only an effort to realize the spiritual in a human organization.[21]

Does it mean that if state is not religion neutral, then non-Muslim citizens will face discrimination? The Qur'ān specifically in the context of non-Muslims directs believers to "observe justice (i'dilū) as it is near to piety and Allah consciousness (*al-Māi'dah* 5:8). State has an obligation to protect life, honour, property, rational behaviour, religious and cultural freedom of its non-Muslim citizens.[22] State cannot differentiate between a Muslim and non-Muslim as member of the civil society. However, it does not mean that violating all norms of reason, logic and fairness a person by virtue of being a citizen may be appointed to perform a duty for which he may not meet requisite qualifications, for example, leading prayers in the masjid, or adjudicating Sharī'ah matters without conviction, expertise, knowledge, skill and trust in it. Second, it is in line with the true spirit of democracy to allow the majority law reflects the values the community believes. At the same time, minority has every right to live according to its own faith and values, guaranteed under the Qur'ānic principle of lā ikrāha fi al-dīn (there is no compulsion

21 M. Iqbal, *The Reconstruction of Religious Thought in Islam* (Lahore: Shaikh M. Ashraf, 1977) p. 154-155.

22 Syed Abu'l A'la Mawdūdī, *Islamic Law and Constitution,* Chapter eight "Rights of non-Muslims in an Islamic State," tr. ed. Prof. Khurshid Ahmad (Lahore: Islamic Publications., 1980) pp. 273-300.

in religion). However, minority has no right to dictate majority not to legislate public law in keeping with the people's will. Genuine plurality is an integral part of the Islamic system.

Religious equality

The Islamic political order subsumes not only religious freedom but considers religious liberty within and outside the Islamic state as an inalienable right of its citizen. We are not aware of any other ideological or "religious" state, which would be committed to the inalienable right to faith and practice for people of other faiths, to the extent of taking up arms for restoration of their rights. The Qur'ān declares that "[t]hose who were unjustly expelled from their homes for no other reason than their saying 'Allah is our Lord.' If Allah was not to repel some through others, monasteries and churches and synagogues and masajid, wherein the name of Allah is much mentioned would certainly have been pulled down. Allah will certainly help those who will help Him" (*al-Ḥajj*: 22:40). By mentioning specifically four places of worship namely, churches, synagogues, temples or monasteries and masājid, the Qur'ān has left no ambiguity in the minds of its readers that if religious liberty is denied to the followers of other religions, it is for the Islamic state to take all necessary steps for the restoration of their rights.

This protection of "religious" freedom is not a favour to anyone but an obligation of an ideological Islamic state. Any one who will read the Qur'ān and the Prophet's hadith will discover for himself that the Prophet has gone to the extent of saying: "Beware! Whosoever is cruel and hard on such people (non-Muslims), or curtails their rights or burden them with more than they can endure, or realize anything from them against their free will, I shall myself be a complainant against such a person on the Day of Judgment."[23]

Muslim and Islamic state

Modern Muslim political discourse often draws a line between an Islamic and a Muslim state. The former, it says, implement rigorously

---

23 Abu Dā'ūd, *Sunan*, "*Kitab al-Jihād*", quoted by Mawdūdi, *Islamic Law*, p. 279.

the Sharīʿah penalties and punishments while the later is a Muslim majority state ruled by not-so-good or ideal Muslim rulers. Only three out of fifty-seven O.I.C. member states call themselves Islamic. Others call themselves kingdoms (mamālik), people's republics or simply an emirate ruled by a chief (amīr). On a closer look, the difference does not appear substantial for three simple reasons:

In the case of the earlier Muslim history, the political authority embodied the so-called "religious" and "political" functions. The rightly guided caliphs were also knowledgeable mujtahidīn (jurists) in matters of law. With the Umayyad political take over, the state still in principle remained Islamic, though it was taken over per force (bil istilā) by a mālik (hereditary claimants to power). Second, the state remained Islamic because its laws were based on the Sharīʿah, neither the Umayyads nor the ʿAbbasids or later aspirants for power, suppressed the Sharīʿah laws, though occasionally in a few areas they tried to influence the judiciary leading to an obvious tension between the two. The Sharīʿah laws, however, determined economic and social life. State appointed chief justice (qāḍi al-quḍā) as well as local judges, who adjudicated matters according to one or another recognized school of law. It is historically incorrect to think that with the change of the caliphate to mulūkiyah, the law of land changed and Islamic laws confined to personal laws of the Muslims. Conferment of Islamic laws to the so-called "Muslim personal law" was an imposition by the overseas colonialists, who occupied Muslim lands.

Third, a formal and strong link between the less pious (exceptions allowed) and observant ruler and the people remained through the institution of Friday sermons in which a prayer was made for the monarch for being supposedly "shadow of Allah on earth," a statement which calls for a critical look, nevertheless speaks for the Islamic character of state.

Then what is the problem? Why do we have this ongoing political discourse from Yazid's time to the British raj in Pakistan and elsewhere? Mawdūdi and before him others, like Rashid Rida, pleaded for an Islamic state in order to bring back those essential features and characteristics, which were suppressed, modified or replaced by certain other features under the kings and monarchs in the past centuries.

Mawdūdī in his *Khilāfat wa Mulūkiyat* has tried to address the issue at three levels. First, he tries to identify in the Qur'ān and the Prophet's Sunnah the normative foundations of an Islamic political and social order. It is here that theoretical and applied dimensions of concept of sovereignty, vicegerency, limits of obedience to the authorities, rights and obligations of the public servants, and more importantly, the role of the shūrā (interactive decision making) and implementation of social justice ('adl) is deliberated.

Having dilated on the intellectual and normative foundations and the framework of an Islamic political order, Mawdūdi compares the post-rightly guided caliphate period with the ideal contained in the Qur'ān and the Sunnah. He finds certain obvious deviations from the ideal. Making a departure from the romantic and traditionalist interpretation of history re-enforced at the intellectual level by Shibli Nu'māni (1847-1914) in his classic *al-Māmūn* (1887), Mawdūdī applies principles of historical criticism in understanding the causes of transition from the caliphate to monarchy. Source criticism in the Islamic intellectual tradition had been the feature of the Muslim scholars from early days, encouraged by the Prophet himself. However, the romantic approach in history and conservative traditionalism did not encourage intellectuals to develop a critique of the monarchial period of the after-fall caliphate.

Mawdūdī breaks this "taboo" but with extreme respect for such personalities, while being critical of their policies and decisions, which became instrumental in changing the course of events and the trend of society. He bases his analysis on the touchstone of the truth provided by the Qur'ān and the Sunnah.

This critical work highlights causes and reasons for the transition from ideal to the incidental, which shows a departure from certain basic norms such as decision making done on the shūrā principle, direct election or selection of the ruler based on ahliyah (capability and qualifications) and not on hereditary succession and public accountability of the expenditure of funds. Despite the preceding three shortcomings, independence of judiciary and the institutions of iftā (legal opinion) and qaḍā (judicial edicts) and madāris (schools) were practically engines of change thanks to their ongoing practice of ijtihād (independent) in various areas of life which helped in broadening the Sharīʿah application in economy, social and financial matters as well as in art and architecture.

The social norms, economic practices, family system and personal laws, inheritance law, evidence law, as prescribed by the Qur'ān and the Sunnah continued to operate even under the greatest usurpers of political power. This peculiar situation resulted into a legal dilemma for the jurists. Even scholars like Imām Ibn Taymiyah (1263-1328) hesitated in endorsing rebellion against a Muslim ruler who may have obvious weakness but who maintains public prayers and takes care of the people's welfare.

The issue became more complex with the political decline, disintegration of Muslim political authority and rise of European imperialism in the eighteenth and nineteenth centuries. The oppressive colonizers, who in the secular European tradition imposed secular laws on Muslim lands, replaced not-so-good-Muslim rulers. The abolition of the Ottoman caliphate turned out to be the last blow to the concept of the global Islamic state and Muslim Ummah.

The new challenge was perhaps no less serious than the earlier one. The basic issues at conceptual and applied levels though were not completely new, the European secular model concentrated on the people's sovereignty along with the final authority of the crown or the President in certain cases.

The source of law for the European nations was mainly the pronouncement of the crown or customary law in which their religious scriptures had practically no role to play. The distribution of power in the legislative bodies was based on secular principles and on show of hands. Morality was important but confined to personal realms.

For the Muslims, the pain of colonization added to the already existing concern and desire to revive the Muslim caliphate. The colonizers were generally considered more undesirable than the corrupt Muslim rulers were. Emergence of movements for restoration of Islamic political order was therefore a natural phenomenon in the length and breadth of the Muslim world during this period.

Methodological level

Sayyid Mawdūdīs *Khilāfat wa Mulūkiyat*, in this context, presents a bold step forward in examining critically the past. Unconventional as he is, with openness of mind and with due reverence for the companions of the Prophet ('alayhi as-salām), rising above the bias of sect or madhab (school of thought), he makes a distinction at a methodological level between the norm and deviation, between essential and incidental, central and peripheral, permanent and the changing.

Progress, development and advancement is a dynamic process in which instead of re-inventing a wheel an existing wheel is improved, perfected and made to excel on other wheels. Progress is neither a matter of rejection of the past nor a matter of holding to the past. It calls for capturing the normative foundations and universal principles of good governance while applying an innovative approach in order to discover appropriate viable system of power sharing, realization of justice and peace and observance of human rights of the people in the present and future context.

The post-colonial challenges faced by the Muslim world have been multidimensional. For some elitist Muslim, Western secular political model, thanks to its apparent success in delivering political liberties to the people in Europe and America deserves to be embraced in the Muslim world as well. They hypothesize that the values of freedom of expression, civil society, security and fair play are essentially a heritage of the Muslims; therefore, their adoption does not violate any Islamic norms. They further add that secular political system also provides space for personal religious practices. One can go to church or masjid without any hindrance while at collective and social levels a political order should have no religious interference.

The Islamic revivalist and innovative school of thought represented outspokenly by Mawdūdi, on the contrary, holds that the norms and values contained in the Qur'ān and the Prophet's Sunnah have universal relevance and applicability. Therefore, an Islamic political order is essentially a matter of translation of these norms and values in a progressive political order. An Islamic state, however, shows no reluctance in adapting processes and measure, which does not conflict with the Islamic norms and values.

The conceptual confusion that a state may be called Muslim instead of Islamic is perhaps due to a basic error in defining a Muslim. Some people think that like the neighbouring Indian Hindus a person is also Muslim by virtue of being born in a Muslim family. Two basic conditions as manifested in the confusion of faith and to be fulfilled by anyone who wants to be Muslim, are namely acceptance of undisputed authority and sovereignty of Allah, and second, total acceptance of the Prophetic conduct and behavior as the model to be imitated. If a person with his apparent Muslim name acts contrary to both the above requirements, his Islam becomes doubtful. A "Muslim State" which does not subscribe to the above two basic principles can be neither Muslim nor Islamic.

Similarly, Islamic state versus Muslim state dichotomy appears to be based on certain misgivings. For example, it is assumed that the Islamic state is utopian and idealist while a Muslim state stands for a pragmatic, liberal and westernized socio-political order with ceremonial observance of Islam. This is a contradiction in terms. A Muslim is Muslim only when he or she observes Islam. It is true for the state as well. It has to be de jure Islamic, and in the process of evolution becomes a de facto Islamic state. It is ideal but viable and a manifest reality.

In the Jewish tradition, a Jew is defined as one born of a Jewish mother. A Jew remains a Jew whether he is Karl Marx, Sigmund Freud or Martin Buber or a terrorist Menachem Begin or a confirmed atheist. This is not so with Islam. Islam means conscious acceptance of obligations and responsibilities as a Muslim. Simply gene, race or cast, as in Hinduism, does not inherit Islam for example. Similarly, an Islamic state, being ideological refers to a conscious, dynamic process of becoming. Its identity lies in its Islamicity. Thus, a Muslim state cannot be other than a de-jure Islamic state.

An apparently very intelligent point is made that if we call a state Islamic, we will end up in differences of opinions on all policy matters. But if we call a state Muslim it will only mean it is Muslim by name, though it may not follow and implement Islamic teachings. We fail to understand the logic of this self-contradictory position. If the intention of a people is not to observe and apply Islam in state why to call it even Muslim? In fact, in Islam difference of opinion, contrary to many other faiths, is welcome. Islam assumes that research-based differences of opinion are a pre-requisite to people's progress. We are not aware of any constitution of a country, which does not provide for more than one interpretation. Does it mean that since there is room for difference of opinion therefore constitutions should be a set aside? Or, if in a criminal case lawyers differ in their interpretation of law, should the law be suspended. Possibility of different interpretations is a sign of maturity and dynamism. The secret of progress and development lies in constructive disagreement, critical views and an ongoing educative process through intellectual interaction. If we stop people from disagreeing on various issues, we may create worse kind of a totalitarian society or a "secular theocracy". Islam rejects this exclusivist approach of the secularists and wants its followers to interpret the Qur'ān and the Sunnah, with proper tools, in order to find solutions for emerging problems in a growing and developing socio-political order. Since scriptural texts are interpreted with the help of a scientifically developed methodology, which makes use of lexicography, external and internal criticism, understanding the context, identification of the core and the periphery, the cause ('illah) and the wisdom (ḥikmah), specific and general and so on, the textual study provides a variety of possible applications in solution of emerging problems. This process is dynamic and not static. It is progressive and not retrogressive. It is modern and futuristic and not backward and conservative.

Return to the scriptural foundations in the West, on the contrary, has a different hermeneutical history. The Jewish and Christian fundamentalists are known for their return to scriptural foundations in the name of literalism and fundamentalism. The doctrine of the inerrancy of the Bible led to literal application; consequently no rational, critical analyses of the Bible was allowed by those who called for going back to the Bible.

In the Islamic framework, the whole enterprise is different. The call for going back to the Qur'ān whether by Ibn Taymiyah

(1263-1328) or Iqbal and Mawdūdī simply means liberatir Muslim mind from the traditional corpus of law "fiqh wa al Ç and conduct of fresh interpretation of the texts of the Qur' the Sunnah in order to address modern and contemporary issues through ijtihād. As a methodology, it is not to be confused with imitation and adoption of Western secular culture and law in the name of modernity, post-modernity or enlightenment. It stands for use of professional skills in discerning the intent and purpose of the manifest and implied legal commands, directions and teachings of the Qur'ān and the Sunnah and discovering their relevance and application in an emergent situations. It is not a free lance, personal opinion but a professional exercise of reasoned judgment founded on the two non-variable principles namely the Qur'ān and the Sunnah. The process being dynamic leads to an ever-expanding meaning of the same text. While the text remains non-variable, concentration on its meaning should reveal new dimensions.

Mawdūdī, like Ibn Taymiyah, is concerned with the institution of the state and the supremacy of the Islamic Sharī'ah. The caliphate for him provides an historical model, successfully exercised in Madinah. He wants to capture the spirit of this ideal and glorious period, in order to evolve a new and modern setup, with Sharī'ah as its source of inspiration. The use of the term Madīnah as the model of a viable Islamic state never stand for a literal reproduction of society and state as it once was. On the other hand, it means learning from this experience while using most modern available means for the development of a Sharī'ah-based political order capable of meeting the problems of our time and translating their eternal and universal values into contemporary idiom and context. It is the technology of the times, which is to be harnessed in the service of principles and values, therein lie the dynamism of the Islamic model.

The lesson from the Madīnah model is that the most efficient means of the age have to be harnessed to better the statecraft. We need to capture its spirit and make our system more efficient in order to follow the model of al-Khulafā al-Rāshidīn. A warning, however, is needed in areas where the Qur'ān and the Sunnah are specific; there is no scope of wild interpretations in the name of modernity and innovation. Ijtihād is a dynamic process aimed at discerning guidance from the Qur'ān and the Sunnah to reach solutions for modern problems, not to subvert its teachings to pander to modernity whims.

Some secularists also assert that the state is not supposed to make a people pious and ethical; it is the individual conviction, which makes a people moral. The problem with this approach, in our view, is twofold. First, it does not elaborate what it means by piety. Even if piety for some means wearing a specific kind of dress or speaking in a civil tone, state does have a role in it. If piety means observance of ethical conduct in economy, political policies, educational system, cultural activities, social relations and everyday transactions, then state cannot leave these matters for the individual judgment.

If state has no role or authority in policy-making on economic, educational, cultural and social matters, society shall end up in a state of anarchy. This does not reduce the importance of personal piety and individual conscience. Nevertheless, family, education, society and state are the four stakeholders, which have equal importance in building an ethical vision and moral conduct and behaviour of citizens. That is why the Qur'ān makes state responsible for ensuring implementation of ethical and moral measures (ma'rūf) in economy, in family, and application of justice ('adl) and equity in social, economic, political and legal matters.

The concept that "religion" is a personal relationship between a person and his or her God is not new either. This was common among the Greek, Romans, Indians, and the Jewish and Christian religious traditions. Islam is perhaps the only faith, which has taken a social approach and not an individual-centred approach of one's salvation. Piety, birr (goodness) and taqwa (Allah-consciousness), while intensely personal and of internalized nature, have a distinct and quantifiable manifestation in human behaviour. To that extent, they represent measurable, behavioural social categories and not confined to an individual heart. "Righteousness does not consist in turning your face toward the East or the West. True righteousness consists in believing in Allah and the Last Day, the Angels, the Book and the Prophets and in giving away one's property in love of Him to one's relatives, the orphans, the poor, and the wayfarer, and to those who ask for help, and in freeing the necks of slaves and in establishing prayer and dispersing Zakāh. True righteousness is attained by those who are faithful in their promise once they have made it and by those who remain steadfast in adversity and affliction, and at the time of battle (between truth and falsehood). Such are the truthful ones, such are the Allah fearing". (*al-Baqarah* 2:177). This Qur'ānic definition of what is virtue, righteousness and moral conduct (taqwā), not only specifies its nature but also provides a scale and measure for quantification and quality assurance of human behaviour and conduct. It is not true with reference to Islam, to say that virtue and ethical attitudes is something abstract, invisible, non-measurable and non-tangible. Individual as much as civil society and state are responsible for establishment of an ethical and moral social order embodying virtue and righteousness at individual and collective levels.

If state policies do not take care of contracts and promises it makes, if it does not take care of minimizing the gap between those who have and those who have not, if it does not use the same scale in dispensing justice to the poor and the rich, the polity becomes a mockery. The state, the society as well as the individual are to share in the burden, of immorality and unethical behaviour. Therefore, in the context of Islamic morality, "religious" values are not a domain of the individual alone nor relative and left to the personal will of an individual and his or her motivation. State and society have legal, constitutional, and moral obligations to make sure that good (ma'rūf) prevails and evil and excess (munkar) are eradicated from state, society and individual's behaviour. State is a major player in implementing Islamic moral norms, laws and values in society as stated very clearly in the Qur'ān "Those if We give them authority in land would establish Ṣalāh (prayers), Zakāh (poor-due) and enjoin what is good and forbid what is wrong..."
(*al-Ḥajj 22: 41*).

State in the Islamic thought, therefore, is not value neutral, neither secular nor theocratic. It is morality-centered, not situational or relativistic but representative of universal values of justice, peace, equity, fraternity, coherence or in the single term *tawhīdi*. The foundational role of shūrā (mutual consultation) or interactive decision-making does not allow state to turn into kingship. It does not welcome conservatism, dogmatism, kingship, and authoritarianism. It has the potential to address socioeconomic problems humanity is facing today.

Khilāfat wa Malūkiyat, is more than a systematic treatment of the issue from a historical critical view point: it is an exercise in discovering Islamic foundations of a modern democratic order. Mawdūdi is critical of the so-called classical and glorious periods of the Umayyad, 'Abbasid, Fātimīd, Mamlūk, 'Uthmāniyah or even Mughal periods and consider them as a clear violation of the political norms of the Qur'ān and the Sunnah. To him, mulūkīyah is a deviation from the historical paradigm of the Khilāfah al-Rāshidah. This makes him a champion of an Islamic political order, which he calls as "theo-democracy."

Striking at the very roots of dictatorial and hereditary monarchical systems, Mawdūdi addresses the core issue of the real source of political authority. In the Western secular democratic model, the electoral college, at a hypothetical level, enjoys ultimate authority. In Islamic framework of thought, the doctrine of tawhīd (monotheism) implies that the real sovereign is Allah. People are the instrument for the realization of the Islamic ethical and political values. They have to seek guidance from these primary sources in the development of modern solutions, legislature, and strategic need to respond to change.

While kingship represents concentration of power in a person, Islamic political order empowers morality and law for the realization of peace, harmony and justice in society. Sharī'ah (divine commands) should not be confused with the corpus of Islamic law, developed in different periods by the jurists (fuqahā) and proclaimed as law of land in various parts of the world. Islamic political order is founded, as underscored by Mawdūdi, on the Qur'ānic principle of sh*ūrā*, ijm*ā*' and ijtih*ā*d through an ongoing interaction at different levels in society. The will and aspirations of the people interact with the guiding principles of the Sharī'ah in order to improvise viable solutions needed for development, progress and sustainability of a society.

His concept of al-Khilāfah appears at variance with the historical view of the caliphate put forth by Rashid Ridā or Abdul Kalām and others. His concept of popular caliphate focuses on a dynamic role of the people, elected representatives and legislators in creation of a just and moral social order. This fresh approach of power sharing by the competent and capable persons focuses on qualitative aspects of the political order and transcends the quantitative character of secular democratic order.

Khilāfat wa Malūkiyat paves the way for a representative political order wherein supremacy of law, norms, and values prevails over the classical Greek or even modern Western view of the simple majority rule.

Misconceptions about the Islamic state develop when intellectuals try to read in the Muslim history clash and conflict, which existed in the European Christian context. They try to discover imaginary conflict between religious and secular, sacred and profane in Islam while this dichotomy is non-existent in the case of Islam.

In conclusion, we can say that kingship (mulūkīyah)[24] or dictatorships are alien concepts in Islam. Islamic state is neither theocracy nor secular democracy. It has its own norms and values, which invalidate separation between state and "religion" or between the sacred and profane. It is not a reproduction of the so-called 'Abbasid or Umayyad rulers. Islamic state stands for a shūrāwi (consultative), ādil (just), and an ethical sociopolitical order of its own.

---

24 Al-Dhahabi, *Manāqib*, p. 30.

Chapter One

The Political Teachings of the Qur'ān

1. The worldview

To understand the polity the Qur'ān creates, it is import to reflect on how it visualizes the universe from the perspective of political philosophy. This should give us the following points:

a) Allah the Exalted is the Creator of this whole universe including humans and the natural resources humans make use of in this world.

وَهُوَ الَّذِي خَلَقَ السَّمَاوَاتِ وَالأَرْضَ بِالْحَقِّ

And He it is who has created the heavens and the earth in truth.
(al-Anʿām 6:73)

قُلِ اللهُ خَالِقُ كُلِّ شَيْءٍ وَهُوَ الْوَاحِدُ الْقَهَّارُ

Say: "Allah is the creator of everything. He is the One, the Irresistible."
(al-Raʿd 13:16)

يَا أَيُّهَا النَّاسُ اتَّقُواْ رَبَّكُمُ الَّذِى خَلَقَكُم مِّنْ نَّفْسٍ وَّاحِدَةٍ وَّخَلَقَ مِنْهَا
زَوْجَهَا وَبَثَّ مِنْهُمَا رِجَالاً كَثِيرًا وَّنِسَآءً

O people! Fear your Lord Who created you from a single being and out of it created its mate; and out of the two spread many men and women. Fear Allah in Whose name you plead for rights, and heed the ties of kinship. Surely, Allah is ever watchful over you.
(al-Nisā' 4:1)

هُوَ الَّذِى خَلَقَ لَكُمْ مَّا فِى الأَرْضِ جَمِيعاً

It is He who has created for you all that is on earth.
(al-Baqarah 2:29)

هَلْ مِنْ خَالِقٍ غَيْرُ اللهِ يَرْزُقُكُم مِّنَ السَّمَآءِ وَالْأَرْضِ

Is there any Creator, apart from Allah, Who provides you're your sustenance out of the heavens and earth?
(*Fāṭir 35:3*)

أَفَرَأَيْتُم مَّا تُمْنُونَ. أَأَنْتُمْ تَخْلُقُونَهُ أَمْ نَحْنُ الْخَالِقُونَ. نَحْنُ قَدَّرْنَا بَيْنَكُمُ الْمَوْتَ
وَمَا نَحْنُ بِمَسْبُوقِينَ. عَلَى أَن نُّبَدِّلَ أَمْثَالَكُمْ وَنُنشِئَكُمْ فِي مَا لَا تَعْلَمُونَ.
وَلَقَدْ عَلِمْتُمُ النَّشْأَةَ الْأُولَى فَلَوْلَا تَذَكَّرُونَ. أَفَرَأَيْتُم مَّا تَحْرُثُونَ. أَأَنتُمْ تَزْرَعُونَهُ
أَمْ نَحْنُ الزَّارِعُونَ. لَوْ نَشَاءُ لَجَعَلْنَاهُ حُطَامًا فَظَلْتُمْ تَفَكَّهُونَ. إِنَّا لَمُغْرَمُونَ.
بَلْ نَحْنُ مَحْرُومُونَ. أَفَرَأَيْتُمُ الْمَاءَ الَّذِي تَشْرَبُونَ. أَأَنتُمْ أَنزَلْتُمُوهُ مِنَ الْمُزْنِ
أَمْ نَحْنُ الْمُنزِلُونَ. لَوْ نَشَاءُ جَعَلْنَاهُ أُجَاجًا فَلَوْلَا تَشْكُرُونَ. أَفَرَأَيْتُمُ النَّارَ
الَّتِي تُورُونَ. أَأَنتُمْ أَنشَأْتُمْ شَجَرَتَهَا أَمْ نَحْنُ الْمُنشِؤُونَ.

Did you ever consider the sperm that you emit?
Do you create a child out of it, or are We its Creators?
It is We Who ordained death upon you and We are not to be frustrated.
Had We so wished, nothing could have hindered Us from replacing you by others like yourselves, or transforming you into beings you know nothing about.
You are well aware of the first creation; then, do you learn no lesson from it?
Have you considered the seeds you till?
Is it you or We Who makes them grow?
If We so wished, We could have reduced your harvest to rubble, and you would have been left wonder-struck to exclaim: "We have been penalized; nay; we have been undone!"
Did you cast a good look at the water that you

drink?
Is it you who brought it down from the clouds or is it We Who brought it down?
If We had so pleased, We could have made it bitter. So why do you not give thanks?
Did you consider the fire that you kindle?
Did you make its tree grow or was it We Who made it grow?
(al-Wāqi'ah 56:58-72)

b) Allah is the Creator of His creation, Sovereign and the Controller.

لَهُ مَا فِي السَّمَاوَاتِ وَمَا فِي الْأَرْضِ وَمَا بَيْنَهُمَا وَمَا تَحْتَ الثَّرَى.

To Him belongs all that is in the heavens and all that is in the earth, and all that is in between, and all beneath the soil.
(Ṭā-Hā 20 :6)

وَلَهُ مَن فِي السَّمَاوَاتِ وَالْأَرْضِ كُلٌّ لَّهُ قَٰنِتُونَ.

To Him belongs all who are in the heavens and all who are on the earth: All are in obedience to Him.
(*al-Rūm 30:26*)

وَالشَّمْسَ وَالْقَمَرَ وَالنُّجُومَ مُسَخَّرَاتٍ بِأَمْرِهِ، أَلاَ لَهُ الْخَلْقُ وَالأَمْرُ، تَبَارَكَ اللَّهُ رَبُّ الْعَالَمِينَ.

Who created the sun, and the moon, and the stars, making them all subservient to His command? Lo! His is the creation and His is the command. Blessed is Allah, the Lord of the whole Universe.
(*al-A'rāf 7:54*)

يُدَبِّرُ الْأَمْرَ مِنَ السَّمَآءِ إِلَى الْأَرْضِ.

He governs from the heavens to the earth.
(al-Sajdah 32:5)

c) To none but Allah belongs the sovereignty of this universe; there is none to share His powers.

أَلَمْ تَعْلَمْ أَنَّ اللّٰهَ لَهُ مُلْكُ السَّمَاوَاتِ وَالأَرْضِ

Are you not aware that the dominion of the heavens and the earth belongs to Allah.
(al-Baqarah 2:107)

وَلَمْ يَكُن لَّهُ شَرِيكٌ فِي الْمُلْكِ

Nor has taken any partner in His kingdom.
(al-Furqān 25:2)

لَهُ الْحَمْدُ فِى الْأُولَى وَالْآخِرَةِ وَلَهُ الْحُكْمُ وَإِلَيْهِ تُرْجَعُونَ۔

His is the Praise in this world and in the Hereafter. His is the Command and to Him will all of you be returned.
(al-Qaṣaṣ 28:70)

إِنِ الْحُكْمُ إِلَّا لِلّٰهِ۔

Judgement lies with Allah alone.
(al-An'ām 6:57)

مَا لَهُم مِّنْ دُونِهِ مِنْ وَّلِيٍّ وَلَا يُشْرِكُ فِى حُكْمِهِ أَحَدًا.

The creatures have no other guardian than Him; He allows none to share His authority.
(al-Kahf 18:26)

يَقُولُونَ هَل لَّنَا مِنَ الأَمْرِ مِن شَيْءٍ، قُلْ إِنَّ الأَمْرَ كُلَّهُ لِلّٰهِ.

Tell them: "Truly, all power of decision rests solely with Allah.
(āl 'Imrān 3:154)

لِلّٰهِ الْأَمْرُ مِن قَبْلُ وَمِن بَعْدُ.

All power belongs to Allah both before and after.
(al-Rūm 30:4)

لَهُ مُلْكُ السَّمَاوَاتِ وَالْأَرْضِ وَإِلَى اللهِ تُرْجَعُ الْأُمُورُ.

His is the dominion of the heavens and the earth, and to Him are all matters referred (for judgment).
(al-Ḥadīd 57: 5)

أَفَمَن يَخْلُقُ كَمَن لَّا يَخْلُقُ أَفَلا تَذَكَّرُونَ.

Is then the One Who creates like one who does not create? Will you not, then, take heed?
(al-Nahl 16:17)

أَمْ جَعَلُوا لِلّهِ شُرَكَاء خَلَقُوا كَخَلْقِهِ فَتَشَابَهَ الْخَلْقُ عَلَيْهِمْ.

Then have those whom they associate with Allah in His Divinity ever created anything like Allah did?
(al-Ra'd 13:16)

قُلْ أَرَأَيْتُمْ شُرَكَاءَكُمُ الَّذِينَ تَدْعُونَ مِن دُونِ اللهِ، أَرُونِي مَاذَا خَلَقُوا مِنَ الْأَرْضِ أَمْ لَهُمْ شِرْكٌ فِي السَّمَاوَاتِ، أَمْ آتَيْنَاهُمْ كِتَابًا فَهُمْ عَلَى بَيِّنَةٍ مِّنْهُ بَلْ إِنْ يَّعِدُ الظَّالِمُونَ بَعْضُهُم بَعْضًا إِلَّا غُرُورًا. إِنَّ اللهَ يُمْسِكُ السَّمَاوَاتِ وَالْأَرْضَ أَن تَزُولَا، وَلَئِن زَالَتَا إِنْ أَمْسَكَهُمَا مِنْ أَحَدٍ مِّن بَعْدِهِ إِنَّهُ كَانَ حَلِيمًا غَفُورًا.

Say to them (O Prophet): "Have you ever seen those of your associates upon whom you call apart from Allah? Show me, what have they created in the earth? Or do they have any partnership (with Allah) in the heavens? Or have We given them a Book so that they have a clear proof (for associating others with Allah in His Divinity)?" Nay, what these wrong-doers promise each other is nothing but delusion.

Surely Allah holds the heavens and the earth, lest they should be displaced there, for if they were displaced none would be able to hold them after Him. Surely, He is Most Forbearing, Most Forgiving.
(Fāṭir 35:40-41)

d) All attributes of sovereignty and powers are vested in Allah; there is none to share them in this universe: He alone overpowers everything. Free from deficiency and error, He is conscious of every moment. None can dare go out of His dominion and control; cause and consequence flow from Him; none but He can cause hurt or give profit. Without His authorization – nothing happens. Nor anyone without His permission can plead for any person. He can punish and forgive anyone. He is answerable to no one. His decree is non-stoppable; nobody can ward it off. All these attributes of power are His alone.

وَهُوَ الْقَاهِرُ فَوْقَ عِبَادِهِ وَهُوَ الْحَكِيمُ الْخَبِيرُ.

He has the supreme hold over His servants. He is All-Wise, All-Aware.
(al-An'ām 6:18)

عَالِمُ الْغَيْبِ وَالشَّهَادَةِ الْكَبِيرُ الْمُتَعَالِ.

He knows both what is hidden and what is manifest. He is the Supreme One, the Most High.
(al-Ra'd 13:9)

الْمَلِكُ الْقُدُّوسُ السَّلَامُ الْمُؤْمِنُ الْمُهَيْمِنُ الْعَزِيزُ الْجَبَّارُ الْمُتَكَبِّرُ.

He: the Kind, the Holy, the All-Peace, the Giver of security, the Overseer, the Most Mighty, the Overpowering.
(al-Ḥashr 59:23)

الْحَيُّ الْقَيُّومُ لَا تَأْخُذُهُ سِنَةٌ وَلَا نَوْمٌ، لَهُ مَا فِي السَّمَاوَاتِ وَمَا فِي الْأَرْضِ،

مَن ذَا الَّذِي يَشْفَعُ عِنْدَهُ إِلاَّ بِإِذْنِهِ، يَعْلَمُ مَا بَيْنَ أَيْدِيهِمْ وَمَا خَلْفَهُمْ.

(Allah) Ever-Living, the Self-subsisting by Whom all subsist, there is no God but He. Neither slumber seizes Him, nor sleep; to Him belongs all that is in the heavens and all that is in the earth. Who is there who might intercede with Him save with His leave? He knows what lies before them and what is hidden from them.
(al-Baqarah 2:255)

تَبَارَكَ الَّذِي بِيَدِهِ الْمُلْكُ وَهُوَ عَلَى كُلِّ شَيْءٍ قَدِيرٌ.

Blessed is He in whose Hand is the dominion of the Universe, and Who has power over everything.
(al-Mulk 67:1)

بِيَدِهِ مَلَكُوتُ كُلِّ شَيْءٍ وَإِلَيْهِ تُرْجَعُونَ.-

Holy is He Who has full control over everything, and to Him you shall all be recalled.
(Yā Sīn 36:83)

وَلَهُ أَسْلَمَ مَن فِي السَّمَاوَاتِ وَالأَرْضِ طَوْعًا وَكَرْهًا.

...all that is in the heavens and the earth is in submission to Him — willingly or unwilling.
(āl 'Imrān 3:83)

إِنَّ الْعِزَّةَ لِلّٰهِ جَمِيعًا هُوَ السَّمِيعُ الْعَلِيمُ.

Indeed all honour is Allah's He is All-Hearing, All-Knowing.
(Yūnus 10:65)

قُلْ فَمَن يَمْلِكُ لَكُم مِّنَ اللهِ شَيْئًا إِنْ أَرَادَ بِكُمْ ضَرًّا أَوْ أَرَادَ بِكُمْ نَفْعًا.

Say to them: "Who can be of any avail to you against Allah if He should intend to cause you any harm or confer upon you any benefit?
(al-Fatḥ 48:11)

وَإِن يَمْسَسْكَ اللّٰهُ بِضُرٍّ فَلاَ كَاشِفَ لَهُ إِلاَّ هُوَ وَإِن يُرِدْكَ بِخَيْرٍ فَلاَ رَآدَّ لِفَضْلِهِ يُصَيبُ بِهِ مَن يَشَاء مِنْ عِبَادِهِ وَهُوَ الْغَفُورُ الرَّحِيمُ.

If Allah afflicts you with any hardship, none other than He can remove it: and if He wills any good for you none can aver His Bounty. He bestows good upon whomsoever of His servants He wills. He is All-Forgiving, All-Merciful.
(Yūnus 10:107)

وَإِن تُبْدُواْ مَا فِي أَنفُسِكُمْ أَوْ تُخْفُوهُ يُحَاسِبْكُمْ بِهِ اللّٰه، فَيَغْفِرُ لِمَن يَشَاء وَيُعَذِّبُ مَن يَشَاء وَاللّٰهُ عَلَى كُلِّ شَيْءٍ قَدِيرٌ.

Whether you disclose whatever is in your hearts or conceal it, Allah will call you to account for it and will then forgives whomsoever He wills, and chastise whomsoever He wills. Allah has power over everything.
(al-Baqarah 2:284)

أَبْصِرْ بِهِ وَأَسْمِعْ، مَا لَهُم مِّن دُونِهِ مِن وَلِيٍّ وَلَا يُشْرِكُ فِي حُكْمِهِ أَحَدًا.

How well He sees; how well He hearts! The creatures have no other guardian than Him; He allows none to share His authority.
(al-Kahf 18:26)

قُلْ إِنِّي لَن يُجِيرَنِي مِنَ اللهِ أَحَدٌ وَلَنْ أَجِدَ مِن دُونِهِ مُلْتَحَدًا.

Say: "None can protect me from Allah, nor can I find a refuge apart from Him.
(al-Jinn 72:22)

وَهُوَ يُجِيرُ وَلَا يُجَارُ عَلَيْهِ.

(who is it) that grants asylum, but against Whom no asylum is available?
(al-Mu'minūn 23:88)

إِنَّهُ هُوَ يُبْدِئُ وَيُعِيدُ. وَهُوَ الْغَفُورُ الْوَدُودُ. ذُو الْعَرْشِ الْمَجِيدُ. فَعَّالٌ لِّمَا يُرِيدُ.

He it is Who creates for the first time and He it is Who will create against, and He is the Ever-Forging, the Most Loving — the Lord of the Glorious Throne, the Executor of what He wills.
(al-Burūj 85:13-16)

إِنَّ اللّٰهَ يَحْكُمُ مَا يُرِيدُ.

Indeed Allah decrees as He wills.
(al-Mā'idah 5:1)

وَاللّٰهُ يَحْكُمُ لَا مُعَقِّبَ لِحُكْمِهِ۔

Allah judges and no one has the power to reverse His judgement.
(al-Ra'd 13:41)

لَا يُسْئَلُ عَمَّا يَفْعَلُ وَهُمْ يُسْأَلُونَ.

None shall question Him about what He does, but they shall be questioned.
(al-Anbiyā 21:23)

لَا مُبَدِّلَ لِكَلِمَاتِهِ وَلَن تَجِدَ مِن دُونِهِ مُلْتَحَدًا.

For none may change His words; (and were you to make any change in His words) you will find no refuge from Him.
(al-Kahf 18:27)

أَلَيْسَ اللّٰهُ بِأَحْكَمِ الْحَاكِمِينَ

Is not Allah the Greatest of all sovereigns?
(al-Tīn 95:8)

قُلِ اللَّهُمَّ مَالِكَ الْمُلْكِ تُؤْتِي الْمُلْكَ مَن تَشَاءُ وَتَنزِعُ الْمُلْكَ مِمَّن تَشَاءُ وَتُعِزُّ
مَن تَشَاءُ وَتُذِلُّ مَن تَشَاءُ بِيَدِكَ الْخَيْرُ إِنَّكَ عَلَىٰ كُلِّ شَيْءٍ قَدِيرٌ.

Say: "O Allah, Lord of all dominion! You bestow dominion on whomever You please, and take away dominion from whomever You please, and You exalt whom You please, and abase whom You please, In Your Hands is all good, Surely, You are All-Powerful.
(āl 'Imrān 3:26)

إِنَّ الْأَرْضَ لِلَّهِ يُورِثُهَا مَن يَشَاءُ مِنْ عِبَادِهِ.

The earth is Allah's, He bestows it on those of His servants He chooses.
(al-A'rāf 7:128)

2. The divine governance

Primed by this concept of the universe, the Qur'ān says that the real sovereign of humanity is the same who is the master of the universe and runs its affairs. Because of it, He alone qualifies to rule humans; decree is His and none else's. The difference, however, is that in the universe He enforces His will and calls for no acknowledgement from anyone. Even humans in their unwilled spheres of life (like the physiological functioning of their bodies) are subject to His will as are the particles of matter from the earth to galaxies. In the self-willed sphere of human life He does not enforce His sovereign writ but through revealed books. The last of them is the Qur'ān, which calls them to accept His sovereign will. The Qur'ān has dealt with this subject thoroughly at different places.

a) That the Lord of the universe is the real Lord of humanity and He alone should be accepted as one who creates and nourishes everything (al-Rabb):

قُلْ إِنَّ صَلاَتِي وَنُسُكِي وَمَحْيَايَ وَمَمَاتِي لِلّهِ رَبِّ الْعَالَمِينَ. لاَ شَرِيكَ لَهُ وَبِذَلِكَ أُمِرْتُ وَأَنَاْ أَوَّلُ الْمُسْلِمِينَ. قُلْ أَغَيْرَ اللّهِ أَبْغِي رَبًّا وَهُوَ رَبُّ كُلِّ شَيْءٍ وَلاَ تَكْسِبُ كُلُّ نَفْسٍ إِلاَّ عَلَيْهَا وَلاَ تَزِرُ وَازِرَةٌ وِزْرَ أُخْرَى ثُمَّ إِلَى رَبِّكُم مَّرْجِعُكُمْ فَيُنَبِّئُكُم بِمَا كُنتُمْ فِيهِ تَخْتَلِفُونَ.

Say: "Surely my Prayer, all my acts of worship, and my living and my dying are only for Allah, the Lord of the whole Universe.
He has no associate. Thus have I been bidden, and I am the foremost of those who submit themselves (to Allah)."
Say: "Shall I seek someone other than Allah as Lord when He is the Lord of everything?"
Everyone will bear the consequence of what he does, and no one shall bear the burden of another.
(al-An'ām 6:162-164)

إِنَّ رَبَّكُمُ اللّهُ الَّذِي خَلَقَ السَّمَاوَاتِ وَالأَرْضَ

Surely, your Lord is none other than Allah, Who created the heavens and the earth.
(al-A'rāf 7:54)

قُلْ أَعُوذُ بِرَبِّ النَّاسِ. مَلِكِ النَّاسِ. إِلَهِ النَّاسِ.

Say, "I seek refuge with the Lord of mankind; the King of mankind, The True God of mankind.
(al-Nās 114:1-3)

قُلْ مَن يَرْزُقُكُم مِّنَ السَّمَآءِ وَالأَرْضِ أَمَّن يَمْلِكُ السَّمْعَ والأَبْصَارَ وَمَن يُخْرِجُ الْحَيَّ مِنَ الْمَيِّتِ وَيُخْرِجُ الْمَيَّتَ مِنَ الْحَيِّ وَمَن يُدَبِّرُ الأَمْرَ، فَسَيَقُولُونَ اللّهُ فَقُلْ أَفَلاَ تَتَّقُونَ. فَذَلِكُمُ اللّهُ رَبُّكُمُ الْحَقُّ فَمَاذَا بَعْدَ الْحَقِّ إِلاَّ الضَّلاَلُ فَأَنَّى تُصْرَفُونَ.

Ask them: "Who provides you with sustenance out of the heavens and the earth? Who holds mastery over your hearing and sight? Who brings forth the living from the death and the

death from the living? Who governs all affairs of the Universe? They will surely say: "Allah." Tell them: "Will you, then, not shun (going against reality)? Such, then, is Allah, your true Lord. And what is there after Truth but error? How, then, are you being turned away?
(Yūnus 10:31-32)

وَمَا اخْتَلَفْتُمْ فِيهِ مِن شَيْءٍ فَحُكْمُهُ إِلَى اللهِ.

The judgment on whatever you differ rests with Allah.
(al-Shūrā 42:10)

إِنِ الْحُكْمُ إِلَّا لِلهِ، أَمَرَ أَلَّا تَعْبُدُواْ إِلَّا إِيَّاهُ، ذَلِكَ الدِّينُ الْقَيِّمُ وَلَكِنَّ أَكْثَرَ النَّاسِ لاَ يَعْلَمُونَ.

He has command that you serve none but Him. This is the right way of life, though most people are altogether unaware.
(Yūsuf 12:40)

يَقُولُونَ هَل لَّنَا مِنَ الأَمْرِ مِن شَيْءٍ قُلْ إِنَّ الأَمْرَ كُلَّهُ لِلهِ.

They ask: "Have we any say in the matter? Tell Them: Truly, all power of decision rests solely with Allah.
(āl 'Imrān 3:154)

أَلاَ لَهُ الْخَلْقُ وَالأَمْرُ.

Lo! His is the creation and His is the command.
(al-A'rāf 7:54)

وَالسَّارِقُ وَالسَّارِقَةُ فَاقْطَعُواْ أَيْدِيَهُمَا جَزَاء بِمَا كَسَبَا نَكَالاً مِّنَ اللهِ وَاللهُ عَزِيزٌ حَكِيمٌ. فَمَن تَابَ مِن بَعْدِ ظُلْمِهِ وَأَصْلَحَ فَإِنَّ اللهَ يَتُوبُ عَلَيْهِ إِنَّ اللهَ غَفُورٌ رَّحِيمٌ. أَلَمْ تَعْلَمْ أَنَّ اللهَ لَهُ مُلْكُ السَّمَاوَاتِ وَالأَرْضِ يُعَذِّبُ مَن يَشَاء وَيَغْفِرُ لِمَن يَشَاء وَاللهُ عَلَى كُلِّ شَيْءٍ قَدِيرٌ.

As for the thief – male or female, cut off hands

of both. This is a recompense for what they have done, and an exemplary punishment from Allah. Allah is all- Mighty, all-Wisdom. But he who repents after he has committed wrong, and makes amends, Allah will graciously turn to him. Truly, Allah is all-Forgiving, all-Compassion.
Do you not know that to Allah belongs the dominion of the heavens and the earth? He chastises whom He wills and forgives whom He wills. Allah is all-Powerful.
(al-Mā'idah 5:38-40)

عَسَى أَنْ تَكْرَهُواْ شَيْئًا وَهُوَ خَيْرٌ لَّكُمْ وَعَسَى أَن تُحِبُّواْ شَيْئًا وَهُوَ شَرٌّ لَّكُمْ وَاللّهُ يَعْلَمُ وَأَنتُمْ لاَ تَعْلَمُونَ.

And it is disliked by you; it may well be that you dislike a thing even though it is good for you, and it may well be that you like a thing even though it is bad for you. Allah knows and you do not know.
(al-Baqarah 2:216)

وَاللّهُ يَعْلَمُ الْمُفْسِدَ مِنَ الْمُصْلِحِ.

Allah knows the mischievous from the righteous, and had Allah willed, He would indeed have imposed on you exacting conditions; but He is All-Powerful, Most Wise.
(al-Baqarah 2:220)

يَعْلَمُ مَا بَيْنَ أَيْدِيهِمْ وَمَا خَلْفَهُمْ وَلاَ يُحِيطُونَ بِشَيْءٍ مِّنْ عِلْمِهِ إِلاَّ بِمَا شَاءَ.

He knows what lies before them and what is hidden from them, whereas they cannot attain to anything of His knowledge save what He wills them to attain.
(al-Baqarah 2:255)

وَإِذَا طَلَّقْتُمُ النِّسَاء فَبَلَغْنَ أَجَلَهُنَّ فَلاَ تَعْضُلُوهُنَّ أَنْ يَنْكِحْنَ أَزْوَاجَهُنَّ

إِذَا تَرَاضَوْا بَيْنَهُم بِالْمَعْرُوفِ، ذَٰلِكَ يُوعَظُ بِهِ مَن كَانَ مِنكُمْ يُؤْمِنُ بِاللَّهِ وَالْيَوْمِ الْآخِرِ ذَٰلِكُمْ أَزْكَىٰ لَكُمْ وَأَطْهَرُ وَاللَّهُ يَعْلَمُ وَأَنتُمْ لَا تَعْلَمُونَ.

When you divorce women and they complete their waiting term, do not hinder them from marrying other men if they have agreed to this in a fair manner. That is an admonition to everyone of you who believes in Allah and the Last Day; that is a cleaner and purer way for you. For Allah knows whereas you do not know.
(al-Baqarah 2:232)

يُوصِيكُمُ اللَّهُ فِي أَوْلَادِكُمْ لِلذَّكَرِ مِثْلُ حَظِّ الْأُنثَيَيْنِ، فَإِن كُنَّ نِسَاءً فَوْقَ اثْنَتَيْنِ فَلَهُنَّ ثُلُثَا مَا تَرَكَ، وَإِن كَانَتْ وَاحِدَةً فَلَهَا النِّصْفُ وَلِأَبَوَيْهِ لِكُلِّ وَاحِدٍ مِّنْهُمَا السُّدُسُ مِمَّا تَرَكَ إِن كَانَ لَهُ وَلَدٌ، فَإِن لَّمْ يَكُن لَّهُ وَلَدٌ وَوَرِثَهُ أَبَوَاهُ فَلِأُمِّهِ الثُّلُثُ، فَإِن كَانَ لَهُ إِخْوَةٌ فَلِأُمِّهِ السُّدُسُ مِن بَعْدِ وَصِيَّةٍ يُوصِي بِهَا أَوْ دَيْنٍ، آبَاؤُكُمْ وَأَبْنَاؤُكُمْ لَا تَدْرُونَ أَيُّهُمْ أَقْرَبُ لَكُمْ نَفْعًا، فَرِيضَةً مِّنَ اللَّهِ إِنَّ اللَّهَ كَانَ عَلِيمًا حَكِيمًا.

Thus, does Allah command you concerning your children: the share of the male is like that of two females. If (the heirs of the deceased are) more than two daughters, they shall have two-thirds of the inheritance, and if there is only one daughter, she shall have half the inheritance. If the deceased has any offspring, each of his parents shall have a sixth of the inheritance; and if the deceased has no child and his parents alone inherit him, then one-third shall go to his mother; and if the deceased has brothers and sisters, then one-sixth shall go to his mother. All these shares are to be given after payment of the bequest he might have made or any debts outstanding against him. You do not know which of them, your parents or your children, are more beneficial to you. But these portions have been determined by Allah, for He indeed knows everything, is

cognizant of all beneficent considerations.
(al-Nisā' 4:11)

يَسْتَفْتُونَكَ، قُلِ اللّٰهُ يُفْتِيكُمْ فِي الْكَلاَلَةِ، إِنِ امْرُؤٌ هَلَكَ لَيْسَ لَهُ وَلَدٌ وَلَهُ أُخْتٌ فَلَهَا نِصْفُ مَا تَرَكَ وَهُوَ يَرِثُهَآ إِن لَّمْ يَكُن لَّهَا وَلَدٌ، فَإِن كَانَتَا اثْنَتَيْنِ فَلَهُمَا الثُّلُثَانِ مِمَّا تَرَكَ وَإِن كَانُواْ إِخْوَةً رِّجَالاً وَنِسَاء فَلِلذَّكَرِ مِثْلُ حَظِّ الأُنثَيَيْنِ، يُبَيِّنُ اللّٰهُ لَكُمْ أَن تَضِلُّواْ وَاللّٰهُ بِكُلِّ شَيْءٍ عَلِيمٌ.

People ask you to pronounce a ruling concerning inheritance from those who have left behind no lineal heirs (*kalālah*). Say: "Allah pronounces for you the ruling: should be a man die childless but have a sister, she shall have one half of what he has left behind; and should the sister die childless, (but have a brother), he shall inherit her. And if the heirs are two sisters, they shall have two-third of what he has left behind. And if the heirs are two sisters and brothers, then the male shall have the share of two females. Allah makes (His commandments) clear to you lest you go astray. Allah has full knowledge of everything.
(al-Nisā 4:176)

وَأُوْلُواْ الأَرْحَامِ بَعْضُهُمْ أَوْلَى بِبَعْضٍ فِي كِتَابِ اللّٰهِ إِنَّ اللّٰهَ بِكُلِّ شَيْءٍ عَلِيمٌ.

But those related by blood are nearer to one another according to the Book of Allah. Allah has knowledge of everything.
(al-Anfāl 8:75)

إِنَّمَا الصَّدَقَاتُ لِلْفُقَرَاء وَالْمَسَاكِينِ وَالْعَامِلِينَ عَلَيْهَا وَالْمُؤَلَّفَةِ قُلُوبُهُمْ وَفِي الرِّقَابِ وَالْغَارِمِينَ وَفِي سَبِيلِ اللّٰهِ وَابْنِ السَّبِيلِ فَرِيضَةً مِّنَ اللّٰهِ وَاللّٰهُ عَلِيمٌ حَكِيمٌ.

The alms are meant only for the poor and the needy and those who are in charge thereof, those whose hearts are to be reconciled, and to free those in bondage, and to help those burdened with debt, and for expenditure in the

Way of Allah and for the wayfarer. This is an obligation from Allah. Allah is all- Knowing, all-Wisdom.
(al-Tawbah 9:60)

يَا أَيُّهَا الَّذِينَ آمَنُوا لِيَسْتَأْذِنكُمُ الَّذِينَ مَلَكَتْ أَيْمَانُكُمْ وَالَّذِينَ لَمْ يَبْلُغُوا الْحُلُمَ مِنكُمْ ثَلَاثَ مَرَّاتٍ، مِن قَبْلِ صَلَاةِ الْفَجْرِ وَحِينَ تَضَعُونَ ثِيَابَكُم مِّنَ الظَّهِيرَةِ وَمِن بَعْدِ صَلَاةِ الْعِشَاءِ، ثَلَاثُ عَوْرَاتٍ لَّكُمْ لَيْسَ عَلَيْكُمْ وَلَا عَلَيْهِمْ جُنَاحٌ بَعْدَهُنَّ، طَوَّافُونَ عَلَيْكُم بَعْضُكُمْ عَلَى بَعْضٍ كَذَلِكَ يُبَيِّنُ اللَّهُ لَكُمُ الْآيَاتِ وَاللَّهُ عَلِيمٌ حَكِيمٌ. وَإِذَا بَلَغَ الْأَطْفَالُ مِنكُمُ الْحُلُمَ فَلْيَسْتَأْذِنُوا كَمَا اسْتَأْذَنَ الَّذِينَ مِن قَبْلِهِمْ كَذَلِكَ يُبَيِّنُ اللَّهُ لَكُمْ آيَاتِهِ وَاللَّهُ عَلِيمٌ حَكِيمٌ.

Believers! At three times let those whom your right hands possess and those of your children who have not yet reached puberty ask leave of you before entering your quarters: before the Morning Prayer and when you take off your clothes at noon, and after the Night Prayer. These are the three times of privacy for you. If they come to you at other times then there is no sin for them nor for you, for you have to visit one another frequently. Thus does Allah clearly explain His directives to you. Allah is all-Knowing, all-Wisdom.
And when your children attain puberty let them ask leave to come to you like their elders used to ask leave. Thus does Allah clearly explain to you His signs. He is all-Knowing, all-Wisdom.
(al-Nūr 24:58-59)

يَا أَيُّهَا الَّذِينَ آمَنُوا إِذَا جَاءَكُمُ الْمُؤْمِنَاتُ مُهَاجِرَاتٍ فَامْتَحِنُوهُنَّ، اللَّهُ أَعْلَمُ بِإِيمَانِهِنَّ فَإِنْ عَلِمْتُمُوهُنَّ مُؤْمِنَاتٍ فَلَا تَرْجِعُوهُنَّ إِلَى الْكُفَّارِ، لَا هُنَّ حِلٌّ لَّهُمْ وَلَا هُمْ يَحِلُّونَ لَهُنَّ وَآتُوهُم مَّا أَنفَقُوا، وَلَا جُنَاحَ عَلَيْكُمْ أَن تَنكِحُوهُنَّ إِذَا آتَيْتُمُوهُنَّ أُجُورَهُنَّ وَلَا تُمْسِكُوا بِعِصَمِ الْكَوَافِرِ وَاسْأَلُوا مَا أَنفَقْتُمْ وَلْيَسْأَلُوا مَا أَنفَقُوا، ذَلِكُمْ حُكْمُ اللَّهِ يَحْكُمُ بَيْنَكُمْ وَاللَّهُ عَلِيمٌ حَكِيمٌ.

> Believers! When believing women come to you as Emigrants (in the cause of faith), examine them. Allah fully knows (the truth) concerning their faith. And when you have ascertained them to be believing women, do not send them back to the unbelievers. Those women are no longer lawful to the unbelievers, nor are those unbelievers lawful to those (believing) women. Give their unbelieving husbands whatever they have spent (as bridal-dues); and there is no offence for you to marry those women if you give them their bridal-dues. Do not hold on to your marriage with unbelieving women: as for the return of the bridal-due you gave to your unbelieving wives and the unbelievers may ask for the return of the bridal-due they had given to their believing wives. Such is Allah's command. He judges between you. Allah is all Knowing, most Wise.
> *(al-Mumtaḥinah 60:10)*

3. Allah's legal governance

For these reasons, the Qur'ān makes a decisive statement that people should obey Allah the Exalted and His laws followed. To leave Him and follow others or one's own self (nafs) is shirk (polytheism) and thus prohibited.

إِنَّا أَنْزَلْنَا إِلَيْكَ الْكِتَابَ بِالْحَقِّ فَاعْبُدِ اللهَ مُخْلِصًا لَّهُ الدِّينَ.

> (O prophet), it is We Who have revealed this Book to you with Truth. So serve only Allah, consecrating your devotion to Him.
> *(al-Zumar 39:2)*

قُلْ إِنِّي أُمِرْتُ أَنْ أَعْبُدَ اللهَ مُخْلِصًا لَّهُ الدِّينَ. وَأُمِرْتُ لِأَنْ أَكُونَ أَوَّلَ الْمُسْلِمِينَ.

Tell them, (O Prophet): "I am bidden to serve Allah, consecrating my devotion to Him, and I am bidden to be the first of those who surrender to Him.
(al-Zumar 39:11-12)

وَلَقَدْ بَعَثْنَا فِي كُلِّ أُمَّةٍ رَّسُولاً أَنِ اعْبُدُواْ اللّهَ وَاجْتَنِبُواْ الطَّاغُوتَ.

We raised a Messenger in every community (to tell them): "Serve Allah and shun the Evil One."[1]
(al-Naḥl 16:36)

وَمَا أُمِرُوا إِلَّا لِيَعْبُدُوا اللَّهَ مُخْلِصِينَ لَهُ الدِّينَ حُنَفَاءَ.

Yet all they had been commanded was that they serve Allah, with utter sincerity, devoting themselves exclusively to Him.
(al-Bayyinah 98:5)

اتَّبِعُواْ مَا أُنزِلَ إِلَيْكُم مِّن رَّبِّكُمْ وَلاَ تَتَّبِعُواْ مِن دُونِهِ أَوْلِيَاء.

(O people), follow what has been revealed to you from your Lord and follow no masters other than Him.
(al-A'rāf 7:3)

وَلَئِنِ اتَّبَعْتَ أَهْوَآءَهُمْ بَعْدَ مَا جَآءَكَ مِنَ الْعِلْمِ مَا لَكَ مِنَ اللَّهِ مِن وَلِيٍّ وَلَا وَاقٍ.

Were you indeed to follow the vain desires of people after the true knowledge has come to you, none will be your supporter against Allah, and none will have the power to shield you from His punishment!
(al-Ra'd 13:37)

---

1 Ṭāghūt is one who rebels against Allah and is worshipped beside Allah, irrespective of the fact whether he is worshipped by force or willingly. It also does not matter if he is a human or a devil or an idol or else. Abū Ja'far Muḥammad ibn Jarīr al-Ṭabri, *al-Jāmi' al-Bayān fi Tāwīl al-Qur'ān* (Cairo: al-Matba'h al Amiryah, 1324 A.H.) vol. 3, p.13.

ثُمَّ جَعَلْنَاكَ عَلَىٰ شَرِيعَةٍ مِّنَ الْأَمْرِ فَاتَّبِعْهَا وَلَا تَتَّبِعْ أَهْوَآءَ الَّذِينَ لَا يَعْلَمُونَ.

And then We sent you, (O Prophet), on a clear high road in religious matter. So follow that and do not follow the desires o those who do not know.
(al-Jāthiyah 45:18)

الطَّلَاقُ مَرَّتَانِ فَإِمْسَاكٌ بِمَعْرُوفٍ أَوْ تَسْرِيحٌ بِإِحْسَانٍ، وَلاَ يَحِلُّ لَكُمْ أَن تَأْخُذُواْ مِمَّا آتَيْتُمُوهُنَّ شَيْئًا إِلاَّ أَن يَخَافَا أَلاَّ يُقِيمَا حُدُودَ اللّٰه، فَإِنْ خِفْتُمْ أَلاَّ يُقِيمَا حُدُودَ اللّٰهِ فَلاَ جُنَاحَ عَلَيْهِمَا فِيمَا افْتَدَتْ بِهِ، تِلْكَ حُدُودُ اللّٰهِ فَلاَ تَعْتَدُوهَا وَمَن يَتَعَدَّ حُدُودَ اللّٰهِ فَأُوْلَـئِكَ هُمُ الظَّالِمُونَ.

Divorce can be pronounced twice: then, either honourable retention or kindly release should follow. (While dissolving the marriage tie) it is unlawful for you to take back anything of what you have given to your wives unless both fear that they may not be able to keep within the bounds set by Allah. Then, if they fear that they might not be able to keep within the bounds set by Allah, there is no blame upon them for what the wife might give away of her property to become released from the marriage tie. These are the bounds set by Allah; do not transgress them. Those of you who transgress the bounds set by Allah are indeed the wrong-doers.
(al-Baqarah 2:229)

يَا أَيُّهَا النَّبِيُّ إِذَا طَلَّقْتُمُ النِّسَآءَ فَطَلِّقُوهُنَّ لِعِدَّتِهِنَّ وَأَحْصُوا الْعِدَّةَ، وَاتَّقُوا اللّٰهَ رَبَّكُمْ لَا تُخْرِجُوهُنَّ مِن بُيُوتِهِنَّ وَلَا يَخْرُجْنَ إِلَّا أَن يَأْتِينَ بِفَاحِشَةٍ مُّبَيِّنَةٍ، وَتِلْكَ حُدُودُ اللّٰهِ وَمَن يَتَعَدَّ حُدُودَ اللّٰهِ فَقَدْ ظَلَمَ نَفْسَهُ، لَا تَدْرِى لَعَلَّ اللّٰهَ يُحْدِثُ بَعْدَ ذَلِكَ أَمْرًا.

O Prophet, when you divorce women, divorce them for their waiting-period, and compute the waiting period accurately, and hold Allah

your Lord in awe. Do not turn them out of their homes (during the waiting period) nor should they go away (from their homes) – unless they have committed a manifestly evil deed. Such are the bounds set by Allah; and he who transgresses the bounds set by Allah commits a wrong against himself. You do not know: maybe Allah will cause something to happen to pave the way (for reconciliation).
(al-Ṭalāq 65:1)

فَمَن لَّمْ يَجِدْ فَصِيَامُ شَهْرَيْنِ مُتَتَابِعَيْنِ مِن قَبْلِ أَن يَتَمَاسَّا، فَمَن لَّمْ يَسْتَطِعْ فَإِطْعَامُ سِتِّينَ مِسْكِينًا ذَٰلِكَ لِتُؤْمِنُوا بِاللَّهِ وَرَسُولِهِ، وَتِلْكَ حُدُودُ اللَّهِ وَلِلْكَافِرِينَ عَذَابٌ أَلِيمٌ.

And he who does not find a slave (to free), shall fast for two months consecutively before they may touch other, and he who is unable to do so shall feed sixty needy people.
All this is in order that you may truly believe in Allah and His Messenger. These are the bounds set by Allah; and a grievous chastisement awaits the unbelievers.
(al-Mujādilah 58:4)

وَمَن لَّمْ يَحْكُم بِمَا أَنزَلَ اللَّهُ فَأُولَـٰئِكَ هُمُ الْكَافِرُونَ.

And those who do not judge by what Allah has revealed are indeed the unbelievers.
(al-Mā'idah 5:44)

وَمَن لَّمْ يَحْكُم بِمَا أَنزَلَ اللَّهُ فَأُولَـٰئِكَ هُمُ الظَّالِمُونَ.

And those who do not judge by what Allah has revealed are indeed the wrong-doers.
(al-Mā'idah 5:45)

وَمَن لَّمْ يَحْكُم بِمَا أَنزَلَ اللَّهُ فَأُولَـٰئِكَ هُمُ الْفَاسِقُونَ.

And those who do not judge by what Allah has revealed are indeed the transgressors.
(al-Mā'idah 5:47)

أَفَحُكْمَ الْجَاهِلِيَّةِ يَبْغُونَ، وَمَنْ أَحْسَنُ مِنَ اللهِ حُكْمًا لِّقَوْمٍ يُوقِنُونَ.

(If they turn away from the Law of Allah) do they desire judgement according to the Law of Ignorance? But whose judgement can be better than Allah's for those who have certainly of belief?
(al-Mā'idah 5:50)

أَلَمْ تَرَ إِلَى الَّذِينَ يَزْعُمُونَ أَنَّهُمْ آمَنُواْ بِمَا أُنزِلَ إِلَيْكَ وَمَا أُنزِلَ مِن قَبْلِكَ يُرِيدُونَ أَن يَتَحَاكَمُواْ إِلَى الطَّاغُوتِ وَقَدْ أُمِرُواْ أَن يَكْفُرُواْ بِهِ، وَيُرِيدُ الشَّيْطَانُ أَن يُضِلَّهُمْ ضَلاَلاً بَعِيدًا.

(O Messenger), have you not seen those who claim to believe in the Book which has been revealed to you and in the Books revealed before you and yet desire to submit their disputes to the judgment of ṭaghūt (the Satanic authorities who decide independently of the law of Allah), whereas they had been asked to reject it. Satan seeks to make them drift far away from the Right Path.
(al-Nisā' 4:60)

4. The Messenger's position

The Divine laws, which the preceding Āyāt (verses) call for compliance, are given to humanity through Allah's Messenger, who communicates His guidance to fellow humans and explicates them by his mouth and deeds. Thus, the Messenger implements God's legal sovereignty and for that reason alone, his obedience is Allah's obedience. Allah enjoins the believers to accept what the Messenger enjoins them to do or forbids them not to do. Even a fraction of uneasiness that one may feel in one's heart in following the Prophet can compromise one's belief.

وَمَا أَرْسَلْنَا مِن رَّسُولٍ إِلاَّ لِيُطَاعَ بِإِذْنِ اللهِ.

(And tell them that) We never sent a Messenger but that he should be obeyed by the leave of Allah.
(al-Nisā' 4:64)

مَّنْ يُطِعِ الرَّسُولَ فَقَدْ أَطَاعَ اللّٰهَ.

He who obeys the Messenger thereby obeys Allah.
(al-Nisā' 4:80)

وَمَن يُشَاقِقِ الرَّسُولَ مِن بَعْدِ مَا تَبَيَّنَ لَهُ الْهُدَى وَيَتَّبِعْ غَيْرَ سَبِيلِ الْمُؤْمِنِينَ نُوَلِّهِ مَا تَوَلَّى وَنُصْلِهِ جَهَنَّمَ وَسَآءَتْ مَصِيرًا.

As for him who sets himself against the Messenger and follows a path other than that of the believers even after true guidance had become clear to him, We will let him go to the way he has turned to, and We will cast him into Hell – an evil destination-
(al-Nisā' 4:115)

وَمَا آتَاكُمُ الرَّسُولُ فَخُذُوهُ وَمَا نَهَاكُمْ عَنْهُ فَانتَهُوا، وَاتَّقُوا اللّٰهَ إِنَّ اللّٰهَ شَدِيدُ الْعِقَابِ.

So accept whatever the Messenger gives you, and refrain from whatever he forbids you. And fear Allah: verily Allah is Most Stern in retribution.
(al-Ḥashr 59:7)

فَلاَ وَرَبِّكَ لاَ يُؤْمِنُونَ حَتَّىَ يُحَكِّمُوكَ فِيمَا شَجَرَ بَيْنَهُمْ ثُمَّ لاَ يَجِدُواْ فِي أَنفُسِهِمْ حَرَجًا مِّمَّا قَضَيْتَ وَيُسَلِّمُواْ تَسْلِيمًا.

But no, by the Lord, they cannot become true believers until they seek your arbitration in all matters on which they disagree among themselves, and then do not find the least vexation in their hearts over your judgement, and accept it in willing submission.
(al-Nisā' 4:65)

5. Supreme law

The Qur'ān declares Allah's and His Messenger's say as supreme law that the believers can only comply with and not violate. A Muslim is not free to make independent decisions where Allah and His Messenger have given their verdict. Anything contrary to it is opposite to belief.

وَمَا كَانَ لِمُؤْمِنٍ وَلَا مُؤْمِنَةٍ إِذَا قَضَى اللهُ وَرَسُولُهُ أَمْرًا أَن يَكُونَ لَهُمُ الْخِيَرَةُ مِنْ أَمْرِهِمْ، وَمَن يَعْصِ اللهَ وَرَسُولَهُ فَقَدْ ضَلَّ ضَلَالًا مُّبِينًا.

It does not behove a believer, male or female, that when Allah and His Messenger have decided an affair they should exercise their choice. And whoever disobeys Allah and His Messenger has strayed to manifest error.
(al-Aḥzāb 33:36)

وَيَقُولُونَ آمَنَّا بِاللهِ وَبِالرَّسُولِ وَأَطَعْنَا ثُمَّ يَتَوَلَّى فَرِيقٌ مِّنْهُم مِّن بَعْدِ ذَلِكَ وَمَا أُولَئِكَ بِالْمُؤْمِنِينَ. وَإِذَا دُعُوا إِلَى اللهِ وَرَسُولِهِ لِيَحْكُمَ بَيْنَهُمْ إِذَا فَرِيقٌ مِّنْهُم مُّعْرِضُونَ.

They say, "We believe in Allah and in the Messenger, and we obey", but thereafter a faction of them turns away (from obedience). These indeed are not believers.
When they are called to Allah and His Messenger that he may judge (the disputes) among them, a faction of them turns away.
(al-Nūr 24:47-48)

إِنَّمَا كَانَ قَوْلَ الْمُؤْمِنِينَ إِذَا دُعُوا إِلَى اللهِ وَرَسُولِهِ لِيَحْكُمَ بَيْنَهُمْ أَنْ يَقُولُوا سَمِعْنَا وَأَطَعْنَا وَأُولَئِكَ هُمُ الْمُفْلِحُونَ.

When those that believe are called to Allah and His Messenger in order that he (that is, the Messenger) may judge their disputes

> among them, nothing becomes them but to say: "We hear and we obey." Such shall attain true success.
> *(al-Nūr 24:51)*

6. Al-Khilāfah

The Qur'ān describes the best governance for humans as one that accepts Allah's and His messengers' legal superiority, and abdicates their right to govern in deference to the Real Sovereign and accept their role as Khilāfah (vicegerent). Obviously, in this caliphal capacity his powers, whether explicatory, judicial, or administrative will be governed by the limits set in paragraphs 3, 4 and 5 above.

وَأَنزَلْنَا إِلَيْكَ الْكِتَابَ بِالْحَقِّ مُصَدِّقًا لِّمَا بَيْنَ يَدَيْهِ مِنَ الْكِتَابِ وَمُهَيْمِنًا
عَلَيْهِ فَاحْكُمْ بَيْنَهُم بِمَا أَنزَلَ اللّٰهُ وَلاَ تَتَّبِعْ أَهْوَاءهُمْ عَمَّا جَاءكَ مِنَ الْحَقِّ.

> Then We revealed the Book to you, (O Mu*h*ammad), with Truth, confirming whatever of the Book was revealed before, and protecting and guarding over it. Judge, then, in the affairs of men in accordance with the Law that Allah has revealed, and do not follow their desires in disregard of the Truth which has come to you.
> *(al-Mā'idah 5:48)*

يَا دَاوُودُ إِنَّا جَعَلْنَاكَ خَلِيفَةً فِى الْأَرْضِ فَاحْكُمْ بَيْنَ النَّاسِ بِالْحَقِّ وَلَا تَتَّبِعِ
الْهَوَى فَيُضِلَّكَ عَن سَبِيلِ اللّٰهِ.

> (We said to him): "O David, we have appointed you vicegerent on earth. Therefore, rule among people and do not follow (your) desire lest if should lead you astray from Allah's Path.
> *(Ṣād 38:26)*

7. The nature of the caliphate

The Khilāfah (caliphate), as expounded by the Qur'ān, underscores the fact that they should use whatever Allah has gifted to humans in the permissible limits. Thus, humans are not unboundedly autonomous in their use but are the deputies of the Real Master.

وَإِذْ قَالَ رَبُّكَ لِلْمَلَآئِكَةِ إِنِّي جَاعِلٌ فِي الأَرْضِ خَلِيفَةً.

> Just think when your Lord said to the angels: "Lo! I am about to place a vicegerent on earth."
> *(al-Baqarah 2:30)*

وَلَقَدْ مَكَّنَّاكُمْ فِي الأَرْضِ وَجَعَلْنَا لَكُمْ فِيهَا مَعَايِشَ.

> We assuredly established you in the earth and arranged for your livelihood in it.
> *(al-A'rāf 7:10)*

أَلَمْ تَرَ أَنَّ اللهَ سَخَّرَ لَكُمْ مَّا فِي الأَرْضِ.

> Have you not seen how Allah has subjected to you all that is in the earth?
> *(al-Ḥajj 22:65)*

وَاذْكُرُوا إِذْ جَعَلَكُمْ خُلَفَآءَ مِن بَعْدِ قَوْمِ نُوحٍ.

> And do call to mind when He made you successors after the people of Noah.
> *(al-A'rāf 7:69)*

وَاذْكُرُوا إِذْ جَعَلَكُمْ خُلَفَآءَ مِن بَعْدِ عَادٍ.

> And call to mind when after 'Ād He made you their successors.
> *(al-A'rāf 7:74)*

عَسَى رَبُّكُمْ أَنْ يُهْلِكَ عَدُوَّكُمْ وَيَسْتَخْلِفَكُمْ فِي الأَرْضِ فَيَنظُرَ كَيْفَ تَعْمَلُونَ.

> (Moses) said: "Your Lord will soon destroy your enemy and make you rulers in the land.

Then He will see how you act.
(al-A'rāf 7:129)

ثُمَّ جَعَلْنَاكُمْ خَلَائِفَ فِي الْأَرْضِ مِنْ بَعْدِهِم لِنَنْظُرَ كَيْفَ تَعْمَلُونَ.

Now We have appointed you as their successors in the earth to see how you act.
(Yūnus 10:14)

This Khilāfah (caliphate) will qualify itself to be valid and just only when it subordinates itself to the will of the real Master. Any violated act that concretizes itself into an autonomous system of governance free from the Divine ordination will be rebellious and not a caliphal manifestation.

هُوَ الَّذِي جَعَلَكُمْ خَلَائِفَ فِي الْأَرْضِ، فَمَن كَفَرَ فَعَلَيْهِ كُفْرُهُ، وَلَا يَزِيدُ الْكَافِرِينَ كُفْرُهُمْ عِندَ رَبِّهِمْ إِلَّا مَقْتًا وَلَا يَزِيدُ الْكَافِرِينَ كُفْرُهُمْ إِلَّا خَسَارًا.

It is He Who made you vicegerents in the earth. So whoever disbelieves will bear the burden of his unbelief. The unbelievers' unbelief adds nothing but Allah's wrath against them. The unbelievers' unbelief adds nothing but their own loss.
(Fāṭir 35:39)

أَلَمْ تَرَ كَيْفَ فَعَلَ رَبُّكَ بِعَادٍ. إِرَمَ ذَاتِ الْعِمَادِ. الَّتِي لَمْ يُخْلَقْ مِثْلُهَا فِي الْبِلَادِ. وَثَمُودَ الَّذِينَ جَابُوا الصَّخْرَ بِالْوَادِ. وَفِرْعَوْنَ ذِي الْأَوْتَادِ. الَّذِينَ طَغَوْا فِي الْبِلَادِ.

Have you not seen how your Lord dealt with 'Ād of Iram, known for their lofty columns, the like of whom no nation was ever created in the lands of the world? And how did He deal with Thamūd, who hewed out rocks in the valley? And with Pharaoh of the tent pegs who transgressed in the countries of the world.
(al-Fajr 89:6-11)

اِذْهَبْ إِلَى فِرْعَوْنَ إِنَّهُ طَغَى. فَقُلْ هَل لَّكَ إِلَى أَنْ تَزَكَّى. وَأَهْدِيَكَ إِلَى رَبِّكَ فَتَخْشَى. فَأَرَاهُ الْآيَةَ الْكُبْرَى. فَكَذَّبَ وَعَصَى. ثُمَّ أَدْبَرَ يَسْعَى. فَحَشَرَ فَنَادَى. فَقَالَ أَنَا رَبُّكُمُ الْأَعْلَى.

And directed him: "Go to Pharaoh, he has rebelled, and say to him: 'Are you willing to be purified, that I may direct you to your Lord and then you hold Him in awe?" "Then Moses (went to Pharaoh and) showed him the Great Sign; but he denied it as false and disobeyed, and then he turned back to have recourse to his craftiness, and gathered his people and declared: "I am the supreme lord of you all." *(al-Nāzi'āt 79:17-24)*

وَعَدَ اللهُ الَّذِينَ آمَنُوا مِنكُمْ وَعَمِلُوا الصَّالِحَاتِ لَيَسْتَخْلِفَنَّهُم فِي الْأَرْضِ كَمَا اسْتَخْلَفَ الَّذِينَ مِن قَبْلِهِمْ وَلَيُمَكِّنَنَّ لَهُمْ دِينَهُمُ الَّذِى ارْتَضَى لَهُمْ وَلَيُبَدِّلَنَّهُم مِّنْ بَعْدِ خَوْفِهِمْ أَمْنًا، يَعْبُدُونَنِى لَا يُشْرِكُونَ بِى شَيْئًا وَمَنْ كَفَرَ بَعْدَ ذٰلِكَ فَأُوْلَئِكَ هُمُ الْفَاسِقُونَ.

Allah has promised those of you who believe and do righteous deeds that He will surely bestow power on them in the land even as He had bestowed power on those that preceded them. And that that He will firmly establish their religion, which He has been pleased to choose for you, and He will replace with security the state of fear that they are in. Let them serve Me and associate none with Me in My divinity. Whoso thereafter engages in unbelief, such indeed are the ungodly. *(al-Nūr 24:55*

8. The collective Khilāfah

a) A person, a family, or a class of people cannot lay claim to this caliphate unless it is givening to them by the community of believers. Surah *al-Nūr*:55 "*layastakhli.fan.na.hum fil arḍ*" is self-evident. According to its import, every member of the believers' community has an equal share in the Khilāfah (caliphate). No person or group has the right to usurp the caliphal rights of the believers and invest his person with them. Nor can anyone arrogate to himself this caliphate in the name of a prerogative received from Allah. This distinguishes Islamic caliphate from monarchy, class-based government and theocracy, giving it thus a democratic face of its own kind.

b) But what stands it apart from Western democracy is its essence. Western democracy is built on popular sovereignty while in the democratic caliphate of Islam people themselves agree to Allah's sovereignty and willingly restrict their powers within the confines of Allah-given laws.

9. The limit of obeying the state

The state that comes up out of the effort to run this caliphate can only be given loyalty in matters that fall within the realm of m'arūf (goodness). Thus, in violating the Sharī'ah there is neither obedience nor cooperation.

يَآ أَيُّهَا النَّبِيُّ إِذَا جَآءَكَ الْمُؤْمِنَاتُ يُبَايِعْنَكَ عَلَى أَنْ لَّا يُشْرِكْنَ بِاللّٰهِ شَيْئًا وَلَا يَسْرِقْنَ وَلَا يَزْنِينَ وَلَا يَقْتُلْنَ أَوْلَادَهُنَّ وَلَا يَأْتِينَ بِبُهْتَانٍ يَفْتَرِينَهُ بَيْنَ أَيْدِيهِنَّ وَأَرْجُلِهِنَّ وَلَا يَعْصِينَكَ فِي مَعْرُوفٍ فَبَايِعْهُنَّ وَاسْتَغْفِرْ لَهُنَّ اللّٰهَ، إِنَّ اللّٰهَ غَفُورٌ رَّحِيمٌ.

O Prophet, when believing women come to you to and give you their pledge that they will not associate anyone with His divinity, that they will not steal, that they will not commit illicit sexual intercourse, that they will not kill their children, that they will not bring forth a calumny between their hands and feet, and that they will not disobey you in anything known to be good, then accept their allegiance and ask Allah to forgive them. Surely, Allah is Most Forgiving, most Compassionate.
(al-Mumtaḥinah 60:12)

وَتَعَاوَنُواْ عَلَى الْبِرِّ وَالتَّقْوَى وَلاَ تَعَاوَنُواْ عَلَى الإِثْمِ وَالْعُدْوَانِ وَاتَّقُواْ اللّٰهَ، إِنَّ اللّٰهَ شَدِيدُ الْعِقَابِ.

Rather help you one another in acts of righteousness and piety, and do not help one another in sin and transgression. Fear Allah: Surely Allah is severe in retribution.
(al-Mā'idah 5:2)

وَلَا تُطِعْ مِنْهُمْ آثِمًا أَوْ كَفُورًا.

And do not pay any heed to the wicked and the unbelieving.
(al-Dahr 76:24)

10. Shūrā

The whole affairs of this caliphal state from its origination to its effort to restructure life, including the election of its head and the expository and administrative affairs are managed by mutual consultation. Whether this consultation is effectuated through direct or elected representation is not material.

وَأَمْرُهُمْ شُورَى بَيْنَهُمْ.

Who conduct their affairs by consultation.[2]
(al-Shūrā 42:38)

11. The characteristics of its decision-makers

In the elections of those who will run this caliphal state, the following merits have to be sought.

a) They should believe in the principles that subsume this caliphate, for its management cannot be entrusted to its opponents.

وَأَمْرُهُمْ شُورَى بَيْنَهُمْ.

Their affairs are run by mutual consultation.
(al-Shūrā 42:38)

يَآ أَيُّهَا الَّذِينَ آمَنُوٓا أَطِيعُوا اللّٰهَ وَأَطِيعُوا الرَّسُولَ وَأُوْلِى الأَمْرِ مِنْكُمْ.

2 For a detailed exposition of this Āyah, see *Tafhīm al-Qur'ān*, vol. 4, pp. 508-510.

Believers! Obey Allah, and obey the Messenger, and those invested with authority among you. *(al-Nisā 4:59)*

يَآ أَيُّهَا الَّذِينَ آمَنُواْ لاَ تَتَّخِذُواْ بِطَانَةً مِّنْ دُونِكُمْ.

Believers! Do not take for intimate friends those who are not of your kind.[3] *(āl 'Imrān 3:118)*

أَمْ حَسِبْتُمْ أَنْ تُتْرَكُواْ وَلَمَّا يَعْلَمِ اللهُ الَّذِينَ جَاهَدُواْ مِنْكُمْ وَلَمْ يَتَّخِذُواْ مِنْ دُونِ اللهِ وَلاَ رَسُولِهِ وَلاَ الْمُؤْمِنِينَ وَلِيجَةً.۔

Do you imagine that you will be spared without being subjected to any test? Know well that Allah has not yet determined who strove hard (in His cause), and has not taken any others instead of His Messenger and the believers as his trusted allies?[4] *(al-Tawbah 9:16)*

b) That they should not be victimizers, law breakers and sinners, oblivious of Allah in their lives and violators of the limits. Rather, they should be Allah fearing and pious. If an oppressor or a law-violator appropriates Khilāfah to himself, his Imāmah will be invalid in the eyes of Islam.

وَإِذِ ابْتَلَى إِبْرَاهِيمَ رَبُّهُ بِكَلِمَاتٍ فَأَتَمَّهُنَّ، قَالَ إِنِّي جَاعِلُكَ لِلنَّاسِ إِمَامًا، قَالَ وَمِنْ ذُرِّيَّتِي، قَالَ لاَ يَنَالُ عَهْدِي الظَّالِمِينَ.

"Recall when Abraham's Lord tested him in

---

3 The word used is *bitānah*. Abū al-Qāsim Mahmūd ibn 'Umar al-Zamakhshari (d.538 A.H./1144 C.E.) explains it: "A pious biṭanah and walījah is one's close friend and a dear companion whom he trusts and consults for his vital interests." See *al-Kashshāf an Haqā'iq al-Tanzīl* (Cairo: al-Matb'āh al-Bihiyyah, 1343 A.H.) vol. 1, p. 162.

4 In the preceding Āyah, the word used is walījah explained in footnote 3 on the authority of al-Zamakhshari. Its other meaning comes from Abū Qāsim Ḥusayn ibn Muḥammad al-Rāghab al-Asfahāni: "Every person can be called walījah whom someone trusts while he is not from amongst his people. This is a derivative of the Arab proverb *fulā-nun walijah tun fi al-qaūm* – that is, a certain person has intruded himself into these people even though he is not of them. See *al-Mufrā*dāt fi gharīb *al-Qur'ān* (Cairo: al-Matba'h al-Khayriyah 1322 A.H.)

certain matters and when he successfully stood the test, He said: Indeed I am going to appoint you a leader of all people." When Abraham asked: "and is this covenant also for my descendants?" the Lord responded: "My covenant does not embrace the wrong-doers."[5]
(al-Baqarah 2:124)

أَمْ نَجْعَلُ الَّذِينَ آمَنُوا وَعَمِلُوا الصَّالِحَاتِ كَالْمُفْسِدِينَ فِي الْأَرْضِ أَمْ نَجْعَلُ الْمُتَّقِينَ كَالْفُجَّارِ.

Shall We then treat alike those that believe and act righteously and those that create mischief on earth? Or treat alike the God-fearing and the wicked?
(Ṣād 38:28)

وَلَا تُطِعْ مَنْ أَغْفَلْنَا قَلْبَهُ عَنْ ذِكْرِنَا وَاتَّبَعَ هَوَاهُ وَكَانَ أَمْرُهُ فُرُطًا.

And obey not the one whose heart We have permitted to neglect the remembrance of Us, one who follows his own desires, whose case has gone beyond all bounds.
(al-Kahf 18:28)

وَلَا تُطِيعُوا أَمْرَ الْمُسْرِفِينَ. الَّذِينَ يُفْسِدُونَ فِي الْأَرْضِ وَلَا يُصْلِحُونَ.

And do not follow the bidding of those that go to excesses and spread mischief in the land

---

5 The famous *Ḥ*anafi jurist Abū Bakr al-Jassas (d.370 A.H./980 C.E.) explains it as follows: Although the lexicographic meaning of imam stands for any person who is followed, whether in truth or falsehood, but in this Āyah it refers to a person who is entitled to be followed and whose obedience is binding (on others). Thus in this sense, the prophets are invested with Im*ā*mah, followed by the rightly-guided caliphs, the pious, the 'ulamā (religious scholars), and the qāḍīs (judges). Thereafter he says: A cruel person cannot be a prophet nor is it right that he becomes the prophet's successor or a qāḍi or an official liable to be followed in matters of religion ... This Āyah proves that a violater's Im*ā*mah is invalid and he cannot be the caliph. Should he grab this office people are not bound to follow and obey him? (Cairo: al-Matba'h al-Bihiyyah, 1347 A.H.) vol. 1, pp. 79-80.

rather that set things right.
(al-Shu'arā 26:151-152)

إِنَّ أَكْرَمَكُمْ عِندَ اللهِ أَتْقَاكُمْ.

Verily the noblest of you in the sight of Allah
is the most God-fearing of you.
(al-Ḥujurāt 49:13)

c) They should not be simpletons nor ignorant but should be knowledgeable, wise, and understand problems, capable enough mentally and physically to run the caliphal affairs:

وَلاَ تُؤْتُواْ السُّفَهَآءَ أَمْوَالَكُمُ الَّتِى جَعَلَ اللهُ لَكُمْ قِيَامًا.

Do not entrust your properties — which Allah
has made a means of support for you.
(al-Nisā' 4:5)

قَالُوٓاْ أَنَّى يَكُونُ لَهُ الْمُلْكُ عَلَيْنَا وَنَحْنُ أَحَقُّ بِالْمُلْكِ مِنْهُ وَلَمْ يُؤْتَ سَعَةً مِّنَ الْمَالِ، قَالَ إِنَّ اللهَ اصْطَفَاهُ عَلَيْكُمْ وَزَادَهُ بَسْطَةً فِى الْعِلْمِ وَالْجِسْمِ.

They (said: "By what right shall he rule over us
when we are more worthy than he to dominion,
for he is not very wealthy? He said: "Allah has
chosen him over you and has endowed him
abundantly with both intellectual and physical
capacities.
(al-Baqarah 2:247)

وَشَدَدْنَا مُلْكَهُ وَآتَيْنَاهُ الْحِكْمَةَ وَفَصْلَ الْخِطَابِ.

And We strengthened his kingdom, and
endowed him wisdom and decisive judgment.
(Ṣād 38:20)

قَالَ اجْعَلْنِى عَلَى خَزَآئِنِ الأَرْضِ، إِنِّى حَفِيظٌ عَلِيمٌ.

Joseph said: "Place me in charge of the
treasures of the land. I am a good keeper and
know my task well."
(Yūsuf 12:55)

وَلَوْ رَدُّوهُ إِلَى الرَّسُولِ وَإِلَى أُوْلِي الأَمْرِ مِنْهُمْ لَعَلِمَهُ الَّذِينَ يَسْتَنبِطُونَهُ مِنْهُمْ.

Whereas if they were to convey it to either the Messenger or to those from among them entrusted with authority, it would come to the knowledge of those who are competent to investigate it.
(al-Nisā' 4:83)

قُلْ هَلْ يَسْتَوِى الَّذِينَ يَعْلَمُونَ وَالَّذِينَ لَا يَعْلَمُونَ.

Ask them "Are those who know equal to those who do not know?"
(al-Zumar 39:9)

إِنَّ اللهَ يَأْمُرُكُمْ أَنْ تُؤَدُّوا الأَمَانَاتِ إِلَى أَهْلِهَا.

Allah commands you to deliver trusts to those worthy of them.[6]
(al-Nisā' 4:58)

12. The foundational principles of the constitution

The constitution of the Islamic state will rest on the following foundational principles:

a) The command structure

يَآ أَيُّهَا الَّذِينَ آمَنُوا أَطِيعُوا اللهَ وَأَطِيعُوا الرَّسُولَ وَأُوْلِي الأَمْرِ مِنكُمْ، فَإِنْ تَنَازَعْتُمْ فِي شَيْءٍ فَرُدُّوهُ إِلَى اللهِ وَالرَّسُولِ إِنْ كُنتُمْ تُؤْمِنُونَ بِاللهِ وَالْيَوْمِ الآخِرِ.

Believers! Obey Allah ṣubḥanahū wa taʿāla and obey the Messenger, and those invested with authority among you; and then if you were to dispute among yourselves about

6 "This has the meaning that responsible governmental slots should be given to those who qualify for them." See Abū al-Thanā' Shihāb al-Dīn al-Ālūsi, *Ruh al-Maʿāni* (Cairo: Idārah al-Tabāʿah al-Muniriyah, 1345 A.H.) vol. 5, p. 58.

anything refer it to Allah and the Messenger if
you indeed believe in Allah and the Last Day.
(al-Nisā' 4:59)

This Āyah explicates six constitutional aspects:

1. The obedience to Allah and His Messenger has priority over obedience to anything else.

2. Obeying people in authority is conditional to obedience the believers owe to Allah and His Messenger.

3. People-in-authority should be from among the believers.

4. People have the right to express themselves against the government and its functionaries.
5. That in case of a dispute between the people and the government the ultimate arbiter is Allah's law and His Prophet's Sunnah.

6. The caliphal system should have a free institution powerful enough to ward off governmental and people's pressure and decide conflictive issues in the light of Allah's law and His Prophet's Sunnah between the government and the people.

b) The executive prerogatives and powers should necessarily be limited by the *ḥudūd* (boundaries) of Allah as prescribed by Allah's law and His Prophet's Sunnah, which cannot be bypassed in policy formulation or in any executive order that may fall within the definition of deviation from norm or sin. The moment it transgresses the constitutional jurisdiction it disqualifies itself to receive the masses' obedience. Besides, this executive branch must come into being through the consent of the shūrā and work through it as explained above.

The Qur'ān, however, do not give definitive details about the mode of elections or the shūrā; their form can vary in order to cohere with civilizational contingencies.

c) Legislature has to have the structure as well as the nature of a consultative body (see subhead 10), though its lawmaking powers will be prescribed by the limits set under Allah's sovereignty and legal status of the Sunnah (see subhead 3 and 5).

As for the affairs for which clear injunctions have been laid down by Allah and His Prophet or have been circumscribed and bonded by principles laid down by them, the legislature can interpret and explicate them and suggest subordinate rules and regulations for their enforcement but cannot change them. The rest of the human affairs for which no clear-cut instructions are available in the supreme law, lawmakers can make laws consistent with the Islamic spirit and its general principle. The absence of an injunction on such matters in the Qur'ān and the Sunnah by itself is an indication that Allah has left them to the believers' discretion.

d) Judiciary should be free from all kind of interventions and pressures so that it could give its verdict motivated by laws and its spirit of juristic fairness and equity. It has perforce to stay confined to the parameters as defined by the Qur'an and the Sunnah.

فَاحْكُم بَيْنَهُم بِمَا أَنزَلَ اللّٰهُ وَلَا تَتَّبِعْ أَهْوَآءَهُمْ.

Judge, then, in the affairs of men in accordance with the Law that Allah has revealed, and do not follow their desires.
(al-Mā'idah 5:48)

وَلَا تَتَّبِعِ الْهَوَىٰ فَيُضِلَّكَ عَن سَبِيلِ اللّٰهِ.

And do not follow (your) desire lest it should lead you astray from Allah's Path.
(Ṣād 38:26)

وَإِذَا حَكَمْتُم بَيْنَ النَّاسِ أَنْ تَحْكُمُوا بِالْعَدْلِ.

And when you judge between people, judge

with justice.
(al-Nisā' 4:58)

13. The purpose of state

The Islamic state must work for two supreme objectives. First, human life should not suffer from wrong; injustice in all form should be eliminated.

لَقَدْ أَرْسَلْنَا رُسُلَنَا بِالْبَيِّنَاتِ وَأَنزَلْنَا مَعَهُمُ الْكِتَابَ وَالْمِيزَانَ لِيَقُومَ النَّاسُ بِالْقِسْطِ، وَأَنزَلْنَا الْحَدِيدَ فِيهِ بَأْسٌ شَدِيدٌ وَمَنَافِعُ لِلنَّاسِ وَلِيَعْلَمَ اللَّهُ مَن يَنصُرُهُ وَرُسُلَهُ بِالْغَيْبِ، إِنَّ اللَّهَ قَوِيٌّ عَزِيزٌ.

Indeed, We sent Our Messenger with Clear Signs, and sent down with them the Book and the Balance[7] that people may uphold justice. And We sent down iron,[8] wherein there is awesome power and many benefits for people, so that Allah may know who, without even having seen Him, helps Him and His Messengers. Surely Allah is Most Strong, Most Mighty.
(al-Ḥadīd 57:25)

Second, it should establish by persuasion and where necessary by force the system of Ṣalāh (prayers) and Zakāh (poor-due) the pillar of Islamic life. It should encourage righteousness among the masses, as it alone is the purpose behind Islam's arrival and curb evil-doing as Allah hates it most.

---

7 Al-Mizān (balance) means justice as said by Mujāhid and Qatādah. See Ibn Kathīr, *Tafsir al-Qur'ān al-A'zim* (Egypt: Matb'ah Mustaphā Muhammad, 1937) vol. 1, p. 314.

8 Al-*ḥa*dīd (steel) means political power. "It points out to this aspect that if people deviate (from guidance), they should be corrected by the sword (state power)." Abū Bakr Mu*ḥ*ammad ibn Zakaria al-Rāzi, *Mafātih al-Ghayb* (Egypt: *al-Matb'ah al-Sharafiyah*, 1324 A.H.) vol. 8, p. 101.

الَّذِينَ إِنْ مَّكَّنَّاهُمْ فِي الْأَرْضِ أَقَامُوا الصَّلَاةَ وَآتَوُا الزَّكَاةَ وَأَمَرُوا بِالْمَعْرُوفِ وَنَهَوْا عَنِ الْمُنكَرِ وَلِلَّهِ عَاقِبَةُ الْأُمُورِ.

(Allah will certainly help) those who, were We to bestow authority on them in the land, will establish prayers, render Zakāh (poor-due), enjoin good, and forbid evil. The end of all matters rests with Allah.
(al-Ḥajj 22:41)

14. Fundamental rights

Muslims or non-Muslims who accept its sovereignty have the following basic rights that are obligatory for the state to uphold:[9]

a) Preservation of life

وَلاَ تَقْتُلُواْ النَّفْسَ الَّتِي حَرَّمَ اللّهُ إِلاَّ بِالحَقِّ.

Do not kill any person whom Allah has forbidden to kill, except with right.
(al-Isrā' 17:33)

b) Preservation of the right to own

لاَ تَأْكُلُواْ أَمْوَالَكُمْ بَيْنَكُمْ بِالْبَاطِلِ.

Do not usurp one another's possessions by false means.
(al-Baqarah 2:188,
al-Nisā 4:29)

c) The right to personal dignity

يَا أَيُّهَا الَّذِينَ آمَنُوا لَا يَسْخَرْ قَوْمٌ مِّنْ قَوْمٍ عَسَى أَنْ يَكُونُوا خَيْرًا مِّنْهُمْ وَلَا نِسَاءٌ مِّنْ نِّسَاءٍ عَسَى أَنْ يَكُنَّ خَيْرًا مِّنْهُنَّ، وَلَا تَلْمِزُوا أَنْفُسَكُمْ وَلَا تَنَابَزُوا بِالْأَلْقَابِ، بِئْسَ الِاسْمُ الْفُسُوقُ بَعْدَ الْإِيمَانِ، وَمَنْ لَّمْ يَتُبْ فَأُولَئِكَ هُمُ الظَّالِمُونَ. يَا أَيُّهَا الَّذِينَ آمَنُوا اجْتَنِبُواْ كَثِيرًا مِّنَ الظَّنِّ، إِنَّ بَعْضَ الظَّنِّ إِثْمٌ

9 For a greater discussion on fundamental rights, see my book *Tafhimāt*, (Lahore: Islamic Publication, 1996) vol. 3, pp. 248-268. Sixteenth print.

وَلَا تَجَسَّسُواْ وَلَا يَغْتَب بَّعْضُكُم بَعْضًا، أَيُحِبُّ أَحَدُكُمْ أَنْ يَأْكُلَ لَحْمَ أَخِيهِ
مَيْتًا فَكَرِهْتُمُوهُ وَاتَّقُوا اللهَ، إِنَّ اللهَ تَوَّابٌ رَّحِيمٌ.

Believers, let not a group (of men) scoff at another group, it may well be that the latter (at whom they scoff) are better than they; nor let a group of women scoff at another group, it may well be that the latter are better than they. And do not taunt one another, nor revile one another by nicknames. It is an evil thing to again notoriety for ungodliness after belief. Those who do not repent are indeed the wrongdoers.
Believers, avoid being excessively suspicious, for some suspicion is a sin. Do not spy, nor backbite one another. Would any of you like to eat the flesh of his dead brother? You would surely detest it. Have fear of Allah. Surely Allah is much prone to accept repentance, is Most Compassionate.
(al-Ḥujurāt 49:11-12)

d) The right to privacy

لَا تَدْخُلُواْ بُيُوتًا غَيْرَ بُيُوتِكُمْ حَتَّى تَسْتَأْنِسُوا.

Enter not houses other than your own houses until you have obtained the permission of the inmates of those houses.
(al-Nūr 24:27)

وَلَا تَجَسَّسُوا وَلَا يَغْتَب بَّعْضُكُم بَعْضًا.

Do not spy, nor backbite one another.
(al-Ḥujarāt 49:12)

e) The right to raise voice against excesses

لَا يُحِبُّ اللهُ الْجَهْرَ بِالسُّوءِ مِنَ الْقَوْلِ إِلَّا مَنْ ظُلِمَ.

Allah does not like speaking evil publicly unless one has been wronged.
(al-Nisā 4:148)

f) **Amr bil maʿrūf wa nihi ʿan al-munkar – the right to enjoin good and forbid wrong.** This includes the right to question and criticize people in power.

لُعِنَ الَّذِينَ كَفَرُواْ مِنْ بَنِى إِسْرَائِيلَ عَلَى لِسَانِ دَاوُودَ وَعِيسَى ابْنِ مَرْيَمَ، ذَٰلِكَ بِمَا عَصَوْا وَّكَانُواْ يَعْتَدُونَ. كَانُواْ لاَ يَتَنَاهَوْنَ عَنْ مُّنكَرٍ فَعَلُوهُ لَبِئْسَ مَا كَانُواْ يَفْعَلُونَ.

Those of the Children of Israel who took to unbelief have been cursed by the tongue of David and Jesus, the son of Mary, for they rebelled and exceeded the bounds of right. They did not forbid each other from committing the abominable deeds they committed. Evil indeed was what they did.
(al-Māʾidah 5:78-79)

أَنْجَيْنَا الَّذِينَ يَنْهَوْنَ عَنِ السُّوءِ وَأَخَذْنَا الَّذِينَ ظَلَمُواْ بِعَذَابٍ بَئِيسٍ بِمَا كَانُواْ يَفْسُقُونَ.

We delivered those who forbade evil and afflicted the wrongdoers with a grievous chastisement because of their exceeding the bounds (their evil doing).
(al-Aʿrāf 7:165)

كُنْتُمْ خَيْرَ أُمَّةٍ أُخْرِجَتْ لِلنَّاسِ تَأْمُرُونَ بِالْمَعْرُوفِ وَتَنْهَوْنَ عَنِ الْمُنكَرِ وَتُؤْمِنُونَ بِاللّٰهِ.

You are the best nation brought forth for humanity. You enjoin what is right and forbid what is wrong, and believe in Allah.
(āl ʿImrān 3:110)

g) The right to form group

The caliphal state allows such freedoms provided these are employed in the spread of goodness and not for discord and divisions in society.

وَلْتَكُن مِّنكُمْ أُمَّةٌ يَدْعُونَ إِلَى الْخَيْرِ وَيَأْمُرُونَ بِالْمَعْرُوفِ وَيَنْهَوْنَ عَنِ الْمُنكَرِ وَأُوْلَـئِكَ هُمُ الْمُفْلِحُونَ. وَلاَ تَكُونُواْ كَالَّذِينَ تَفَرَّقُواْ وَاخْتَلَفُواْ مِن بَعْدِ مَا جَاءهُمُ الْبَيِّنَاتُ وَأُوْلَـئِكَ لَهُمْ عَذَابٌ عَظِيمٌ.

And from amongst you there must be a party who will call people to all that is good and will enjoin the doing of all that is right and will forbid the doing of all that is wrong. It is they, who will attain true success.
And do not be like those who fell into factions and became opposed to one another after clear guidance had come to them. A mighty chastisement awaits them.
(āl 'Imrān 3:104-105)

h) The right to freedom of conscience and belief

لاَ إِكْرَاهَ فِي الدِّينِ.

There is no compulsion in religion.
(al-Baqarah 2:256)

أَفَأَنتَ تُكْرِهُ النَّاسَ حَتَّى يَكُونُواْ مُؤْمِنِينَ.

Will you, then, force people into believing?
(Yūnus 10:99)

وَالْفِتْنَةُ أَشَدُّ مِنَ الْقَتْلِ.

(For though killing is sinful) wrongful persecution is even worse than killing.[10]
(al-Baqarah 2:191)

10 Fitnah means to force someone to change his religion. See Ibn Jarīr, *al-Jāmi'...*, vol 2, p. 111.

i) The right of protection against religious hurt

وَلاَ تَسُبُّواْ الَّذِينَ يَدْعُونَ مِنْ دُونِ اللهِ.

Do not revile those other than Allah whom they invoke.
(al-An'ām 6:108)

Explaining it, the Qur'ān says that academic discussion on religious beliefs is allowed subject to well articulation and due respect.

لَا تُجَادِلُوا أَهْلَ الْكِتَابِ إِلَّا بِالَّتِي هِيَ أَحْسَنُ.

Argue not with the People of the Book except in the fairest manner.
(al-'Ankabūt 29:46)

j) The right to be held responsible for one's own wrong and not for other's wrong.

وَلاَ تَكْسِبُ كُلُّ نَفْسٍ إِلَّا عَلَيْهَا، وَلاَ تَزِرُ وَازِرَةٌ وِزْرَ أُخْرَى.

Everyone will bear the consequence of what he does, and no one shall bear the burden of another.[11]
(al-An'ām 6:164)

k) The right to demand fair legal proceedings

No person shall be prosecuted unless there is evidence for it and the legalities are met with.

إِنْ جَآءَكُمْ فَاسِقٌ بِنَبَإٍ فَتَبَيَّنُوا أَنْ تُصِيبُوا قَوْمًا بِجَهَالَةٍ فَتُصْبِحُوا عَلَى مَا فَعَلْتُمْ نَادِمِينَ.

11 Anyone who wrongs is responsible for its doing. No other (person) will be held accountable for it. Nor can anyone else's wrong be thrown on him other than his own." Ibn Jarir, *al-Jāmi'...*, vol. 8, p. 83.
For the Qur'ānic Āyahs, also see *al-Isrā'*:15, *al-Fāṭir*:18, *al-Zumar*:7, *al-Najam*:38.

When an ungodly person brings to you a piece of news, carefully ascertain its truth, lest you should hurt a people unwittingly and thereafter repent at what you did.
(al-Ḥujarāt 49:6)

وَلاَ تَقْفُ مَا لَيْسَ لَكَ بِهِ عِلْمٌ.

Do not follow that of which you have no knowledge.
(al-Isrā' 17:36)

وَإِذَا حَكَمْتُم بَيْنَ النَّاسِ أَنْ تَحْكُمُواْ بِالْعَدْلِ.

And when you judge between people, judge with justice.
(al-Nisā' 4:58)

l) The restitution of the right to basic needs

وَفِي أَمْوَالِهِمْ حَقٌّ لِّلسَّآئِلِ وَالْمَحْرُومِ.

And in their wealth there was a rightful share for him who would ask and for the destitute.
(al-Dhāriyāt 51:19)

m) Equal treatment for all citizens

The state must treat its subjects equally, with no discrimination amongst them.

إِنَّ فِرْعَوْنَ عَلَا فِي الْأَرْضِ وَجَعَلَ أَهْلَهَا شِيَعًا يَّسْتَضْعِفُ طَآئِفَةً مِّنْهُمْ يُذَبِّحُ
أَبْنَآءَهُمْ وَيَسْتَحْيِي نِسَآءَهُمْ، إِنَّهُ كَانَ مِنَ الْمُفْسِدِينَ.

Indeed Pharaoh transgressed in the land and divided its people into sections. One group of them the humiliated, and slew their sons and spared their daughters. Truly, he was among the mischief-makers.
(al-Qaṣaṣ 28:4)

15. The government right as against the citizens

In the caliphal administration, the state has the following rights over the citizens:

a) Its obedience is binding

أَطِيعُواْ اللهَ وَأَطِيعُواْ الرَّسُولَ وَأُوْلِي الأَمْرِ مِنْكُمْ.

Obey Allah and obey the Messenger, and those invested with authority among you.
(al-Nisā' 4:59)

b) That they should abide by the laws and must not cause disorder.

لاَ تُفْسِدُواْ فِي الأَرْضِ بَعْدَ إِصْلاَحِهَا.

Make no mischief on the earth after it has been set in good order.
(al-A'rāf 7:85)

إِنَّمَا جَزَآءُ الَّذِينَ يُحَارِبُونَ اللهَ وَرَسُولَهُ وَيَسْعَوْنَ فِي الأَرْضِ فَسَادًا أَنْ يُقَتَّلُوا أَوْ يُصَلَّبُوا أَوْ تُقَطَّعَ أَيْدِيهِمْ وَأَرْجُلُهُم مِّنْ خِلاَفٍ أَوْ يُنْفَوْا مِنَ الأَرْضِ ذَلِكَ لَهُمْ خِزْيٌ فِي الدُّنْيَا وَلَهُمْ فِي الآخِرَةِ عَذَابٌ عَظِيمٌ.

Those who wage war against Allah and His Messenger, and go about the earth spreading mischief[12] – indeed their recompense is that they either be done to death, or be crucified, or have their hands and feet be cut off from the opposite sides or they be banished from the land. Such shall be their degradation in this world; and a mighty chastisement lies in store for them in the World to Come.
(al-Mā'idah 5:33)

---

12 The jurists almost have consensus that "war against Allah and His Messenger" means those who indulge in acts of highway robbery and organized crimes or arm themselves to create law and order in the nation. See *al-Jassās*, *Aḥkām* ..., vol. 2, p. 493.

c) That they should cooperate in its good works.

وَتَعَاوَنُواْ عَلَى الْبِرِّ وَالتَّقْوَى.

Help one another in acts of righteousness and piety, and do not help one another in sin and transgression.
(al-Mā'idah 5:2)

d) That they should come to the assistance of the government in defending the state.

يَآ أَيُّهَا الَّذِينَ آمَنُواْ مَا لَكُمْ إِذَا قِيلَ لَكُمُ انْفِرُواْ فِي سَبِيلِ اللهِ اثَّاقَلْتُمْ إِلَى الأَرْضِ أَرَضِيتُمْ بِالْحَيَاةِ الدُّنْيَا مِنَ الآخِرَةِ، فَمَا مَتَاعُ الْحَيَاةِ الدُّنْيَا فِي الآخِرَةِ إِلاَّ قَلِيلٌ. إِلَّا تَنْفِرُواْ يُعَذِّبْكُمْ عَذَابًا أَلِيمًا وَّيَسْتَبْدِلْ قَوْمًا غَيْرَكُمْ وَلاَ تَضُرُّوهُ شَيْئًا، وَاللهُ عَلَى كُلِّ شَيْءٍ قَدِيرٌ. إِلاَّ تَنْصُرُوهُ فَقَدْ نَصَرَهُ اللهُ إِذْ أَخْرَجَهُ الَّذِينَ كَفَرُواْ ثَانِيَ اثْنَيْنِ إِذْ هُمَا فِي الْغَارِ إِذْ يَقُولُ لِصَاحِبِهِ لاَ تَحْزَنْ إِنَّ اللهَ مَعَنَا، فَأَنْزَلَ اللهُ سَكِينَتَهُ عَلَيْهِ وَأَيَّدَهُ بِجُنُودٍ لَّمْ تَرَوْهَا وَجَعَلَ كَلِمَةَ الَّذِينَ كَفَرُواْ السُّفْلَى، وَكَلِمَةُ اللهِ هِيَ الْعُلْيَا، وَاللهُ عَزِيزٌ حَكِيمٌ. انْفِرُواْ خِفَافًا وَثِقَالاً وَّجَاهِدُواْ بِأَمْوَالِكُمْ وَأَنْفُسِكُمْ فِي سَبِيلِ اللهِ، ذَلِكُمْ خَيْرٌ لَّكُمْ إِنْ كُنْتُمْ تَعْلَمُونَ.

Believers! What is amiss with you that when it is said to you: "March forth in the cause of Allah," you cling heavily to the earth? Do you prefer the worldly life to the Hereafter? Know well that all the enjoyment of this world, in comparison with the Hereafter, is trivial.
If you do not march forth, Allah will chastise you grievously and will replace you by another people, while you will in no way be able to harm Him. Allah has power over everything.
It will matter little if you do not help the Prophet, for Allah surely helped him when the unbelievers drove him out of his home and he was but one of the two when they were in the cave, and when he said to his companion: "Do not grieve. Allah is with us. Then Allah caused His tranquility to descend upon him, and

supported him with hosts you did not see, and He humbled the word of the unbelievers. As for Allah's Word, it is inherently uppermost. Allah is all-Powerful all-Wisdom.
March forth whether light or heavy, and strive in the way of Allah with your belongings and your lives. That is best for you if you only knew it.
(al-Tawbah 9:38-41)

16. The principles of external politics

For the foreign policy of this Islamic state, the Qur'ān has the following guidelines:

a) To observe respect for agreements made with other nations

Should it become necessary to annul agreement, the other nation must be informed of your intent.

وَأَوْفُواْ بِالْعَهْدِ، إِنَّ الْعَهْدَ كَانَ مَسْؤُولًا.

And fulfill the covenant, for you will be called to account regarding the covenant.
(al-Isrā' 17:34)

وَأَوْفُواْ بِعَهْدِ اللّٰهِ إِذَا عَاهَدتُّمْ وَلاَ تَنْقُضُواْ الأَيْمَانَ بَعْدَ تَوْكِيدِهَا وَقَدْ جَعَلْتُمُ
اللّٰهَ عَلَيْكُمْ كَفِيلًا، إِنَّ اللّٰهَ يَعْلَمُ مَا تَفْعَلُونَ. وَلاَ تَكُونُواْ كَالَّتِي نَقَضَتْ غَزْلَهَا
مِنْ بَعْدِ قُوَّةٍ أَنْكَاثًا، تَتَّخِذُونَ أَيْمَانَكُمْ دَخَلاً بَيْنَكُمْ أَنْ تَكُونَ أُمَّةٌ هِيَ أَرْبَى
مِنْ أُمَّةٍ، إِنَّمَا يَبْلُوكُمُ اللّٰهُ بِهِ، وَلَيُبَيِّنَنَّ لَكُمْ يَوْمَ الْقِيَامَةِ مَا كُنتُمْ فِيهِ تَخْتَلِفُونَ.

And fulfill the covenant which you have made with Allah and do not break your oath after having firmly made them, and after having made Allah your witness. Surely, Allah knows all that you do.
And do not become like the woman who, after having painstakingly spun her yarn, caused it to disintegrate into pieces. You resort to oaths

as instruments of mutual deceit so that one people might take greater advantage than another might, although Allah puts you to the test through this. Surely, on the Day of Resurrection He will make clear the Truth concerning the matters over which you differed.
(al-Naḥl 16:91-92)

فَمَا اسْتَقَامُواْ لَكُمْ فَاسْتَقِيمُواْ لَهُمْ، إِنَّ اللّٰهَ يُحِبُّ الْمُتَّقِينَ.

Behave in a straight manner with them so long as they behave with you in a straight manner for Allah loves the God-fearing.
(al-Tawbah 9:7)

إِلَّا الَّذِينَ عَاهَدتُّم مِّنَ الْمُشْرِكِينَ ثُمَّ لَمْ يَنقُصُوكُمْ شَيْئًا وَلَمْ يُظَاهِرُواْ عَلَيْكُمْ أَحَدًا فَأَتِمُّواْ إِلَيْهِمْ عَهْدَهُمْ إِلَى مُدَّتِهِمْ.

In exception to those who associate others with Allah in His Divinity are those with whom you have made treaties and who have not violated their treaties nor have backed up anyone against you. Fulfil your treaties with them till the end of their term.
(al-Tawbah 9:4)

وَإِنِ اسْتَنصَرُوكُمْ فِي الدِّينِ فَعَلَيْكُمُ النَّصْرُ إِلَّا عَلَى قَوْمٍ بَيْنَكُمْ وَبَيْنَهُم مِّيثَاقٌ.

And recall when you were encamped at the nearer end of the valley (of Badr) and they were at the farther end and their caravan was below you (along the seaside). Had you made a mutual appointment to meet in an encounter, you would have declined.
(al-Anfāl 8:42)

وَإِمَّا تَخَافَنَّ مِن قَوْمٍ خِيَانَةً فَانبِذْ إِلَيْهِمْ عَلَى سَوَاءٍ، إِنَّ اللّٰهَ لاَ يُحِبُّ الخَائِنِينَ.

And if you fear treachery from any people (with whom you have a covenant) then publicly throw their covenant at them. Allah does not love the treacherous.[13]
(al-Anfāl 8:58)

b) Honesty and righteousness in human affairs

وَلاَ تَتَّخِذُواْ أَيْمَانكُمْ دَخَلاً بَيْنَكُمْ.

Do not make your oaths a means of deceiving one another.[14]
(al-Naḥl 16:94)

c) International justice

وَلاَ يَجْرِمَنَّكُمْ شَنَآنُ قَوْمٍ عَلَى أَلَّا تَعْدِلُواْ، اِعْدِلُواْ هُوَ أَقْرَبُ لِلتَّقْوَى.

And do not let the enmity of any people move you to deviate from justice. Act justly, that is nearer to Allah-fearing.
(al-Mā'idah 5:8)

d) To respect geopolitics of the nonaligned nations

وَدُّواْ لَوْ تَكْفُرُونَ كَمَا كَفَرُواْ فَتَكُونُونَ سَوَآءً فَلاَ تَتَّخِذُواْ مِنْهُمْ أَوْلِيَآءَ حَتَّى
يُهَاجِرُواْ فِي سَبِيلِ اللهِ فَإِنْ تَوَلَّوْا فَخُذُوهُمْ وَاقْتُلُوهُمْ حَيْثُ وَجَدتُّمُوهُمْ، وَلاَ
تَتَّخِذُواْ مِنْهُمْ وَلِيًّا وَلاَ نَصِيرًا.

They wish that you should disbelieve just as they disbelieved so that you may all be alike. Do not, therefore, take allies from them until

13 It means that the news about your intent to annul of the agreement with the other party should be broken to them so that both the parties have equal information. And if you undertake any action against the other, they should not have the feeling that you betrayed them. (*al-Jassās, Aḥkām...*, vol. 3, p. 83).

14 "That is: do not formalize agreements with the intention to deceive the other party to believe you because of your protestations while your intention is to betray the later at a favourable moment." (al-Ṭabari, *al-Jāmi'...*, vol. 14, p. 112).

they emigrate in the Way of Allah; but they turn their backs (on emigration), seize them and slay them wherever you come upon them. Take none of them for your ally or helper.

إِلَّا الَّذِينَ يَصِلُونَ إِلَىٰ قَوْمٍ بَيْنَكُمْ وَبَيْنَهُم مِّيثَاقٌ أَوْ جَآؤُوكُمْ حَصِرَتْ صُدُورُهُمْ أَن يُقَاتِلُوكُمْ أَوْ يُقَاتِلُوا قَوْمَهُمْ وَلَوْ شَآءَ اللَّهُ لَسَلَّطَهُمْ عَلَيْكُمْ فَلَقَاتَلُوكُمْ فَإِنِ اعْتَزَلُوكُمْ فَلَمْ يُقَاتِلُوكُمْ وَأَلْقَوْا إِلَيْكُمُ السَّلَمَ فَمَا جَعَلَ اللَّهُ لَكُمْ عَلَيْهِمْ سَبِيلًا.

Unless it be such of them who seek refuge with a people who are joined with you by a covenant, or those who come to you because their hearts shrink from fighting either against you or against their own people. Had Allah so willed, He would certainly have given them power over you and they would have fought against you. If they leave you alone and do not fight against you and offer you peace, then Allah does not permit you to harm them.
(al-Nisā' 4:89-90)

e) **Peace loving**

وَإِنْ جَنَحُواْ لِلسَّلْمِ فَاجْنَحْ لَهَا.

If they incline to peace, incline you as well to it.
(al-Anfāl 8:61)

f) **To avoid creating mischief on earth and to establish one's supremacy.**

تِلْكَ الدَّارُ الْآخِرَةُ نَجْعَلُهَا لِلَّذِينَ لَا يُرِيدُونَ عُلُوًّا فِي الْأَرْضِ وَلَا فَسَادًا، وَالْعَاقِبَةُ لِلْمُتَّقِينَ.

As for the Abode of the Hereafter, We shall assign it exclusively for those who do not seek glory on earth nor want to cause mischief. The

God-fearing shall have the best end.
(al-Qaṣaṣ 28:83)

g) Friendly attitude toward non-aggressive nations.

لَا يَنْهَاكُمُ اللّٰهُ عَنِ الَّذِينَ لَمْ يُقَاتِلُوكُمْ فِي الدِّينِ وَلَمْ يُخْرِجُوكُمْ مِّنْ دِيَارِكُمْ أَنْ تَبَرُّوهُمْ وَتُقْسِطُوا إِلَيْهِمْ، إِنَّ اللّٰهَ يُحِبُّ الْمُقْسِطِينَ.

Allah does not forbid that you be kind and just to those who did not fight against you because of religion, nor drove you out of your homes. Surely, Allah loves those who are equitable.
(al-Mumtaḥinah 60:8)

h) Reciprocal attitude of goodness

هَلْ جَزَآءُ الْإِحْسَانِ إِلَّا الْإِحْسَانُ.

Can the reward of goodness be any other than goodness?
(al-Raḥmān 55:60)

i) Not to exceed while responding to a hurt caused by others.

فَمَنِ اعْتَدَى عَلَيْكُمْ فَاعْتَدُوا عَلَيْهِ بِمِثْلِ مَا اعْتَدَى عَلَيْكُمْ وَاتَّقُوا اللّٰهَ وَاعْلَمُوا أَنَّ اللّٰهَ مَعَ الْمُتَّقِينَ.

Thus, if someone has attacked you, attack him just as he attacked you, and fear Allah and remain conscious that Allah is with those who guard against violating the bounds set by Him.
(al-Baqarah 2:194)

وَإِنْ عَاقَبْتُمْ فَعَاقِبُوا بِمِثْلِ مَا عُوقِبْتُمْ بِهِ، وَلَئِنْ صَبَرْتُمْ لَهُوَ خَيْرٌ لِّلصَّابِرِينَ.

> If you take retribution, then do so in proportion to the wrong done to you. But if you can bear such conduct with patience, indeed that is best for the steadfast.
> *(al-Naḥl 16:126)*

> وَجَزَآءُ سَيِّئَةٍ سَيِّئَةٌ مِّثْلُهَا فَمَنْ عَفَا وَأَصْلَحَ فَأَجْرُهُ عَلَى اللهِ إِنَّهُ لَا يُحِبُّ الظَّالِمِينَ. وَلَمَنِ انتَصَرَ بَعْدَ ظُلْمِهِ فَأُوْلَئِكَ مَا عَلَيْهِم مِّنْ سَبِيلٍ. إِنَّمَا السَّبِيلُ عَلَى الَّذِينَ يَظْلِمُونَ النَّاسَ وَيَبْغُونَ فِي الْأَرْضِ بِغَيْرِ الْحَقِّ أُوْلَئِكَ لَهُم عَذَابٌ أَلِيمٌ.

> The recompense of evil is evil the like of it. But he who forgives and makes amends, his reward lies with Allah. Surely He does not love the wrong-doers. There is no blame against him who avenges himself after he has been wronged.
> Blame attaches only to those who subject people to wrong and commit excesses on earth. A painful chastisement awaits them.
> *(al-Shūrā 42:40-42)*

17. The characteristics of an Islamic state

The profile of the Islamic state emerging from the preceding sixteen points drawn from the Qur'an is as follows:

1. This state comes into being with a conscious commitment of a free people to surrender themselves to the will of Allah and accept al-Khilāfah in place of sovereignty [located in a single being or a group, or people in general] binding themselves to enforce Allah-given laws as enunciated in the Qur'ān and exemplified by the Prophet ('alayhi as-salām).
2. This state agrees in principle with the notion that sovereignty rests with Allah. But in concretizing this concept its route

is altogether different as instead of authorizing a priestly class to play the caliphal role, it entitles the believers under its territories to exercise vicegerency [and establish justice within the divine parameters].

3. It agrees with present-day democratic dispensation that to form, change and run the government belongs to the people alone but then it stops here. It denies them absolute sovereign will to shape its internal and external policies and to use its material and natural resources as they desire. It binds them to the supremacy of Allah and His law so that the state could function within specified parameters, which can be tempered with neither by its judiciary nor legislature nor people unless they decide to forego Islam by breaking their pledge.

4. It is an ideological state and as such, those who believe in its ideology can only run it. Others can stay as its citizens with all those civic rights that Muslims have provided they abide by its laws.

5. This state is not defined by race, colour, language or geography but by certain principles, which can be accepted by anyone living anywhere on the planet, and thus by accepting those principles can enter this system without facing any discrimination. No matter whether established in Africa or America, Europe or Asia and whether by blacks or whites or yellow, any governance that comes into being because of such principles will be Islamic.

   There is no hitch to such a state to evolve into a global Islamic order. But even if there is more than one such state in different parts of the world they could be still described as equally Islamic. Such states would be free from nationalistic rivalries and would have brotherly cooperation with one another, with the potential to turn into a federal global state.

6. Such an Islamic state would subordinate politics to morality, relegating selfish interests to piety and Allah-consciousness. It is moral excellence of a person, his mental and physical abilities, which determine the qualifying criterion for a seat in the shūrā as well as among the government functionaries.

   Likewise, every segment of its internal system has to be subsumed by trust, honesty and across the broad justice for all. Its foreign policy has to be run by absolute openness, respect for agreements, truthfulness, peaceful coexistence, justice and fair play.

7. This state is not ordained to act as a police officer with the exclusive task of maintaining law and order and patrolling the borders. In fact, it is a purposive state, which has to enforce social justice, spread goodness, and eradicate evil.

8. The Islamic state has to create equal opportunities and accord equal rights and status to its citizens. It has to ensure supremacy of law, cooperation in goodness and withhold support to evil. Besides, it must instill in its citizens and functionaries a sharpened sense of accountability before Allah; stress on obligations rather then clamouring for rights; convergence of individuals, state, and society on one objective; creating a moral environment and making sure that the basic necessities of life are not denied to anyone are some of the primary concerns of this state.

9. The Islamic system creates such a balance between the individual and state that neither the state by its powers can reduce the individual to a helpless subject nor can the individual by his unbounded freedoms become headstrong and start opposing the collective good.

On the one hand, this state provides fundamental rights to its citizens; and on the other, it binds the government not to bypass the supreme law and instead subject itself to shūrā (consultative body). This equation helps in creating a favourable environment in which there is ample space for the individual to grow in his human potential. At the same time, it binds the individual to a moral code of conduct to obey the government that abides by the laws of Allah, to cooperate with it in acts of goodness, to avoid tampering with the system, and to stand for its defence by his or her wealth and life.

Chapter Two

Principles of Islamic Governance

In the last chapter, we described the political teachings of the Qur'ān. The Prophetic mission was to translate them into life situations. The society that came into being after the advent of Islam and the state that emerged in the wake of Hijrah (emigration) rested on these teachings. The distinguishing features of this Islamic governance, which stood it apart from other systems, were the following:

1. Supremacy of the divine law

The primary principle of this state acknowledges sovereignty as a divine prerogative. The system of governance which sprouts up from this principle is al-Khilāfah (the caliphate), is run by the believers. Bonded as it is to divine laws as sourced in the Qur'ān and the Prophetic Sunnah, it is not free to function autocratically. The following Āyāt (verses) in this respect are clear:

> Believers! Obey Allah and obey the Messenger, and those invested with authority among you; and then if you were to dispute among yourselves about anything, refer it to Allah and the Messenger if you indeed believe in Allah and the Last Day; that is better and more commendable in the end.
> *(al-Nisā 4:59)*

> (And tell them that) We never sent a Messenger but that he should be obeyed by the leave of Allah. If whenever they wronged themselves they had come to you praying to Allah for forgiveness, and had the Messenger prayed for their forgiveness, they would indeed have found Allah All-Forgiving, All-Compassionate.
> *(al-Nisā 4:64)*

But no, by your Lord, they cannot become true believers until they seek your arbitration in all matters on which they disagree among themselves, and then do not find the least vexation in their hearts over your judgement, and accept it in willing submission.
(al-Nisā 4:65)

He who obeys the Messenger thereby obeys Allah; as for he who turns away, We have not sent you as a keeper over them!
(al-Nisā 4:80)

(O Messenger), We have revealed to you this Book with the Truth so that you may judge between people in accordance with what Allah has shown you. So do not dispute on behalf of the dishonest.
(al-Nisā 4:105)

Surely, We revealed the Torah, wherein there is Guidance and Light. Thereby did Prophets – who had submitted themselves (to Allah) – judge for the Judaized folk; and so did the scholars and jurists. They judged by the Book of Allah for they had been entrusted to keep it and bear witness to it. So, (O Jews), do not fear human beings but fear Me, and do not barter away My signs for a trivial gain. Those who do not judge by what Allah has revealed are indeed the unbelievers.
(al-Mā'idah 5:44)

And therein, We had ordained for them: "A life for a life, and an eye for an eye, and a nose for a nose, and an ear for an ear, and a tooth for a tooth, and for all wounds, like for like. But whosoever foregoes it by way of charity, it will be for him an expiation." Those who

do not judge by what Allah has revealed are indeed the wrongdoers.
And We sent, Jesus, the son of Mary, after those Prophets, confirming the truth of whatever there still remained of the Torah. And We gave him the Gospel wherein is Guidance and Light, and which confirms the truth of whatever there still remained of the Torah, and a Guidance and Admonition for the God-fearing.
Let the followers of the Gospel judge by what Allah has revealed therein, and those who do not judge by what Allah has revealed are the transgressors.
(al-Mā'idah 5:46-47)

(O people), follow what has been revealed to you from your Lord and follow no masters other than Him. Little are you admonished!
(al-'Arāf 7:3)

Those whom you serve beside Him are merely idle names that you and your fathers have fabricated, without Allah sending down any sanction for them. All authority to govern rests only with Allah. He has commanded that you serve none but Him. This is the Right Way of life, though most people are altogether unaware.
(Yūsuf 12:40)

Say: "Obey Allah and obey the Messenger. But if you turn away, then (know well) that the Messenger is responsible for what he has been charged with and you are responsible for what you have been charged with. But if you obey him, you will be guided to the Right Way. The Messenger has no other responsibility but

to clearly convey (the command)."
Allah has promised those of you who believe and do righteous deeds that He will surely bestow power on them in the land as He bestowed power on those that preceded them, and that He will firmly establish their religion which He has been pleased to choose for them, and He will replace with security the state of fear that they are in. Let them serve Me and associate none with Me in My Divinity. Whoso thereafter engages in unbelief, such indeed are the ungodly.
(al-Nūr 24:54-55)

It does not behove a believer, male or female, that when Allah and His Messenger have decided an affair they should exercise their choice. And whoever disobeys Allah and His Messenger has strayed to manifest error.
(al-Aḥzāb 33:36)

Whatever (from the possessions of the townspeople) Allah has bestowed on His Messenger belongs to Allah, and to the Messenger, and to his kinsfolk, and to the orphans, and to the needy, and to the wayfarer so that it may not merely circulate between the rich among you. So accept whatever the Messenger gives you, and refrain from whatever he forbids you. And fear Allah: verily Allah is Most Stern in retribution.
(al-Ḥashr 59:7)

The Prophet ('alayhi as-salām) has explicated this principal feature of the Islamic state on different occasions.

عَلَيْكُمْ بِكِتَابِ اللهِ، اَحِلُّوا حَلَا لَهُ وَحَرِّمُوا حَرَامَهُ.

To abide by the Book of Allah is binding on you. Follow the things it has allowed and discard the things it has proscribed.[1]

إِنَّ اللّٰهَ فَرَضَ فَرَائِضَ فَلَا تُضِيعُوهَا وَحَرَّمَاتٍ فَلَا تَنْتَهِكُوهَا وَحَدَّ حُدُودًا فَلَا تَعْتَدُوهَا وَسَكَتَ عَنْ اَشْيَآءٍ مِنْ غَيْرِ نِسْيَانٍ فَلَا تَبْحَثُوا عَنْهَا.

Allah has assigned certain obligatories, do not waste them; [He has] ordained certain prohibitions, do not violate them; [He has] drawn certain boundaries, do not transgress them; and for certain things He has observed silence without being amnesiac, do not probe them.[2]

مَنِ اقْتَدىٰ بِكِتَابِ اللّٰهِ لَا يَضِلُّ فِي الدُّنْيَا وَلَا يَشْقىٰ فِي الْآخِرَةِ.

He who follows the Book of Allah would not go astray in the world nor would he be damned in the hereafter.[3]

تَرَكْتُ فِيكُمْ اَمْرَيْنِ لَنْ تُضِلُّوا مَا تَمَسَّكْتُمْ بِهِمَا، كِتَابُ اللّٰهِ وَ سُنَّةُ رَسُولِهِ.

I have left [behind] two things, which if you hold fast you will never go astray – Allah's Book and the Sunnah of His Messenger.[4]

مَا اَمَرْتُكُمْ بِهِ فَخُذُوهُ، وَمَا نَهَيْتُكُمْ عَنْهُ فَانْتَهُوا.

Embrace the thing I have enjoined on you,

---

1 Sheikh ʿAli al-Muttaqi, *Kunz al-Ummāl* (Hyderabad: Da'irah al-Maʿārif, 1955) on the authority of al-Tabarāni's, *Mu'ajm al-Kabīr* and Ahmad ibn Hanbal, Musnad, hadith 907, 966.

2 Al-Khatīb al-Tabrizi, *al-Mishkāt al-Masābih,* cited on the authority of Dar Qatni, Bāb al-Aʿtisām bi al-Kitāb wa al-Sunnah; al-Muttaqi, *Kunz*, vol. 1, pp. 981-982.

3 Al-Tabrizi, *al-Mishkāt,* ibid.

4 Ibid. cited on the authority of *al-Muwattā*, *bāb* al-Aʿtisām..., ibid; al-Muttaqi, *Kunz,* vol. 1, pp. 877, 949, 955, 1001.

and stop from the things I have restrained you from.[5]

2. Justice among the people

The second principle on which this state rests called for equal treatment in accordance with the Qur'ān and the Sunnah horizontally as well as vertically – from an ordinary citizen to head of state.

The Qur'ān asked the Prophet to say:

وَأُمِرْتُ لِأَعْدِلَ بَيْنَكُمُ.

And I have been commanded to establish justice among you.
(al-Shūrā 42:15)

Expressed differently, it asked the Prophet ('alayhi as-salām) to say that my commission is to do justice to all; it is not his job to discriminate favouring some and excluding others. My relationship with humans is even. I stand with those who are truthful and just and I am against those who are unjust.

In my faith there are no discriminatory laws – everyone whether native or alien, big or small, noble or of low birth are governed by laws. Ḥaqq (truth) is for everyone and so is falsehood. What is sin is for one is sin for others and so is Ḥarām (disallowed) and Ḥalāl (allowed). My own person is not exception to Allah's laws.

The Prophet himself explains this universal application of the divine laws:

اِنَّمَا هُلِکَ مَنْ كَانَ قَبْلَكُمْ اِنَّهُمْ كَانُوا يُقِيمُونَ الْحَدَّ عَلَى الْوُضِيعُ وَيتْرِكُونَ
الشَّرِيف، وَالَّذِى نفس مُحَمَّد بِيَدِهِ لَوْ ان فَاطِمَةَ (بِنْت مُحَمَّدٌ) فعَلْتْ
ذَالِکَ لِقَطَعْتُ يَدَهَا.

Nations before you were destroyed because they punished people of lesser origin in

5 Al-Muttaqi, *Kunz*, vol. 1, p. 886.

> accordance with law, while they spared individuals of high birth. By Him who holds Muhammad's life, even if Fātimah had committed theft I would have chopped her hand off.[6]
>
> Caliph 'Umar said:
>
> رَأَيْتُ رَسُولَ اللهِ صَلَّى اللهُ عَلَيْهِ وَسَلَّمَ يُقِيدُ مِنْ نَّفْسِهِ.
>
> I have seen myself Allah's Messenger giving justice to others against his own self.[7]

3. Equality among the Muslims

From justice among the people springs another distinguishing feature of this state that speaks of the Muslims' equal rights irrespective of their colour, race, ethnicity, and region. None can have the privileged position over anyone else. The Qur'ān says:

> إِنَّمَا الْمُؤْمِنُونَ إِخْوَةٌ.
>
> Surely, the believers are none but brothers unto one another …
> *(al-Ḥujurāt 49:10)*
>
> يَا أَيُّهَا النَّاسُ إِنَّا خَلَقْنَاكُم مِّن ذَكَرٍ وَأُنثَى وَجَعَلْنَاكُمْ شُعُوبًا وَقَبَائِلَ لِتَعَارَفُوا إِنَّ أَكْرَمَكُمْ عِندَ اللهِ أَتْقَاكُمْ.
>
> Human beings, We created you all from a male and a female, and made you into nations and tribes so that you may know one another. Verily the noblest of you in the sight of Allah is the most God-fearing of you.
> *(al-Ḥujurāt 49:13)*

---

6 Muhammad ibn Ismā'il al-Bukhāri, *al-Jām'i al-Sahih*, "Kitāb al-Ḥudūd," Bāb 11, 12.

7 Abu Yūsuf Yaqūb ibn Ibrāhīm al-Ansāri, *Kitāb al-Kharāj* (Egypt: al-Matb'ah al-Salafiyah, 1325 A.H.); Abū Dā'ud al-Tayālisi, *Musnad* (Hyderabad: Dā'irah al-Ma'ārif, 1321 A.H.) ḥadī th 55.

While explaining this stated principle, the Prophet says:

إِنَّ اللّٰهَ لَا يَنْظُرُ اِلٰى صُوَرِكُمْ وَاَمْوَالِكُمْ وَلٰكِنْ يَّنْظُرُ اِلٰى قُلُوبِكُمْ وَاَعْمَالِكُمْ.

Allah does not look at your faces and wealth but at your heart and deeds.[8]

اَلْمُسْلِمُونَ اِخْوَةٌ، لَا فَضْلُ لِاَحَدٍ عَلٰى اَحَدٍ اِلَّا بِالتَّقْوٰى.

Muslims are brethren to each other. None has superiority over the other save on taqwā (Allah-consciousness). [9]

يَاَيُّهَا النَّاس، اَلَا اِنَّ رَبَّكُمْ وَاحِدٌ، لَا فَضلُ لِعَرَبِي عَلٰى عَجَمِى، وَلَا لِعَجَمِى عَلٰى عَرَبِي، وَلَا لِاَسْوَدٍ عَلٰى اَحْمَرٍ، وَلَا لِاَحْمَرٍعَلٰى اَسْوَدٍ اِلَّا بِالتَّقْوٰى.

O people hear me! Your God is one. Neither the Arab had superiority over the non-Arab ('ajami) nor the non-Arab over the Arab nor the black have precedence over the white nor the white over the black except the righteous ones.[10]

مَنْ شَهِدَ اَنْ لَّآ اِلٰهَ اِلَّا اللّٰهُ وَاسْتَقْبَلَ قِبْلَتَنَا وَصَلّٰى صَلَوَاتِنَا وَاَكَلَ ذَبِيحَتَنَا فَهُوَ الْمُسْلِمُ لَهُ مَا لِلْمُسْلِمِ وَعَلَيْهِ مَا عَلَى الْمُسْلِمِ.

He who testifies that there is no God but Allah, turned his face towards our *qiblah* and made Ṣalāh like us, and ate our dhabīḥah [slaughtered meat] is a Muslim. He has the same right that a Muslim has and has the same obligations that a Muslim has.[11]

---

8 Ahmad ibn Muhammad ibn Kathir, *Tafsir al-Qur'ān al-'Azīm* (Egypt: Matb'ah Mustafā Muhammad, 1937) cited on the authority of Muslim and Ibn Mājah, vol. 4, p. 217.

9 Ibid, cited on the authority of al-Tabarani, vol. 4, p. 217.

10 Mahmud ibn 'Abd Allah al-Husayni al-Alūsi, *Ruh al-Ma'āni,* cited on the authority of al-Bayhaqi and ibn Mardūyah (Egypt: Idārah al-Tab'āh al-Muniriyah, 1345 A.H.) vol. 26, p. 148.

11 Al-Bukhāri, *al-Jā m'i*, "Kitāb al-Ṣalāh," Bāb 28.

الْمُؤْمِنُونَ تَتَكَافَأُ دِمَآؤُهُمْ، وَهُمْ يَدٌ عَلَى مِنْ سِوَاهُم، وَيَسْعَى بِذِمَّتِهِمْ اَدْنَاهُمْ.

The believers are equal in their blood; they are one as opposed to others. And even an ordinary person among them can take responsibility on their behalf.[12]

لَيْسَ عَلَى الْمُسْلِمِ جِزْيَةٌ.

A Muslim is not liable to jizyah.[13]

4. The government's responsibility and accountability

The fourth principle on which this state rests pertains to the government and its powers and the revenues in the exchequer. The Qur'ān declares the three as trust belonging to Allah and Muslims, which is not assignable to the people who are not God-fearing, honest and just. Nor can the trustees for their ends violate the trust. The trustees are accountable to Allah and the believers. The Qur'ān says:

إِنَّ اللهَ يَأْمُرُكُمْ أَنْ تُؤَدُّوا الْأَمَانَاتِ إِلَى أَهْلِهَا وَإِذَا حَكَمْتُم بَيْنَ النَّاسِ أَنْ تَحْكُمُوا بِالْعَدْلِ إِنَّ اللهَ نِعِمَّا يَعِظُكُم بِهِ إِنَّ اللهَ كَانَ سَمِيعًا بَصِيرًا ـ

Allah commands you to deliver trusts to those worthy of them; and when you judge between people, judge with justice. Excellent is the admonition Allah gives you. Allah is All-Hearing, All-Seeing.
(al-Nisā 4:58)

The Prophet ('alayhi as-salām) says:

اَلَا كُلُّكُمْ رَاعٍ وَّكُلُّكُمْ مَّسْئُولٌ عَنْ رَعِيَّتِهِ، فَالْإِمَامُ الْأَعْظَمُ الَّذِى عَلَى النَّاسِ رَاعٍ وَّهُوَ مَسْئُولٌ عَنْ رَعِيَّتِهِ ـ

Beware, everyone among you is a ra'iy (having responsibility for others) and everyone is

12 Abū Dā'ūd, *Musnad*, "Kitāb al-Diyāt," Bāb 11; "Nasā'i, *al-Sunan,* "Kitāb al-Qasāmah," Bāb 10, 14.
13 Abū Dā'ūd, *Musnad*, "Kitāb al-Imārah," Bāb 34.

answerable about his subjects. And the chief among the Muslims who rules is also a ra'iy and answerable for his subjects.[14]

مَا مِن والٍ يلى رَعْيَةٍ مِنَ الْمُسْلِمِينَ فَيَمُوتُ وَهُوَ غَاشَ لَهُمْ اَلَا حَرَّمَ اللّٰهُ عَلَيْهِ الْجَنَّة.

Any ruler who spearheads the affairs of his subjects among the Muslims and dies while he used to cheat them [in performing his job and ill-spent public money] Allah will proscribe paradise (Jannah) on him.[15]

مَا مِن اميرٍ يلى اَمَرَ الْمُسْلِمِينَ ثُمَّ لَا يَجْهَدُ لَهُمْ وَلَا ينْصِحُ الا لَمْ يَدْخُلْ مَعَهُمْ فِى الْجَنَّةِ.

A ruler who assumes governmental responsibilities and then withholds commitment to his job and lacks sincerity he would not go to Jannah along with the Muslims.[16]

The Prophet ('alayhi as-salam) spoke to Abū Dharr:

يَا اَبَاذَر اِنَّکَ ضَعِيفٌ وَاِنَّهَا اَمَانَةٌ وَاِنَّهَا يَوْم الْقِيَامَةِ خزى وَنِدَامَةٌ اِلَّا مَنْ اَخَذَ بِحَقِّهَا وَادّى الَّذِى عَلَيْهِ فِيهَا.

O Abū Dharr, you are a weak person and the governmental assignment is a trust (given to him). On the Day of Judgment, it will bring disgrace and shame except for him who fulfils its demands and discharges his obligation that comes from it rightly.[17]

مَنْ اَخونِ الْخِيَانَةَ تِجَارَةُ الْوَالِى فِى رَعِيَّتِهِ.

---

14 Al-Bukhāri, *al-Jām'i,* "Kitab al-Ahkām," Bāb 1; Muslim, *al-Jām'i,* "Kitāb al-Imārah," Bāb 5.

15 Ibid, Muslim, *al-Jām'i,* "Kitab al-Imān," Bāb 61, "Kitāb al-Imārah," Bāb 5.

16 Muslim, *al-Jām'i,* Bāb 5.

17 Al-Muttaqi, *Kunz*, vol. 6, ḥadīth 68, 122.

A ruler who does business with his subjects commits a worst usurpation.[18]

مَنْ وَلِيَ لَنَا عملًا وَلَمْ تكُنْ لَهُ زَوْجَةٌ فَلْيَتَّخذْ زَوْجَةً، وَمَنْ لَّمْ يَكُنْ لَهُ خَادِمٌ فَلْيَتَّخَذْ خَادِمًا، اَوَلَيْسَ لَهُ مسكنٌ فَلْيَتَّخذْ مسكناً، اَوَلَيْسَ لَهُ دَابَّةٌ فَلْيَتَّخذ دَابَّةً، فَمَنْ اَصَابَ سِوَىٰ ذَالِکَ فَهُوَ غَالٌّ اَوْ سَارِقٌ.

A person who holds office in our government and has no wife may marry; if he has no servant, may have one (to himself); if he has no house, may have one; if he has no mount (to ride), may have one. Anyone who exceeds it, he is a usurper or a thief.[18]

Says Abū Bakr:

مَنْ يَكُنْ اَمِيرًا فَاِنَّهُ مَنْ اَطْوَلَ النَّاسِ حِسَابًا وَاغلظَه عَذَابًا، وَمَنْ لَا يَكُون اَمِيرًا فَاِنَّهُ مَنْ ايسر النَّاسِ حِسَابًا وَاَهْوَنَهُ عَذَابًا لِاَنَّ الْامَرَاء اَقْرَبَ النَّاسِ مَنْ ظلمَ الْمَؤْمِنِين وَمَنْ يظْلِمِ الْمُؤْمِنِينَ فَاِنَّمَا يَخْفِرُاللّٰهَ

He who is a ruler will have a severe reckoning and he will have the possibility of a great chastisement. And he who is not a ruler will face a light accountability; for him is the likelihood of a lesser punishment, since the rulers (and the functionaries) have greater chances of committing excesses on the Muslims. And he who puts Muslims to hardship indulges in treason against Allah.[19]

'Umar says:

لَوْ هَلَکَ حَملٌ مِنْ وَلَدِ الضَّانِ ضِيَاعًا بِشَاطِئ الْفَرَات خَشِيتُ اَنْ يَسْئَلْنِي اللّٰهُ.

18 Ibid, ḥadīth 346.
19 Ibid, vol. 5, ḥadīth 2505.

If a goat's offspring dies on the bank of the river Euphrates, I feel scared for being questioned by Allah.[20]

5. Shūrā

The fifth important principle on which this state rests pertains to the electoral consensus on the caliph's election obtained through mutual consultation and the people's consent. The caliph thus elected will run its affairs through consultation.

The Qur'ān enjoins:

وَأَمْرُهُمْ شُورَى بَيْنَهُمْ.

who conduct their affairs by consultation.
(al-Shūrā 42:38)

وَشَاوِرْهُمْ فِي الأَمْرِ.

And take counsel from them in matters of importance.
(āl 'Imrān 3:159)

'Ali is reported to have said he asked the Messenger of Allah that if after him they had a problem for which the Qur'ān had no injunction nor had they heard anything from him, what should they do?[21]
The Prophet replied:

شَاوَرُوا فِيهِ الْفُقَهَآءِ وَالْعَابِدِينَ وَلَا تَمْضُوا فِيهِ بِرأيٍ خَاصَّةٍ.

Consult fuqahā (jurists) and the pious people and do not make a decision on the opinion of one particular individual.

20 Ibid, ḥadīth 2512.

21 Al-Tabarāni, *al-Aust.* In this hadith, the pious people are those who worship Allah and are not free to do anything they want. To think that it means seeking consultation with those who pray a lot and ignore other attributes of ahl al-Ra'iy will be unjustified.

Says 'Umar:

مَنْ دَعَا إِلَى إِمَارَةِ نَفْسِهِ أَوْ غَيْرَهُ مِنْ غَيْرِ مَشْوَرَةٍ مِنَ الْمُسْلِمِينَ فَلَا يَحِلُّ لَكُمْ أَنْ لَّا تَقْتُلُوهُ.

He who invites people to his imārah (governance) or to somebody else's without consultations with the Muslims then it is not right for you if you do not kill him.[22]

In another report, 'Umar says:

لَا خِلَافَةَ إِلَّا عَنْ مَشْوَرَةٍ.

Without consultation, there is no caliphate.[23]

6. Obedience in goodness (ma'rūf)

The sixth principle on which this state rests pertains to compliance with and obedience to the government, with a caveat that in evil none had the right to demand obedience. Put differently, it meant that the obedience to the government and its functionaries is valid only their decrees have their basis in the Qur'ān and the Sunnah. They do not have the right to call for compliance if the order they make violate the divine injunctions nor are the people bound to obey them.

In the Qur'ān even the bai'ah (allegiance oath) given to the Prophet was conditional on obedience in m'arūf (goodness).

وَلَا يَعْصِينَكَ فِي مَعْرُوفٍ.

And that they will not disobey you in anything known to be good.
(al-Mumtaḥinah 60:12)

---

22 Al-Muttaqi, *Kunz*, vol. 5, ḥadīth 2577. This saying of 'Umar means that imposing one's self on the people (as head of the Islamic State) is a capital sin, and the Muslim Ummah should not accept it.

23 Ibid, ḥadīth 2354.

Said the Prophet ('alayhi as-salām):

السَّمعُ وَالطَّاعَةُ عَلَى الْمَرْءِ الْمُسْلِمِ فِيمَا اَحَبَّ اَوْ كَرِهَ مَالَمْ يُؤمرُ بِمَعْصِيَةٍ فَإِذَا اُمِرَ بِمَعْصِيَةٍ فَلَا سَمْعٌ وَلَا طَاعَةٌ.

A Muslim is bound to listen and obey his amīr even when he dislikes his decree unless asked to do wrong. And when asked to do wrong, there is no listening and obedience.[24]

لَا طَاعَةَ فِى مَعْصِيَةِ اللّٰهِ، اِنَّمَا الطَّاعَةُ فِى الْمَعْرُوفِ.

There is no obedience when it involves violation of the commands of Allah. Obedience is only in what is ma'rūf.[25]

This subject has repeatedly occurred in the Prophetic sayings. At some places, he said he who deviates from Allah's path, for him there is no obedience. At other places, he said when it violates Allah's injunctions there is no obedience for anyone.

He also said:

لَا طَاعَةَ لِمَنْ عَصَى اللّٰهَ.

He who does not comply with Allah's command for him there is no obedience (from the people).

Likewise, he said:

مَنْ اَمَرَكُمْ مِنَ الْوِلَاةِ بِمَعْصِيَةٍ فَلَا تُطِيعُوهُ.

If a (state) functionary ordains someone to do wrong, do not obey him.[26]\

24 Al-Bukhari, *al-Jām 'i*, "Kitāb al-Ahkām," Bāb 4; Muslim, *al-Jāmi '*, "Kitāb al-Imārah," Bāb 8; Abū Dā'ūd, *Musnad*, "Kitāb al-Jihād," Bāb 95; Nasa'i, *al-Sunan*, "Kitāb al-Bai'ah," Bāb 33; Ibn Mājah, *al-Sunan*, Bāb al-Jihād, bāb 40.

25 Muslim, *al-Jāmi '*, "Kitab al-Imārah," bāb 8; Abū Dā'ūd, *Musnad*, "Kitab al-Jihād," Bāb 95; Nasa'i, *al-Sunan*, "Kitāb al-Bai'ah," Bāb 33.

26 Al-Muttaqi, *Kunz*, vol. 6, ḥadīth 293-296, 299,301.

In one of his addresses, Abū Bakr said:

مَنْ ولی اَمْرَ اُمَّةِ مُحَمَّدٍ صَلَی اللّٰهُ عَلَيْهِ وَسَلَّمَ شَيْئًا فَلَمْ يَقُمْ فِيهِمْ بِكِتَابِ اللّٰهِ فَعَلَيْهِ بُهلةُ اللّٰهِ.

He who has been made responsible for any matter pertaining to Muhammad sal.lal lahu 'alayhi wa-sallam (peace and salutations be on him) and did not follow the Book of Allah while performing his duty, upon him is Allah's curse.[27]

On this basis, he declared in his very first official address as the caliph:

اِطِيعُونِی مَآ اَطَعْتُ اللّٰهَ وَرَسُولَهُ فَاِذَا عَصَيْتُ اللّٰهَ وَرَسُولَهُ فَلَا طَاعَةٌ لِی عَلَيْكُمْ.

Obey me as long as I obey Allah and His Messenger. And when I disobey Allah and His Messenger, you are free not to obey me.[28]

'Ali said:

حَقٌّ عَلَى الْاِمَامِ اَنْ يَّحْكُمُ بِمَآ اَنْزَلَ اللّٰهُ وَاَنْ يُؤَدِّی الْامَانٰةَ، فَاِذَا فَعَلَ ذَالِکَ فَحَقٌّ عَلَى النَّاسِ اَنْ يَسْمعُوا لَهُ وَاَنْ يُطِيعُوا وَاَنْ يَجِيبُوا اِذَا دُعُوا.

It is the duty of a Muslim ruler to run the affairs of the state in the light of the laws revealed by Allah and prove his custodianship of the trust (reposed in him). If he continues discharging his obligation in this way, then the people are bound to listen to him and obey. And when he calls them to his assistance, they should respond.[29]

---

27 Ibid, vol. 5, ḥadīth 2505.

28 Ibid, ḥadīth 2282. In another report, Abū Bakr's words are "If I disobey Allah, you disobey me." See *Kunz*, vol. 5, ḥadīth 2330.

29 Ibid, vol. 5, ḥadīth 2531.

On yet another occasion, 'Ali said:

مَا اَمَرْتُكُمْ بِهِ مِنْ طَاعَةِ اللّٰهِ فَحَقٌّ عَلَيْكُمْ طَاعَتِى فِيمَا اَحْبَبْتُمْ وَمَا كَرَّهْتُمْ،
وَمَا اَمَرْتُكُمْ بِهِ مَنْ مَّعْصِيَةِ اللّٰهِ فَلَا طَاعَةٌ لَا حَدٍ فِى الْمَعْصِيَةِ، الطَّاعَةُ فِى
الْمَعْرُوفِ، الطَّاعَةُ فِى الْمَعْرُوفِ، الطَّاعَةُ فِى الْمَعْرُوفِ.

In obeying Allah the Exalted you are obliged to do as I tell you irrespective of the fact whether you like it or not. And if I enjoin you to do something in violation of Allah's injunction, then in sin there is no obedience for you. Only in goodness is compliance, only in goodness is compliance, only in goodness is compliance.[30]

7. Forbiddance of power aspirations

This state also believes that for high-powered jobs in general and the caliphal office in particular he who aspires and struggles for them disqualifies to have them.

The Qur'ān says:

تِلْكَ الدَّارُ الْآخِرَةُ نَجْعَلُهَا لِلَّذِينَ لَا يُرِيدُونَ عُلُوًّا فِي الْأَرْضِ وَلَا فَسَادًا.

As for the abode of the Hereafter, We shall assign it exclusively for those who do not seek glory on earth nor want to cause mischief.
(*al-Qaṣaṣ* 28: 83)

The Prophet ('alayhi was-salām) said:

اِنَّا وَاللّٰهِ لَا نُوَلِّى عَلٰى عَمَلِنَا هٰذَا اَحَدًا سَئَلَهُ اَوْ حَرِصَ عَلَيْهِ.

By Allah, we do not assign our government's office to him who seeks it and lusts for it.[31]

---

30 Ibid, ḥadīth 2587.

31 Al-Bukhari, *al-Jām'i*, "*Kitāb al-Ahkām*", Bāb 7; Muslim, *al-Jām'i*, "*Kitab al-Imārah*", Bāb 3.

إِنَّ اَخْوَنَكَمْ عِنْدَنَا مَنْ طَلَبَه.

> To us, he who asks for (public office) among you is the greatest of all usurpers. [32]

اِنَّا لَا نَسْتَعْمِلُ عَلٰى عَمَلِنَا مَنْ اَرَادَه.

> We do not appoint anyone in our government as *āmil* (functionary) who aspires for it.[33]

يَا عَبْدَالرَّحْمٰن بِنْ سَمْرَةٍ، لَا تَسْئَلْ الْاَمَارَةِ فَاِنَّکَ اِذَا اُوتِيتهَا عَنْ مَسْئَلَةٍ
وَكِلْتَ اِلَيْهَا، وَاِن اُوتِيتهَا عَنْ غَيْرمَسْئَلَةٍ اُعِنَتْ عَلَيْهَا.

> O Abdul-Rahmān ibn Samurah, do not ask for a job in the government because if it is granted to you in response to your aspiring for it, you will be consigned to it by Allah. And if you got it without asking for it, Allah will help you in performing your responsibilities.[34]

8. The purpose of the state

In this state the ruler and his administration are bound to implement the Islamic agenda without any change in it. It shall spread goodness and extirpate evil according to Islam's moral standards. The Qur'ān spells out the justification for an Islamic state:

الَّذِينَ إِنْ مَّكَّنَّاهُمْ فِي الْأَرْضِ أَقَامُوا الصَّلَاةَ وَآتَوُا الزَّكَاةَ وَأَمَرُوا بِالْمَعْرُوفِ
وَنَهَوْا عَنِ الْمُنكَرِ.

> (Allah will certainly help) those who, were We to bestow authority on them in the land,

---

32 Abū Dā'ūd, *Musnad*, "*Kitāb al-Imārah*", Bāb 2.

33 Al-Muttaqi, *Kunz*, vol. 6, ḥadīth 206.

34 Al-Muttaqi, *Kunz*, vol. 6, ḥadīth 69. One may ask if this is the Islamic principle, then why did Prophet Yūsuf ask the king for the job. In fact, he was then residing in a non-Islamic country. He sensed that even if he had asked for the highest job in the land it would be given to him which he could use for the spread of Allah's dīn. Otherwise, he thought, the chance to invite that non-Muslim nation to Allah's way would be lost. Since this was an exceptional situation, the general Islamic principle cannot be applied to it.

> will establish Prayers, render Zakāh, enjoin good, and forbid evil. The end of all matters rests with Allah.
> *(al-Ḥajj 22:41)*

> The Qur'ān says:

> وَكَذَلِكَ جَعَلْنَاكُمْ أُمَّةً وَسَطًا لِّتَكُونُواْ شُهَدَاء عَلَى النَّاسِ وَيَكُونَ الرَّسُولُ عَلَيْكُمْ شَهِيدًا.

> And it is thus that We appointed you to be the community of the middle way so that you might be witnesses to all mankind and the Messenger might be a witness to you.
> *(al-Baqarah 2:143)*

> كُنتُمْ خَيْرَ أُمَّةٍ أُخْرِجَتْ لِلنَّاسِ تَأْمُرُونَ بِالْمَعْرُوفِ وَتَنْهَوْنَ عَنِ الْمُنكَرِ وَتُؤْمِنُونَ بِاللّهِ.

> You are now the best nation brought forth for mankind. You enjoin what is right, forbid wrong, and believe in Allah.
> *(āl 'Imrān 3:110)*

The Qur'ān also describes the assignment given to Muhammad ('alayhi as-salām) and the prophets before him:

> أَنْ أَقِيمُوا الدِّينَ وَلَا تَتَفَرَّقُوا فِيهِ.

> Establish this religion and do not split up regarding it.
> *(al-Shūrā 42:13)*

The Prophet's whole struggle against non-Islamic forces was wedded to the objective of making the whole life surrendered to Allah's will.
(al-Anfāl 8: 39)

Like the rest of the peoples of the past prophets, Allah has also enjoined on Muslims to follow steadfastly Allah, and realign their lives on the divine pattern (al-Bayyanah: 5). That is why the Prophetic state bonded itself to the supreme task of restructuring life in the light of the divine guidance and desisted allowing infusion of non-Islamic elements into it so that duplicitous attitudes in Muslim society are averted. The Prophet warned his companions and his successors:

مَنْ اَحْدَثَ فِي اَمْرِنَا هٰذَا مَالَيْسَ مِنْهُ فَهُوَ رَدٌّ.

> He who deduces something from our religion that does not belong to its genus [of ideas and spirit] is worth contempt.[35]

اِيَّاكُمْ وَمُحْدَثَاتِ الْاُمُورِ، فَاِنَّ كُلَّ مُحْدَثَةٍ بِدْعَةٍ وَّكُلَّ بِدْعَةٍ ضَلَالَة.

> Beware, stay away from novelties (in religion) for every novelty is a bid'ah (wrong) and every bid'ah is a deviation.[36]

مَنْ وَقَّرَ صَاحِبَ بِدْعَةٍ فَقَدْ اَعَانَ عَلٰى هَدَمِ الْاِسْلَام.

> He who respected the one who introduces bid'ah, helped in demolishing Islam.[37]

مُبْتَغٌ فِي الْاِسْلَامِ سُنَّةَ الْجَاهِلِيَّة.

> We also come across this prophetic statement to the effect that Allah dislikes three persons most. Among them is one who desires to graft jāhiliyah on Islam.[38]

35 Al-Tabrizi, *al-Mishkāt,* "bi al-Kitāb wa al-Sunnah," Bāb al-Ahtasām.
36 Ibid.
37 Ibid.
38 Ibid.

9. The right and obligation of "amr bi al-ma'rūf wa nahi 'an al-munkar"

Last among the principal features of this state that assured its right direction was binding its citizen to the task of exhorting good and avoid evil, to support the spread of goodness in society and do utmost in rooting out evil and in chartering the state towards the well-being of its people.

The Qur'ānic institutions are as under:

وَتَعَاوَنُواْ عَلَى الْبرِّ وَالتَّقْوَى وَلاَ تَعَاوَنُواْ عَلَى الإِثْمِ وَالْعُدْوَانِ.

Help you one another in acts of righteousness and piety, do not help one another in sin and transgression.
(al-Mā'idah 5:2)

يَا أَيُّهَا الَّذِينَ آمَنُوا اتَّقُوا اللَّهَ وَقُولُوا قَوْلًا سَدِيدًا.

Believers, fear Allah, and speak the truth.
(al-Aḥzāb 33:70)

يَا أَيُّهَا الَّذِينَ آمَنُواْ كُونُواْ قَوَّامِينَ بِالْقِسْطِ شُهَدَاء لِلّهِ وَلَوْ عَلَى أَنفُسِكُمْ أَوِ الْوَالِدَيْنِ وَالأَقْرَبِينَ.

Believers! Be upholders of justice, and bearers of witnesses to Truth for the sake of Allah, even though it may be against yourselves or against parents and kinsmen…
(al-Nisā' 4:135)

الْمُنَافِقُونَ وَالْمُنَافِقَاتُ بَعْضُهُم مِّن بَعْضٍ يَأْمُرُونَ بِالْمُنكَرِ وَيَنْهَوْنَ عَنِ الْمَعْرُوفِ وَيَقْبِضُونَ أَيْدِيَهُمْ نَسُواْ اللّهَ فَنَسِيَهُمْ إِنَّ الْمُنَافِقِينَ هُمُ الْفَاسِقُونَ. وَعَدَ اللهِ الْمُنَافِقِينَ وَالْمُنَافِقَاتِ وَالْكُفَّارَ نَارَ جَهَنَّمَ خَالِدِينَ فِيهَا هِيَ حَسْبُهُمْ وَلَعَنَهُمُ اللّهُ وَلَهُمْ عَذَابٌ مُّقِيمٌ. كَالَّذِينَ مِن قَبْلِكُمْ كَانُواْ أَشَدَّ مِنكُمْ قُوَّةً وَأَكْثَرَ أَمْوَالاً وَأَوْلاَدًا فَاسْتَمْتَعُواْ بِخَلاقِهِمْ فَاسْتَمْتَعْتُم بِخَلاَقِكُمْ كَمَا اسْتَمْتَعَ الَّذِينَ

مِن قَبْلِكُمْ بِخَلاَقِهِمْ وَخُضْتُمْ كَالَّذِي خَاضُواْ أُوْلَـئِكَ حَبِطَتْ أَعْمَالُهُمْ فِي الدُّنْيَا وَالآخِرَةِ وَأُوْلَئِكَ هُمُ الْخَاسِرُونَ. أَلَمْ يَأْتِهِمْ نَبَأُ الَّذِينَ مِن قَبْلِهِمْ قَوْمِ نُوحٍ وَعَادٍ وَثَمُودَ وَقَوْمِ إِبْرَاهِيمَ وِأَصْحَابِ مَدْيَنَ وَالْمُؤْتَفِكَاتِ أَتَتْهُمْ رُسُلُهُم بِالْبَيِّنَاتِ فَمَا كَانَ اللّهُ لِيَظْلِمَهُمْ وَلَـكِن كَانُواْ أَنفُسَهُمْ يَظْلِمُونَ. وَالْمُؤْمِنُونَ وَالْمُؤْمِنَاتُ بَعْضُهُمْ أَوْلِيَاء بَعْضٍ يَأْمُرُونَ بِالْمَعْرُوفِ وَيَنْهَوْنَ عَنِ الْمُنكَرِ وَيُقِيمُونَ الصَّلاَةَ وَيُؤْتُونَ الزَّكَاةَ وَيُطِيعُونَ اللّهَ وَرَسُولَهُ أُوْلَـئِكَ سَيَرْحَمُهُمُ اللّهُ إِنَّ اللّهَ عَزِيزٌ حَكِيمٌ.

The hypocrites, be they men or women, all are alike. They enjoin what is evil, and forbid what is good, and withhold their hands from doing. They forgot Allah, so Allah also forgot them. Surely, the hypocrites are wicked.

Allah has promised Hell-Fire to the hypocrites, both men and women, and to the unbelievers. They shall abide in it a sufficient recompense for them. Allah has cursed them, and theirs is a lasting torment.

Your ways are like the ways of those who have gone before you. They were mightier than you in power, and more abundant in riches and children. They enjoyed their lot for a while as you have enjoyed your lot, and you also engaged in idle talk as they did. Their works have come to naught in this world, and in the Hereafter, they are surely the losers.

Have they not heard the accounts of those who came before them – of the people of Noah and ‘Ād and Thamūd, and the people of Abraham and the dwellers of Madyan (Midian), and the cities that were overturned? Their Messengers came to them with Clear Signs. Then, it was not Allah Who caused them any wrong; they rather wronged themselves.

The believers, both men and women, are allies of one another. They enjoin good, forbid evil, establish Prayer, pay Zakāh, and obey Allah and His Messenger. Surely, Allah will show mercy to them. Allah is All-Mighty, All-Wise. *(al-Tawbah 9:67-71)*

الآمِرُونَ بِالْمَعْرُوفِ وَالنَّاهُونَ عَنِ الْمُنكَرِ وَالْحَافِظُونَ لِحُدُودِ اللهِ.

Who enjoin what is good and forbid what is evil, and who keep the limits set by Allah. *(al-Tawbah 9:112)*

The Prophet's pronouncements on the subject are as follows:

مَنْ رَأىٰ مِنْكُمْ مُنْكِرًا فَلْيُغَيِّرْهُ بِيَدِهِ فَإنْ لَّمْ يَسْتَطِعْ فَبِلِسَانِهِ فَإنْ لَّمْ يَسْتَطِعْ فَبِقَلْبِهِ وَذَالِكَ اَضْعَفُ الْإِيمَان.

He who sees a wrong should bolt it out by hand. If he cannot do it, he should seek its change through his word of mouth. If he cannot do even this much, then he should condemn it in his heart (thinking it bad and harbouring desire to prevent it). And this will be the weakest state of imān (faith).[39]

ثُمَّ إنَّهَا تَخْلُفُ مِنْ بَعْدِهِمْ خُلُوفٌ يَقُولُونَ مَالَا يَفْعَلُونَ وَيَفْعَلُونَ مَالَا يُؤْمَرُونَ، فَمَنْ جَاهَدَهُمْ بِيَدِهِ فَهُوَ مُؤْمِنٌ وَمَنْ جَاهَدَهُمْ بِلِسَانِهِ فَهُوَ مُؤْمِنٌ وَمَنْ جَاهَدَهُمْ بِقَلْبِهِ فَهُوَ مُؤْمِنٌ وَلَيْسَ وَرَآءَ ذَالِكَ حَبَّةُ خَرْدَلٍ مِنَ الْإِيمَان.

After them will come inept people, who will say things but will not act accordingly. And they will do things for which they have not been told. Thus, he who wages jihād against them by hand is a believer (mu'min). And he who wages jihād against them by mouth is

39 Muslim, *al-Jām'i*, "*Kitab al-Imān*," Bāb 20; *Tirmidhi*, Bāb 12; Abū Dā'ūd, *al-Musnad*, "*Kitāb al-Malāham*," Bāb 17; *Ibn Mājah*, Bāb 20, *Abwāb al-Fitan*.

a believer. And he who wages jihād against them in his heart is a believer. And imān less than this have no merit.[40]

اَفضَلُ الْجِهَاد كَلِمَة عَدْلٍ (اَوْحَق) عِنْدَ سَلْطَانٍ جَآئِرٍ.

The best of the jihād is to say a just word (or of truth) before a tyrant ruler.[41]

انَّ النَّاسَ اِذَا رَأَوُا الظَّالِمَ فَلَمْ يَأْخُذُواعَلٰى يَدَيْهِ اَوْشَک اَنْ يَّعُمَّهُمُ اللّٰهُ بِعِقَابٍ مِنْه۔

When people see oppression perpetuated by a tyrant and do not withhold him from doing so, then it will not be surprising if Allah sends punishment on them.[42]

انه سَتَكُونُ بَعْدِى امرَاءَ، مَنْ صَدَّقَهُمْ بِكِذْبِهِمْ وَاَعَانَهِمْ عَلٰى ظُلْمِهِمْ فَلَيْسَ مِنِّى وَلَسْتُ مِنْهُ.

After me, some people will install themselves as rulers, he who supports them in their lies and lend them help in their oppressive acts he is not of me and I am not of him.[43]

سَيَكُون عَلَيْكُمْ اَئِمَّةٌ يَمْلِكُونَ ارزَاقِكَمْ يُحَدِّثُونَكُمْ فَيَكْذِبُونَكُمْ وَيَعْمَلُونَ فَيُسَيِّئُونَ الْعَمِلَ لَا يَرْضون مِنْكُمْ حَتّٰى تَحْسِنُوا قَبِيحَهُمْ وَتَصَدَّقُوا كِذْبَهُمْ فَاَعْطُوهُمُ الْحَقَّ مَا رَضُوا بِهِ فَاِذَا تَجَاوَزُوا فَمَنْ قُتِلَ عَلٰى ذَالِک فَهُوَ شَهِيدٌ.

Soon you will have rulers who will have in their hands your sustenance. They will talk but lies to you and will do but wrongdoing.

40 Muslim, *al-Jām'i,* "Kitāb al-Imān," Bāb 20.

41 Muslim, *al-Jām'i, "Kitāb al-Malāham,"* Bāb 17; *Tirmidhi, "Kitāb al-Fitan,"* Bāb 12; Nasā'i, *al-Sunan, "Kitab al-Bai'ah,"* Bāb 34-35.

42 *Abu Dā'ud, "Kitāb al-Malāham,"* Bāb 17; *al-Tirmidhi, "Kitab al-Fitan,"* Bāb 12.

43 Nasā'i', *al-Sunan, "Kitāb al-Bai'ah,"* Bāb 34-35.

They will not be satisfied with you unless you praise them for their bad deeds and confirm them in their lies. Thus, you talk truth to them as long as they bear with it. Then, if they turn deaf and kill someone as a result thereof, he is a martyr (shahīd).[45]

مَنِ ارْضٰى سُلْطَاناً بِمَا يُسْخِطُ رَبَّهُ خَرَجَ مِنْ دِيْنِ اللهِ.

He who tries to please a ruler by saying something that may annoy his Provider goes out of the pale of Allah's religion.[44]

44 Ibid, ḥadīth 309.

Chapter Three

Al-Khilāfah al-Rāshidah and its Characteristics

In the last pages, we dealt with the Islamic principals of governance, which provided the basis for the caliphal regime after the Prophet's death. The social setup instituted under the Prophet's direct guidance gave everyone a feel as to the nature of the Islamic governance and the difference it makes to his or her lives.

Although the Prophet ('alayhi as-salām) had withheld his decision to nominate his successor but the people knew [by their internalizing the Islamic system] that Islam called for the participatory caliphate (Khilāfah). It was because of such an ambience that post-prophetic period neither saw dynastic kingship installed itself nor did anyone strive for personal hold on power; instead, four successive individuals came into power through people's consent. The Muslims Ummah named their style of governance as al-Khilāfah al-Rāshidah (the rightly guided caliphate), the sole end of their aspirations and ideals.

1. Electoral Khilāfah

To succeed the Prophet, 'Umar proposed Abū Bakr's name, which won for him people's pledge of support.

Before his death, Abū Bakr nominated 'Umar as his successor and after summoning the people to Masjid al-Nabawi addressed them:

> "Are you happy with the person I have nominated as my successor? By Allah, while thinking over the matter, I spared no effort. I have not given succession to any of my relatives but to 'Umar ibn al-Khattāb. So listen to him and follow him."

Responding, people assured Abū Bakr: "We will listen to him and follow him."[1]

In 'Umar's last ḥajj a person said that if 'Umar died, he would give his pledge to a certain person, for Abū Bakr's nomination popped up suddenly and it succeeded.[2]

On hearing it, 'Umar said he would warn people about "those who are planning to seek domination over their affairs." Thus after reaching Mādinah, the first thing he did was to explain the situation that led to Abū Bakr's sudden succession in Saqīfah Bani Sā'dah. Elaborating the matter he said:

> "If I had not taken this course and the gathering had dispersed without resolving the succession issue, people would have made a wrong decision making it difficult for us to accept it or change it later. If [our] act succeeded, it should not serve as a precedent. Among you, there is none to equal the stature and standing of Abū Bakr. Now, any person who gives his pledge to another person without the Muslims' consent, he as well as the nominee, who receives his pledge will qualify himself for execution."[3]

Following the rule he laid out, 'Umar appointed an electoral college to decide the succession issue and said before his death:

---

1 Abū Ja'far Muḥammad ibn Jarīr al-Ṭabari, *Tārikh al-Umum wa al-Malūk*, (Cairo: al-Matb'ah al-Astaqāmah, 1935) vol. 2, p. 618.

2 He was pointing to the event in the Saqifah Bani Sā'idah meeting, when 'Umar suddenly rose and suggested Abū Bakr's name followed by his *bai'ah* to him. There was no consultation prior to his appointment as caliph.

3 Al-Bukhari, *al-Jām'i*, "Kitāb al-Maharbīn," chapter 16; Aḥmad ibn Muḥammad ibn Ḥanbal, *al-Musand* (Cairo: Dār al-Ma'ārif, 1949) vol. 1, ḥadīth 391, third print.

In *al-Musnad*, the Caliph 'Umar's words are: "He who gives his bai'ah (pledge) to someone without consultation with the Muslims has no validity nor of the person who received his bai'ah."

In another report 'Umar's words are "A person whom bai'ah (pledge) is given without consultation for him it is unjustified to accept it." See Ibn Ḥajar, *Fatḥ al-Bāri* (Cairo: al-Matba'h al-Khayriyah, 1325 A.H.) vol. 2, p. 125.

"He who seeks rulership (imārah) without the Muslims' consent should be killed." At the same time, he excluded his son for caliphal nomination so the Khilāfah does not become a dynastic office.[4] His appointed electoral body had six persons who in his view were the most liked and influential in the Islamic Ummah."

After deliberation, the electoral colleges deputed 'Abdul-Raḥmān ibn 'Auf to nominate the caliph. He made mass contact including the hajj caravans to know about their inclination for any particular person. He found that people preferred 'Uthmān to others.[5]

It was on this basis that 'Uthmān was elected for the caliphal office, with people pledging support to him in a mass gathering.

When 'Uthmān met shahādah (martyrdom), some people approached 'Ali to succeed him but he refused saying: "You do not have the right to do so, as this pertains to ahl al-'aqd and ahl al-Badr (people who have wisdom and those who participated in the battle of Badr). Whoever they want to be the caliph will assume the office. Thus, we will get together to consider the issue." [6] In al-Ṭabari's report 'Ali's words are as follows:

> "Giving oath in secret to me will be incorrect. This should have the people's assent."[7]

As death approached 'Ali, people asked him if they could pledge their loyalty to his son al-Hasan. His reply was "I can neither dictate you nor will I stop you. You can make your own choice."[8]

---

4 Al-Ṭabari, *Tārikh*, vol. 1, p. 292; Izzudin abi al-Ḥassan 'Ali ibn Muḥammad al-Jazāri ibn al-Athīr, *al-Kāmil fi al-Tārikh* (Cairo: Idārah al-Taba'tah al-Muniriyah, 1356 A. H.) vol. 3, pp. 34-35; Abū 'Abdullah Muḥammad ibn Sa'd, *al-Ṭabaqāt al-Kubrā* (Beirut: Dār Sādr, 1957) vol. 3, p.1344. Ibn Ḥajar, *Fatḥ...*, vol. 7, p. 49.

5 Al-Ṭabari, *Tārik* , vol. 3, p. 296; Ibn al-Athīr, *al-Kāmil,* vol. 3, p. 36; Ibn Kathīr, *al-Bidāyah*, vol. 7, p. 146.

6 'Abdullah ibn Muslim ibn Qutaybah, *al-Imāmah wa al-Siyāsah*, vol. 1, p. 41 al-Ṭabari, *Tārikh...*, vol. 3, p. 45.

7 Al-Ṭabari, *Tārikh*, vol. 3, p. 45.

8 Al-Ṭabari, *Tārikh*, vol. 4, p. 112; Abū al-Ḥasan 'Ali ibn Ḥusayn ibn 'Ali al-Mas'ūdi, *Murūj al-Dhahab* (Cairo: al-Matbah al-Bihiyyah, 1346 A.H.) vol. 2, p. 12.

A person interrupted him while he was making his last will to his sons urging him to name his successor, which he refused by saying: "I will leave the Muslims in the same state in which Rasūl Allāh (peace be on him) left them."[9]

From these events, it is obvious that the first four caliphs and the ṣaḥābah (companions) viewed caliphate as an elected office, which came into being by consultation among the Muslim people and their free will. In their eyes dynastic monarchy or forcibly captured power did not constitute caliphate: it was kingship. Abū Musā al-Ash'ari articulated the difference between the two in these words:

> "Imārah (that is caliphate) comes into being when it is the outcome of (mutual) consultation. And kingship is obtained by force."[10]

2. Shūrāwi governance

The first four caliphs never decided the governmental issues and lawmaking without consulting people of wisdom and opinion. In *Sunan al-Dārami*, Maymūn ibn Mayhrān says that when faced with a problem Abū Bakr would look for an answer into the Qur'ān first. If he did not find it there, he would probe the prophetic Sunnah for an answer. Failing in that, he would summon the community leading members and the pious ones for advice. Thereafter, whatever opinion emerged he would abide by it.[11] The same went with 'Umar.[12]

In obtaining advice, the four caliphs believed in the shūrā right to express it. While addressing the inaugural session of the shūrā, 'Umar elaborated his policy:

> "My reason to inconvenience you is nothing else but to ask you to share the [heavy] load of executing your affairs that you have placed on my shoulders. I

9 Ibn Kathir, *al-Bidāyah*, vol. 8, pp. 13-14; al-Mas'udi, *Murūj*, vol. 2, p. 42.

10 Ibn Sa'd, *al-Ṭabaqāt*, vol. 4, p. 113.

11 'Abdullah ibn 'Abdul-Raḥmān, *Sunan al-Dārmi*, "Bab al-Futiyā wa mā fih min al-Shaddah."

12 Al-Muttaqi, *Kunz,* vol. 5, ḥadīth 2281.

am from among you. And today, you are the people who will affirm what is right (ḥaqq). Whoever wants to disagree with me may do so, and whoever wants to agree with me may do so. I do not want you to follow my desire."[13]

3. Bayt al-māl a matter of trust

For them, bayt al-māl (public treasury) was a trust from Allah and people, which they were not supposed to spend without justification. When it came to private needs of the caliphs, they were vehemently opposed to it. The difference between the caliphate and kingship was essentially of legitimacy and usurpation. A king feels himself free to spend public money the way he wants whereas a caliph feels himself bound as for him it was an inviolable trust. Once ‘Umar asked Salmān al-Fārsi: "Am I a king or a caliph?" Salmān said forthwith: "If you obtain even a dirham unjustifiably from the people and spend it without a reason, then you are a king and not a caliph."

On another occasion, ‘Umar asked people in a sitting: "By Allah, I am still confused if I am a king or a caliph. If I have become a king, then I am in trouble."

A person said: "Yā Amīr al-Mu'minīn, there is a big difference between the two." ‘Umar asked him to elaborate. He said a caliph takes nothing but with justification and spends nothing but with a reason. By Allah's grace, you are a caliph. As for the king, he does excesses on the people – he receives from one unjustifiably and transfers it to another without his right. [14]

The caliphs' conduct is illustrative of this attitude. Immediately after his induction as caliph, Abū Bakr took to the street, as was his practice with a bundle of cloth on his shoulder to make his living. ‘Umar saw him. Surprised, he asked why he was doing it. His answer was equally surprising – he had to feed his family. ‘Umar discounted it. The caliphal responsibility and earning daily living, he said, cannot go together. He suggested going to Abū ‘Ubaydah, the

13 Abū Yūsuf, *Kitāb,* p. 25.
14 Ibn Sa‘d, *al-Tabaqāt*, vol. 3, pp. 306-307.

head of the public treasury, who keeping in view the living standard of an average muhājir (émigré) granted Abū Bakr subsistence allowance. As said by Abū 'Ubaydah, this allowance would neither be equal to the richest income among the muhājir*ū*n nor would it measure the poorest among them. The amount allocated was thus 4,000 dirham a year. But as his death neared, Abu Bakr willed that out of his legacy 8,000 dirham should be returned to bayt al-māl (treasury). When they brought the amount to 'Umar, he could not help say it: May Allah has His mercy upon Abū Bakr, he has put his successors into a difficult situation.[15]

> Stating the caliph's right in bayt al-māl 'Umar said in one of his speeches:
>
> "In Allah's money there is nothing Ḥalāl (allowed) for me other than a two- piece wear for the summer and a two-piece wear for the winter; that I should take subsistence for my family equal to an average Qurayshi's living. After that, I am just a person among the Muslims."[16]
>
> In another speech, he says:
>
> "As for the (public) money, I do not consider anything right other than three matters: take it with (genuine) reason; give it justifiably (to others); and safeguard it against misuse. My relation with your money is that of an orphan's guardian with his wealth. If I am not dependent, I will desist taking anything out of it. And if I am in need, I will take according to known, acceptable way."[17]

'Ali followed Abū Bakr and 'Umar's tradition by maintaining the same subsistence allowance. Wearing clothes, half up to his knees and that too patched at places,[18] not once in his life he had the means

---

15 Al-Muttaqi, *Kunz*, vol. 5, ḥadīth 2280-2285.
16 Ibn Kathīr, *al-Bidāyah*, vol. 7, p. 134.
17 Abu Yūsuf, *Kitāb*, p. 117.
18 Ibn Sa'd, *al-Ṭabaqāt*, vol. 3, p. 28.

to overcome his poverty. A man came to see him in winter and found him shivering with cold.[19] After his death, his legacy did not exceed seven hundred dirham, which he saving over the years for buying a helping hand to himself.[20]

Never would he buy a thing from someone who knew him lest he charges him less for being amīr al-mu'minīn (commander of the faithful).[21]

When he was up against Mu'āwiyah, people suggested him that he should follow the latter's proactive policy by winning over allies through gifts and awards from bayt al-māl. But he refused: "Are you telling me that I should seek success by wrong means."[22] His elder brother 'Aqīl approached him for a grant from bayt al-māl, but he refused, saying, "Do you want your brother to give you money of the Muslims and go instead to hell fire?"[23]

4. The Responsible governance

What was the concept of these people about governance? As the rulers of the Muslim people, what did they think about their position and responsibilities? And what policy did they pursue for their governments?

They themselves explained their approach towards governance in their speeches from the pulpit. In his post-allegiance speech in the Masjid al-Nabawi, Abū Bakr said:

> "You have made me your ruler (even though I am not the best among you), for which I have no strength unless Allah helps me.

---

19 Ibn Kathīr, *al-Bidayah,* vol. 8, p. 3.

20 Ibid; Ibn Sa'd, *al-Tabaqāt*, vol. 3, p. 38.

21 Ibid; also, Ibn Kathīr, *al-Bidāyah*, vol. 8, p. 3.

22 Ibn abi al-Ḥadid, *Sharh Nahj al-Balāqhah* (Cairo: Dār al-Kutb al-Arabiyah, 1329 A.H.) vol. 1, p. 182.

23 Ibn Qutaybah, *al-Imāmah*, vol. 1, p. 71.
Ibn Ḥajar has written in *al-Isābah* that 'Aqīl had incurred some loan, which 'Ali refused to pay him from bayt al-māl. Thus annoyed, he joined Mu'āwiyah. See *al-Isābah fi Tamyīz al-Ṣaḥābah* (Cairo: Matb'ah Mustaphā Muhammad, 1939) vol. 3, p. 487.

I wanted someone else to bear the load of this office. Even now if you want, you can elect someone else from among the companions of Rasūl Allāh. Your pledge oath to me is no bar in your way.
If you measured me to Rasul Allah's standards and held me to expectations that you had from him, I would surely fail for he was in Allah's protection against the shaytān and the revelation from above. If I stay the course, help me. If I act wrong, straighten me. Truth is trust (amānah) and lie is usurpation.
He who is weak among you is strong before me until I restored his right to him, if Allah wills. And he who is strong among you is weak before me until I obtain from him what is due on him, if Allah wills.
It has never happened that a nation ceases to strive in Allah's way and is not consigned to disgrace imposed on it.
And that a nation has immoralities and that Allah will not subject it to difficulties.
Obey me as long as I bind myself to Allah and His Messenger. And if I divert from Allah and His Messenger's way, then you are free from your pledge to me.
I am a follower and not a new pathfinder."[24]

'Umar says in one of his speeches:

"Nobody, his legitimacy notwithstanding, has the right to demand obedience from people if he follows non-Allah.... O people, I will describe to you the rights you have against me so that you may lay claim against me. You can hold me to account (if I do not give you your rights).
Your right on me is that I should avoid taking from your kharāj and Allah-given fay but lawfully.
And your right on me is that whatever comes to me

24 Al-Ṭabari, *Tārikh*, vol. 2, p. 480; Muḥammad 'Abdul- Mālik ibn Hishām, *al-Sirah al-Nabawiyyah* (Cairo: Matb'ah Mustaphā al-Bābi, 1936) vol. 4, p. 311; al-Muttaqi, *Kunz*, vol. 5, ḥadīth 2261, 2268, 2278, 2291, 2299.

(in the form of kharāj and fay), I should not spend it but with justification."[25]

When Abū Bakr sent 'Amr ibn al-'Āṣ to Syria and Palestine, his instructions were:

"O 'Amr, fear Allah in your hidden and open deeds. Show regard to Him and do not violate Him for He eyes your every deed .... Work for the *ākhirah* (hereafter).
Seek Allah's beneficence for your every deed. Treat your companions as if they were your children. Do not probe people's secrets and deal with them on what is obvious ... Stay the course and people will follow you."[26]

While deputing governors to provinces, 'Umar would say: "I am not appointing you over the Prophet's Ummah that you become the master of their hair and hides. Rather, I put them to your charge so that you establish prayer (Ṣalāh), decide between people with truth (ḥaqq) and give them what you owe them with justice."[27]

In his post-pledge address to the people, 'Uthmān said: "Listen! I am a follower, not a new pathfinder. Know it that after following Allah and His Messenger, there are three things that I pledge to abide by. That I will stick to the ways and means agreed among you before my induction into the caliphate (Khilāfah).
Second, in matters where there are no agreed procedural precedents, I will formulate new ones through consensus with the people of right thinking.
Third, I will not lay my hands on you unless law supports my action."[28]

---

25 Abu Yūsuf, *Kitāb*, p. 117.
26 Al-Muttaqi, *Kunz*, vol. 5, ḥadīth 2313.
27 Al-Ṭabari, *Tarikh*, vol. 3, p. 273.
28 Ibid, p. 446.

Likewise, when 'Ali appointed Qays ibn Sa'd as governor of Egypt, he wrote the following caliphal decree to the people over there.

> "Beware! Your right upon us is that we act according to Allah's Book and His messenger's Sunnah and run your affairs in the light of Allah's guidance and establish the Prophet's Sunnah and do good to you even in your absence."
>
> After having read this decree, Qays ibn Sa'd declared: "If we did not treat you according to the way [announced], then you are free from your pledge to us."[29]
>
> 'Ali wrote to one of his governors:
> "Do not allow veils of separation between yourself and the people. The officials distancing themselves from the people show narrow mindedness and lack of knowledge. By such veils, they obscure themselves from the people's affairs. Small things become bigger and big things become smaller for them. Good turns into bad and bad into good before them. [Eventually] truth intermingles with falsehood."[30]

This was not just a rhetorical speech – he acted on it. The Kūfah bazaars often saw him with a lash in his hand restraining people from wrong and exhorting them to do good. He would visit the marketplace to see if traders were measuring and selling goods properly. Dressed ordinarily, without kingly trappings and security apparatus none would have taken him as the caliph of the Islamic world walking before their very eyes.[31]

> On an occasion 'Umar declared in public:
> "I have not sent my officials to beat you and snatch your belongings from you. Rather, I have sent them to teach you your dīn and the Sunnah of your Prophet.

29 Ibid, pp. 550-551.
30 Ibn Kathīr, *al-Bidāyah,* vol. 8, p. 8.
31 Ibn Kathīr, vol. 8, pp. 4-5.

Anyone who treated otherwise should bring up his complaint to me. By Allah, I will seek revenge from him (the wrongdoer)."

Disturbed, 'Amr ibn al-'Ās (the governor of Egypt) stood up and said: "If a person is the custodian of the Muslim affairs and punishes someone for a wrong, would you still exact vengeance from him?" 'Umar replied: "Yes! By Allah, I have seen Rasūl Allāh exacting vengeance from his person"[32]

On yet another occasion, 'Umar summoned his governors during the ḥajj and while standing asked the milling crowed around him that if they were subjected to miscarriage of justice by any of these officials they should say so. Only one person rose to complaint against 'Amr ibn al-'Ās that he had unjustifiably got him lashed hundred times.

'Umar asked him to seek his revenge from the governor. 'Amr ibn al-'Ās protested that the governors should not be subjected to this humiliation for it would open up the mischief door. But 'Umar said he saw the Prophet taking vengeance from himself. "O man, get up and exact your vengeance." Eventually 'Amr ibn al-'Ās had to pay two ashrafis for each lash to save his back.[33]

5. Supremacy of the Sharī'ah

These caliphs would never exalt themselves over the law. They regarded themselves and common citizenry, including al-dhimma (non-Muslims under Islam's protection), as equal. True, the appointment of the qāḍis lay in the realm of their authority but still their appointees were free in their verdicts against them. One time a dispute arose between 'Umar and Ubayy ibn Ka'b. Both agreed on Zayd ibn Thābit to arbitrate between them. The two came to Zayd who rose to seat 'Umar in his place but the latter declined and sat with Ubayy. When Ubayy made his claim, 'Umar rejected it.

32 Abū Yūsuf, *Kitāb*, p. 115; Abu Da'ud al-Tayā lisi, *al-Musand,* ḥadīth 55; Ibn al-Athīr, *al-Kāmil*, vol. 3, p. 30; al-Tabari, *Tārikh,* vol. 3, p. 273.

33 Abū Yūsuf, *Kitāb*, p. 116.

According to the norm, Zayd should have asked ‘Umar to swear by Allah's name but the latter's high moral and political stature gave him reservations. Seeing him oscillating, ‘Umar himself swore. When the sitting ended, ‘Umar made his prudent observation: “Zayd cannot qualify to be a qādi (judge) until he treats ‘Umar and the commoner alike.”[34]

A similar incident happened between ‘Ali and a Christian whom he saw selling his lost armour in the bazaar of Kūfah. He did not forcibly take his armour from him; instead, he lodged his complaint with the qāḍī. And since he failed to support his claim, the verdict was given against him. [35]

Ibn Khallikān reports that ‘Ali and a non-Muslim came to Qāḍi Shuraih's court for a decision. The latter rose to greet the caliph. Thereupon ‘Ali said: “This is your first injustice.”[36]

6. A government free from ethnicities and prejudices

Islam early period was marked by yet another characteristic: it was free from ethnic and tribalistic prejudices and extended equal status to everyone.

The Prophet's death saw the rise of tribalistic prejudices like a storm. Behind the emergence of false prophetic claims and apostasy, this played a major role, symptomized by the utterance of a follower of Musaylimah who said: “I know Musaylimah is a liar but the Rabi‘yah liar is better then the Mudarr's truthful.” [37]

Supporting another claimant to prophetic claim, Tulayhah an elder of Banū Ghatafān said: “By Allah, I prefer to follow the prophet of my allied tribes over the Qurayshi prophet.” [38]

In Madīnah itself, when Abū Bakr was being inducted, Sa‘d ibn ‘Ubādah avoided giving his pledge to him owing to his tribalistic

34 Abū Bakr Ahmad ibn Ḥusayn al-Bayhaqi, *al-Sunan al-Kubrā* (Hyderabad: Dā'irah al-Ma‘ārif, 1355 A.H.) vol. 10, p. 136.

35 Ibid.

36 Abu'l ‘Abbās Aḥmad ibn Khallikan, *Wafayat al-A‘ayān wa Anba Abna al-Zamān* (Cairo: Maktabah al-Nahdah al-Misriyah, 1948) vol. 2, p. 168.

37 Al-Ṭabari, *Tārikh*, vol. 2, p. 508.

38 Ibid, p. 487.

inclinations. Likewise, Abū Sufyān did not like Abū Bakr's Khilāfah (caliphate) on the same grounds and made offer to 'Ali: "How did a person from a small tribe of the Quraysh become the caliph? If you are willing to oppose him, I would fill the valley with the horsemen and foot soldiers."

But 'Ali refused to be tempted and made him speechless by saying: "Your offer is indicative of your enmity for Islam and the Muslims. I would not like you to bring horsemen and foot soldiers [to my support]. Muslims love one another and wish everyone well, even though they may not be in each other's proximity. On the contrary, the hypocrites cut each other's throats. We consider Abū Bakr capable enough to hold this office. Had he not been legible we would have never put him in this office."[39]

It was to this kind of environment that Abū Bakr and 'Umar responded by giving equal status to every tribe, Muslims and non-Muslims alike. To make it transparent, they gave no preference to their own clans and tribes. This had a healthy effect in containing the situation: all prejudices died down, and the universal spirit of Islam resurfaced in them. In his entire tenure, Abū Bakr gave no office to any person from his clan. 'Umar followed the same practice other than his appointment of Nu'mān ibn 'Adi as collector of taxes in Maysān, a small area close to Baṣrah. He recalled him back after sometime.[40] From this aspect, the two caliphs had an exemplary sense of rectitude.

In his last days, 'Umar developed an acute sense of threat from parochial interests at work in the tribes, which though had ebbed under the revolutionary impact of the Islamic movement were still capable of reasserting themselves and undo the Muslim

---

39 Al-Muttaqi, *Kunz,* vol. 5, ḥadīth 2374; al-Ṭabari, *Tārikh,* vol. 2, p. 449; Abū 'Umar Yūsuf ibn 'Abdullah ibn Muḥammad ibn 'Abd al-Barr, *al-Isti'āb, fi M'arifat al-Ashāb*, vol. 2, p. 689.

40 Nu'mān ibn 'Adiy belongs to the first generation of Muslims. His Islam was older than even 'Umar's. He was among those who left Makkah for 'Abyssinia along with his father 'Adiy. When 'Umar appointed him as a tax collector for Maysān, his wife accompanied him. There he composed a few couplets in his wife's memory, which incidentally had an allusion to liquor. 'Umar did not like it and removed him from the job deciding never to give him an appointment again. See Ibn 'Abd al-Barr, *al-Isti'āb*, vol. 1, p. 296. (Hyderabad: Dāirah al-Ma'ārif, 1336 A.H.); Yāqūt al-Hamāwi, *Mu'jam al-Buldān,* (Beirut: Dār Sādir, 1987) vol. 5, pp. 242-245.

unity. Thus, while discussing the issue of his successor with 'Abd Allah ibn 'Abbās, he disapproved 'Uthmān's candidacy saying: "If I nominate him as my successor he would put Bani abi Mu'ayt (Umayyah) on people's necks, and they will hurt them by violating Allah's commands. By Allah, if I nominated him, 'Uthmān will do it exactly the way [I am saying it]. And should that happen, his clan would perpetuate sins and people will rise to kill him.[41]

So great was his concern that in his last moments he called for 'Ali, 'Uthmān, and Sa'd ibn abi Waqqās and urged them not to mount their relatives on the people's neck in the eventuality of their election as caliph.[42]

Besides, he left the instructions for the six-member electoral shūrā that the elected caliph should bind himself not to give preference to his own clan. [43]

Unfortunately, the third caliph 'Uthmān could not maintain the desired standards. During his reign, he gave Banū Umayyah a large share in the administrative hierarchy along with grants from bayt al-māl (in order to overcome their sense of alienation), which others resented.[44] For him, the Qur'ānic injunction of kindness towards blood relatives called for it. He thus used to say: "'Umar

---

41 Ibn 'Abd al-Barr, *al-Isti'āb*, vol. 2, p. 467; Shah Wali Allah, *Azūlatah al-Khifā*, p. 224.
Some people ask if 'Umar had revelation to make him swear by Allah that what he said was sure to come.
The answer is that any person who has the ability to see beyond the present can forecast the future based on what he sees in the situation and then by arranging its elements logically, can predict with the mathematical precision of two plus two equal to four, without revelation. 'Umar knew that the tribalistic prejudices were deep rooted in the Arabian society. He also knew that even after 25-30 years of Islamic spread, parochialism though subdued could still stage a comeback. Thus, he believed that even a small change made in Abū Bakr's and 'Umar's policy by their successors in favouring their tribes for governmental jobs can trigger parochialism, which none would be able to contain unless by a bloody revolution.

42 Al-Tabari, *Tārikh*, vol. 3, p. 219; also ibn Sa'd, *al-Ṭabaqāt*, vol. 3, pp. 340-344.

43 Ibn Ḥajar, *Fatḥ,* vol. 7, pp. 49-50, al-Ṭabari, *al-Riād al-Nadira fi Manāqib al-'Ashrah,* (Cairo: al-Matb'ah Husayniyah, B. 27 A.H.); vol. 2, p. 76, Ibn Khaldūn, *Kitāb al-'Ibar...*, (Cairo: al-Matba'h al-Kubrā, 1284 A. H.) vol. 2, p. 125., The same report has been cited by Shah Wali Allah.

44 Sa'd, *al-Ṭabaqāt*, vol. 3, p. 64, vol. 5, p. 36.

deprived his relatives for Allah's sake, and I benefit them for Allah's sake."[45]

On one occasion, he said: "In respect of bayt al-māl, Abū Bakr and 'Umar preferred to keep themselves and their relatives starved while I seek compassion (for them)."[46]

'Umar's fear proved true. Rebellion broke loose against him. In the end, not only did he lose his life, it also regenerated tribalistic rivalries into life, burning everything associated with the pious caliphate.

7. Nourishing freedom as a value

Yet another merit of this caliphate was its allowance for criticism and freedom of speech. The caliphs were easily accessible to people. They would sit among the members of the consultative body (shūrā) and join the discussion; they had no party of their own nor did they have an organized opposition. This made the political environment free, enabling shūrā members to express themselves in the light of their belief and conscience. Issues that called for deliberation were placed before the shūrā, decisions were made on the strength of reason free from any group pressure, governmental influence or interest lobbies.

Added to these, they not only faced their people through the shūrā but also five times a day in congregational prayer, every week on Friday, and on the occasions of 'idayn and hajj. Their houses were not in posh areas of privilege; instead, they lived among the people with their doors open for everyone to knock at and seek redress of their problems. They moved in public without the trappings of power, security and maintaining distance. On all such occasions, everybody could pick cause with them and hold them accountable for their alleged misdeeds or neglect of public affairs. They would not only give people space to speak their minds but also encouraged them.

---

45 Al-Ṭabari, *al-Tārikh,* vol. 3, p. 291.
46 Al-Muttaqi, *Kunz,* vol. 5, ḥadīth 2324; Ibn Sa'd, *al-Ṭabaqāt*, vol. 3, p. 64.

Abū Bakr in his first public address asked people to help him if he followed the straight path, and straighten him if he stray the course. In one of his Friday addresses, 'Umar thought of fixing the dower to 400 dirham; a woman rebuked him for lack of authorization from the Qur'ān, which allows a woman to ask for a pile of wealth (qintār) as dower. 'Umar withdrew his opinion forthwith.[47]

On yet another occasion before a large audience Salmān al-Fārsī questioned him on his having two garments while everybody else had one. 'Umar asked his son 'Abd Allah to witness that he gave his share to his father.[48] One time he asked his audience how they would react if he adopted leniency in certain matters. Bishr ibn Sa'd responded we would straighten you up. This made 'Umar happy, applauding Bishr for being a man of merit. [49]

"Uthmān faced the worst criticism, but he never stopped others from criticizing him. He always defended himself in public.

The Khawārij yelled invectives on 'Ali; he always showed forbearance for them. One time they brought five Khawārij to him who openly abused him. A person among them even swore to kill him, but he released all of them. He told his followers to answer their abuses if they wanted to, but avoid bringing them to law unless they caught them in the act to kill him. Mere verbal opposition was no ground for prosecution.[50]

This period of the pious caliphate that we described was a beacon light towards which fuqahā' (jurists), muḥaddithīn (ḥadīth scholars) and common men always looked at with admiration and for guidance and considered it as true Islam in its religious, political, moral, and collective dimensions.

---

47 Ibn Kathir, *Tafsir*, narrated by Abu Ya'lā and Ibn al-Munzir, vol. 1, p. 467.
48 Muhib al-Din al-Tabarai, *al-Riadh*, vol. 2, p. 56; al-Jauzi, *Sirah 'Umar*, p. 127.
49 Al-Muttaqi, Kunz, vol. 5, ḥadīth 2414.
50 al-Sarakhsi, *al-Mabsūt*, vol. 10, p. 125.

Chapter Four

From the Rightly Guided Caliphate to Monarchy

The pious caliphate thus described was not mere political government but in fact the continuation of the prophetic model (*nabūwah*). In other words, it did not confine itself to run the administration, secure peace, and safeguard the frontiers of the state but to go beyond the routine and act as educator, benefactor and guide in the collective life of the Muslims after the prophetic model. It had upon its shoulder the responsibility to implement the holistic Islam in its true essence and to train Muslims to spread its message across the globe. In this, it was not only al-Khilāfah al-Rāshidah (the rightly guided caliphate) but in fact al-Khilāfah al-Murshidah (a caliphate that guides). The term *al-Khilāfah 'alā-minhaj al-nabūwah* expresses these two aspects. Anyone who understands Islam knows that Islam objectifies this kind of state and not a political government (after the secular image).

Now, we will deal with the phases that eventuated into the shift from the caliphate to monarchy. We will also explain how this unfortunate change weaned the state away from the Islamic principles of governance and the catastrophic impact it had on the collective life of the Muslims.

1. The beginning of change

The drift from the caliphate towards monarchical absolutism (mulūkīyah) took place exactly the way 'Umar had apprehended. Close to his death, his heart pined on the possibility that his successors might change the prophetic policy on tribes and relations. During his life, the Prophet ('alayhi as-salām) did not allow anyone from Banū Hāshim other than 'Ali to share the power apparatus. Abū Bakr ignored his tribe as well. 'Umar in his ten-year tenure accommodated only one person from Bani 'Adiy that too in a marginal job but later relieved him. It was because of this policy transparency and non-partisanship that parochial interests remained in check. He feared that any policy shift [on this important aspect of the caliphate] would undermine the Muslim unity and thus the integrity of the state. His advice to his three prospective successors – 'Uthmān, 'Ali and Sa'd ibn abī Waqqāṣ – specifically stressed that they should not mount their tribes and relations on the necks of the Muslims.[1]

Nobody can deny, however, the fact that 'Uthmān's appointees were capable people; their administrative and military skills brought new territories to the Islamic state extending the Muslim domain. But all said, they were not the only ones who had such attributes – there were others as well who had proven their genius in a far better way. Mere ability to perform could not be the reason for giving administrative control of a territory as large as Khurāsān to North Africa to one family along with a high position of a secretary in the central secretariat. This by itself was objectionable, though there were some other reasons, which aggravated the people.

First, the new entrants to power by and large came from the tulaqā' (later-day converts). In other words, they belonged to those Makkan families, which persecuted the Prophet and his message till their last effort. After the Makkan conquest, the Prophet forgave them and they accepted Islam. Al-Walīd ibn 'Uqbah and Marwān ibn al-Ḥakam belonged to this forgiven group. 'Abdullah ibn Sa'd ibn abi Sarah had turned apostate. He was one among those for whom the Prophet's order were to kill them even when found holding the Ka'bah's curtain. 'Uthmān brought him to the Prophet and asked for his clemency which out of regard for 'Uthmān was given to him. With such a crowd around 'Uthmān, people were obviously upset.

Second, such individuals were unsuitable to lead the Islamic movement for even though they had become Muslims, they lacked certain essentials of moral and spiritual training that only the Prophet could have given them. True, they excelled in administrative and military matters but Islam had not come for expansion alone; it was in its essence a movement for goodness whose leadership called for a greater moral calibre than were the military and administrative attributes. Thus in the scale of eminence they were not at par with the companions and the tabi'ūn in moral excellence.

---

1 Abu J'afar Muḥammad ibn Jarir al-Ṭabari, *Tārikh al Umum wa al-Mulūk*, vol. 3, p. 264. For the event, see p. 42 of chapter 3.

Third, some of these people because of their peculiar backgrounds and weeknesses were not qualified enough to be given prominent positions. Their appointment to top slots in the governmental hierarchy gave a bad feeler to Muslims in general.

For example, al-Walīd ibn ʻUqbah accepted Islam in the wake of the Makkan conquest. The Prophet deputed him as zakāt collector to Banū al-Mustaliq. When he reached their territory, he got somehow scared and without making contact with the people there returned to Mādinah. His report to the Prophet of non-compliance by Banū al-Mustaliq obviously infuriated the Prophet. He sent another military expedition to them. But before the calamity could have overtaken them, their elders came to Mādinah and informed the Prophet about al-Walīd not approaching them for the taxes. In fact, as they said, they waited for someone to come and collect Zakāh from them. The Qur'ānic Āyah revealed on the occasion educated the Muslims:

> Believers, when an ungodly person brings to you a piece of news, carefully ascertain its truth, lest you should hurt a people unwittingly and thereafter repent at what you did.[2]

These were the reasons that caused unrest against ʻUthmān. Appointing individuals from the Umayyad in top slots was by itself politically unwise. But what aggravated the situation was that the appointees had some questionable problems. Two policy misformulations, however, had far-reaching impact.

First, he gave Muʻāwiyah a longer tenure in Damascus probably because of his past record in good governance. He was an appointee of ʻUmar. ʻUthmān extended his domain by bringing under his control a large territory from Āylah to Byzantine frontiers and from al-Jazīrah to the coastal areas of the Mediterranean Sea. He

---

2 The exegetes describe *al-Ḥujurāt*: 6 in the backdrop of this episode. See Ibn Kathīr, *Tafsir*...,. Ibn ʻAbd al-Barr also holds that al-Ḥujarāt: 6 relates to al-Walīd ibn ʻUqbah. For this, see *al-Isti'āb*..., vol. 2, p. 603. Taqi al-Din Ahmad ibn Taymiyah is of similar view. See his *Minhaj al-Sunnah al-Nabawiyah* (Egypt: Matbʻah Amiriyah, 1322 A.H.) vol. 3, p. 176.

continued in his office for twelve years in the 'Uthmani caliphate.[3] This factor alone was responsible in his refusal to submit himself to 'Ali's caliphate. By its strategic location, Syria was vital to the security of the Islamic state. On one side, it bordered eastern provinces and on the other, it flanked Western provinces. Seated in the middle the Syrian governor could easily cut them apart. Mu'āwiyah's extended rule over Syria caused alarm in Mādinah.

Second, 'Uthmān brought in Marwān as secretary to the caliphate. Taking use of the caliph's soft disposition and his trust in him, he did a lot of wrong things without the caliph's knowledge, eventually tarnishing the caliphate. Equally troublesome was Marwān's role in spoiling sahābah's good relation with 'Uthmān. He continually worked on this aspect so that instead of seeking advice from the sahābah, the caliph becomes dependent on him.[4] Some aspects of his language did not go well with peoples' sensibilities. Leaving other people aside, the caliph's wife Nā'ilah thought that in causing problems for her husband Marwān's role was pivotal. She even told her husband that if he continued to follow Marwān, he would get him killed. "This man," she said, "has neither regard for Allah, nor does he fear or love Him."[5]

2. The second phase

The Marwān aspect of caliph 'Uthmān's policy was undoubtedly problematic. The fact, however, remains that other than a few judgmental errors, 'Uthman's caliphal role was astoundingly great. Islam made such great a stride in his era that despite dissatisfaction on some of his policies the common Muslims never thought of rising against him.

---

3 Ibn S'ad, *al-Ṭabaqāt*, vol. 7, p. 406; Ibn 'Abd al-Barr, *al-Isti'āb,* vol. 1, p. 253. This region has now four different states and governments – Syria, Lebanon, Jordan and Israel. Their total area even today is the same that we had in Mu'āwiyah's time. In 'Umar's times, there were four governors appointed by him and Mu'āwiyah was one of them. See Imam Ibn Taymiyah, *Yazid ibn Mu'āwiyah* (Karachi: Ibn Taymiyah Academy) pp. 34-35.

4 Ibn Sa'd, *al-Ṭabaqāt*, vol. 5, p. 36, Ibn Kathīr, *al-Bidāyah*, vol. 8, p. 259.

5 Al-Ṭabari, *al-Tārikh*, vol. 3, pp. 396-397; Ibn Kathīr, *al-Bidāyah*, vol. 7, pp. 172-173.

It is true that upset by his governor Sa'īd ibn al-'Āṣ' behaviour in Baṣrah, some people did rise against him but it was a weak response. Abū Mūsā al-Asha'rī called for a new bai'ah to 'Uthman, people thronged to affirm their pledge for the caliph.[6] The rebels knew it; thus instead of an open rebellion, they took the path of conspiracy against him.

The movement against 'Uthmān drew its support from a small pocket of people coming from Egypt, Kūfah, and Baṣrah. They coordinated their efforts by secret communication and planned to reach Madīnah surreptitiously to pressurize the caliph. They had a long litany of allegations against him, mostly unfounded or weak that could have been easily dismissed by reason. And in fact attempts were made to satisfy them. Only two thousands in number they converged on the outskirts of Madīnah. A party they were but they represented no one other than their impulses. They tried to ally 'Ali, Ṭalḥah, and al-Zubayr with them but the three turned them down. 'Ali defended 'Uthmān admirably well in refuting their allegations against the caliph. The Madinese, both ansār and muhājirūn, also refused to join them. But bent as they were on mischief, they eventually entered the capital and demanded the caliph's resignation. 'Uthmān's answer to them was plain and constitutionally right. He was willing to redress their legitimate demands, but he would not resign.[7]

3. The issue of helping relatives from bayt al-māl

Whatever help 'Uthmān extended to his relatives from bayt al-māl was not reprehensible from the Sharī'ah viewpoint. Allah forbid, he never usurped the Muslim money nor did he appropriate what belonged to Allah. But even here his approach, one can say in hindsight, was far from prudence and thus created problems in the people's perception.

When questioned, 'Uthmān explained his position in a meeting convened for discussing his doling out state money to his relatives. Present were 'Ali ibn abī Ṭālib, Sa'd ibn abī Waqqāṣ, Ṭalḥah ibn al-Zubayr, and Mu'āwiyah ibn abī Sufyān.

---

6 Ibn S'ad, *al-Ṭabaqāt*, vol. 3, p. 32-33; al-Ṭabari, *al-Tārikh*, vol. 3; p. Ibn S'ad, *al-Ṭabaqāt,* vol. 3, pp. 372.

7 Ibn Sa'd, *al-Ṭabaqāt*, vol. 3, p. 66.

"My both predecessors adopted a sterner attitude towards their own selves as well as their relatives. But the Messenger of Allah ('alayhi as-salām) used to help his relatives. I belong to a clan facing problems in their living. Thus, in return for the services that I rendered to this government, I took money from it, and I think I have the right (to do so). If you think it was not right, then decide for the return of this money, and I will act accordingly."

All of them agreed that he said the right thing.

"Is it right," they asked, "that you gave money to 'Abdullah ibn Khālid ibn Asīd and Marwān?"

'Uthmān admitted that he had given Marwān 15,000 and Ibn Asīd 50,000 dirham. Thus, he took the amount from the two and returned it to bayt al-māl. The assembly dispersed on a happy note.[8]

From these reports, it is evident that Caliph 'Uthmān's helping out his relatives from bayt al-māl was not inconsistent with the Sharī'ah. As caliph, he was entitled to a certain emolument, which he never took and instead gave to his relatives from that accumulated salary he denied to himself.

Equally true is the fact that he gave his poor relatives loans from bayt al-māl. Occasionally he would use his discretionary powers and gave them grants from the khumus for which no detailed distributive guidance existed in the Sharī'ah. The mischief makers were, however, bent on deepening the impression that he favoured his clan at the expense of public treasury. Obviously, if like Abū Bakr and 'Umar he had helped people other than his relatives, he could have avoided criticism upon himself for this reason alone. Abū Bakr and 'Umar subjected themselves to self restrictions and denied benefit to their relatives, and instead helped others. 'Uthmān did not follow this golden principle and unwittingly gave a chance to the conspirators to instigate circumstances that led to the undoing of his caliphate.

---

8 . Ibid, p. 382; Ibn al-Athīr, *al-Kāmil,* vol. 3, p. 29; Ibn Khaldūn, *Kitāb al-'Ibar,* vol. 2, p. 144.

For forty days, they created a mutinous situation indulging in activities that Mādinah never knew before. They misbehaved with Umm Habībah the Prophet's widow. Disgusted by their unwanted attitude and fearing that they might misbehave with her as well, Sayyidah 'Ā'ishah left for Makkah. While Madīnah stood shocked mired in grief, they killed the caliph. For three days, his body remained without burial; they did not spare his house either and ransacked it.[9]

This was not only a great injustice to 'Uthmān but also to Islam and the rightly guided caliphate. If there had been any weight to their allegation, they would have joined hands with the Ṣaḥābah to persuade the caliph to redress them. In fact, 'Ali had started efforts towards this end and 'Uthmān had promised to remedy the situation.[10] Nevertheless, even if the wrong had not been corrected, the Sharī'ah did not allow rebellion against the caliph and press for his resignation by mere 2,000 miscreants drawn from Baṣrah, Kūfah, and Egypt who had no constituency to speak for. Nor were they empowered by any right to ask for the removal of a caliph, who represented the whole of the Islamic world, who was mandated by *ahl al-hal wa al-'aqd* according to Islamic norms, and whom the Islamic world had accepted as their caliph.[11] They not only made the caliph's blood but also his household permissible for themselves.

Brutal and inhuman as it were, there was an obvious irony to their act, for what they considered as 'Uthmān's sins were not in fact sins to have qualified him for death penalty. In fact, 'Uthmān told them this very thing in one of his speeches to them. The Sharī'ah, he said, allows killing someone in a few specified cases. He had not committed any such crime. Then why were they intent on making

9 For details see al-Ṭabari, *Tārikh,* vol. 3, pp. 376-418; Ibn Kathīr, *al-Bidāyah*, vol. 7, pp. 168-197.

10 . Al-Ṭabari, *Tārikh*, vol. 3, pp. 376-377, 384-385.

11 'Abdullah ibn 'Umar gave the same advice. When the resignation call gained momentum, 'Uthman asked 'Abdullah ibn 'Umar for the way out of the situation. He said, "Do not show Muslim the path that when some people get annoyed with their amīr they dismiss him." See Ibn Sa'd, *al-Ṭabaqāt*, vol. 3, p. 66. 'Uthman repeated this in his response to the allegations framed by the rebels who had surrounded his house: "Did I take over this country by force without consultation of the Muslims that you seek to remove me by sword." Ibn Sa'd, *al-Ṭabaqāt*, vol. 3, p. 68.

his blood permissible for them, he asked.[12] But those who criticized 'Uthmān in the blessed name of the Sharī'ah themselves violated it by killing him.

Here, one should not entertain the notion that the people of Madīnah consented to their savagery. The fact of the matter is that the miscreants' arrival in Madīnah was sudden, least expected by anyone. They took over the city's sensitive points making its residents helpless.[13] Besides, nobody thought they would go to the extent of killing the caliph. So unexpected was the whole thing that the people failed to formulate their response to the conspirators. They even suffered from moral contrition on their failure to come to the caliph's defence.[14] The primary reason being the caliph himself would not allow bloodshed in Madīnah to save his government. He could have summoned the armies from different provinces to smash the rebellion but he refrained from it. From the ansār Zayd ibn Thābit offered unqualified support to defend him. 'Uthmān's response was *amā al-qitāl falā* (bloodshed, no). He gave the same response to Abū Hurayrah and 'Abdullah ibn al-Zubayr. Surprisingly enough, there were at least 700-armed men with him willing to fight for him but he counseled them restrain.[15]

In fact, at this critical juncture, 'Uthmān's chosen path was worthy of a caliph standing him apart from a king, who would have resorted to any means to save his power. He would have let Mādinah raised to the ground, its men and women killed, even the Prophet's masjid demolished, and his wives abused and humiliated. But as a pious caliph, he considered his life trivial to other considerations that a Muslim must hold dear to himself above everything else. He knew how far he could have gone in saving his power. To him, the line of demarcation between personal considerations and the Sharī'ah demand was absolutely known.

4. The third phase

'Uthmān's death engulfed Madīnah in disorder; stricken with fear and lost in grief, they realized to their discomfort that the Ummah has been deprived of a fatherly figure and the Islamic state of its head.

12 Ibn Kathīr, *al-Bidāyah*, vol. 7, p. 179.

13 Ibid, p. 197.

14 Ibn Sa'd, *al-Ṭabaqāt* ,vol. 3, p. 71

15 Ibid, pp. 70-71.

Everybody, including even the outside miscreants, started weighing the situation in the pragmatic context of an empty caliphal office of a state that stretched itself to the Roman frontiers on the one hand and to Yemen, Afghanistan and North Africa on the other. The situation called for an immediate remedy. The caliph had to be elected that too in Madīnah, for it was the centre of the world of Islam and it was here that *ahl al-hal wa al-'aqd* lived, who were decisive in decision-making concerning the appointment of the caliph. There was no reason to tarry the matter further nor was it feasible to approach other parts of the Islamic state further from Madīnah. The Ummah needed a focal point for convergence and consolidation at this hour of distention and strife.

Out of the six Ṣaḥābah (raḍi Allahu 'anhu) 'Umar had preferred over others, four of them were still alive. They were 'Ali, Ṭalḥah, al-Zubayr, and Sa'd ibn abī Waqqāṣ. Among them, 'Ali was the most respected as found out then by 'Abd al-Raḥmān ibn 'Auf.[16]

A class by himself, there was none to measure up to him in the entire Muslim world. A popular vote even according to present electoral standards would have gravitated towards 'Ali.[17] All authentic sources suggest that the Ṣaḥ*ābah* and people from other sectors of Madīnah approached him and said, "This system cannot hold itself without an amīr. For people, the presence of an Imām is a must and we do not have a person more suited to this office than you, either in service to the cause of Islam or in nearness to the Prophet ('alayhi as-salām)."

He refused but the people kept on insisting. So careful he was to the people's consent expressed through bai'ah (oath) that he said: "The oath pledge to me cannot be undertaken in secrecy. Without people's consent it is of no consequence."

Thereafter, in a common gathering in Masjid al-Nabawi ansar and muhajirūn pledged their support to him, with the exception of seventeen to twenty of them who refrained from their pledge.[18]

---

16 Ibn Kathīr, *al-Bidāyah*, vol. 7, p. 146.

17 Imām Aḥmed ibn Ḥanbal says that nobody had more qualifications for the caliphate then 'Ali, see Ibn Kathīr, *al-Bidāyah*, vol. 8, p. 130.

18 Al-Ṭabari, *Tārikh*, vol. 3, pp. 450-452; Ibn 'Abd al-Barr says that in the battle of Ṣiffin 'Ali had 800 such Ṣaḥābah who were present at Ba'yt al-Ridwān with the Prophet. See *al-Isti'āb,* vol. 2, p. 423.

From the preceding, it is obvious that 'Ali's succession to the caliphal office was strictly in accordance with the principles that animated the pious caliphate. He did not seek power by force nor did he make any effort to gain it. People by themselves through mutual consultation brought him into power. A large majority of sahābah took bai'ah at his hand. Later aside from Syria, the rest of the Islamic world agreed to his caliphate.

Some people question the legitimacy of 'Ali's succession to 'Uthmān because of a small discussion over his induction into the caliphal office. The argument however suffers from weakness. If Sa'd ibn 'Ubādah's refrain could not invalidate Abū Bakr's and 'Umar's caliphate how can seventeen-to-twenty refusals to 'Ali's nomination invalidate his caliphate? Besides, the discussion was a mere negative act per se and in no way affected the issue's constitutionality. There was no other candidate the dissenters could have given their pledge. Also, because of the majority verdict in favour of his caliphate, it enjoyed legitimacy and was thus constitutional in the sovereign eye of the Sharī'ah.

By his induction as caliph, the breached Islamic system had the chance to repair itself. But three things frustrated the process of healing and instead pushed it further towards monarchial absolutism.

First, the rebels' involvement in empowering 'Ali as caliph created credibility gap between him and the sahābah. Among them were those who had killed 'Uthmān as well as those who were the motivators and the instigators to this ghastly crime. Thus, their bringing 'Ali to power became the cause for a greater fitnah (mischief).

All said anyone who tries to understand the circumstances that prevailed in Mādinah then, will have the feelings that it was almost impossible to have excluded the miscreants from the electoral process. Nevertheless, it was a right decision to have 'Ali as the caliph. As to bringing the killers of 'Uthmān to justice, it could have only been possible if all the forces had stood in Ali's favour. Thus strengthened, he would have nabbed them in time and the mischief situation averted from further moving to catastrophe.

Second, the self exclusion of certain Ṣaḥābah from giving bai‘ah to ‘Ali, though prompted by good intentions to avoid mischief, became instrumental in catalyzing a graver mischief than they had contemplated. The separatists were prominent Ṣaḥābah; each of them had a hold on the masses; their exclusivist attitude created doubt in many a hearts. The solidarity that it called for in the Muslim ranks failed to take place. And thus, the effort to rehabilitate the pious caliphate sputtered halfway through.

Third, the demand for retribution of the ‘Uthmān blood which the two groups had chartered in their stand with Sayyidah ‘Ā’ishah, Ṭalḥah, and al-Zubayr on one side and Mu‘āwiyah on the other, carried little pith in the constitutional scale. Admittedly, they were highly venerated, towering personalities but they were not operating in a *jahili* system where anyone on anybody's behalf would rise to press his claim for revenge. The ransom demand belonged to the deceased's family. If the administration was lax in apprehending the killers and bringing them to justice, other people could have joined the family members in expediting justice. But under no circumstance they could have solicited justice in their way when the Sharī‘ah did not approve it, especially when they were making their recognition of ‘Ali's caliphate conditional to the fulfillment of their retribution demand.

If ‘Ali lacked legitimacy in their sight, the alleged legality of their demand also had no merit in it. Was he a tribal chief who could have caught anyone he wanted without legal authorization and punished him? Certainly, that was not the case.

Worse was the method the first group adopted. Instead of resorting to Madīnah for lodging their demand where the caliph, the culprits, and the deceased's inheritors were present, they took the road to Baṣrah where they assembled an army for avenging ‘Uthmān's blood. The obvious result was additional 10,000 killed destabilizing the state further. The Sharī‘ah aside, no law code in the world could have upheld their method.

Even more unconstitutional was the second group's attitude led by Mu‘āwiyah, who instead of seeking revenge of Uthmān's blood in his personal capacity rose against Mādinah as governor of

Syria, refusing to submit himself to the Madīnah writ. He should have asked punishment for 'Uthmān's killers through due process of law, but he asked for their deliverance to him so that he could kill them.[19] True, he was a relation of 'Uthmān but that did not accord him legitimacy in the presence of 'Uthmān's immediate family.

Whatever relationship 'Uthmān had, it was with Mu'āwiyah ibn abī Sufyān. The governorship of Syria was not his relations. As governor, he had no right to refuse obedience to the constitutionally elected caliph, whose caliphate everybody else accepted.[20] Nor was he justified to mobilize the regional command against Mādinah.

This issue in its right Sharī'ah context has been discussed by Qāḍī Abū Bakr ibn al-'Arabi in *al-Aḥkām al-Qur'ān*.

> "(After 'Uthmān's shahādah), it would have made no sense to leave people without the imam. Thus, the imamate offer was made to the remainder of the Ṣaḥābah, who constituted the electoral shūrā named by 'Umar. They declined. But 'Ali who deserved it most accepted the offer so that the Ummah could be saved from acrimony and bloodshed. When people gave him their bai'ah the Syrians made it contingent on apprehending the killers of 'Uthmān and subjecting them to retribution. 'Ali persuaded them to enter bai'ah first and then ask for their right as it would be given to them. But they said he was not qualified to receive their bai'ah for they saw 'Uthmān's killers around him all the time.
>
> 'Ali's stand made sense for if he had sought vengeance from 'Uthmān's killers at that point in time the tribes would have risen in their support opening a third battle front for him. Thus, he waited for his government's

---

19 Al-Ṭabari, *Tārikh*, vol. 7, pp. 257-258.

20 This fact is historically proven that after the battle of Ṣiffin the whole Arabian Peninsula and the east and the west sides of Shām, had pledged their loyalty to 'Ali. Only Syria stood opposed to him because of its being under Mu'āwiyah's domain. Thus, the true constitutional position did not suggest lawlessness in the world of Islam where nobody abided by the law. See al-Ṭabari, *Tārikh*, vol. 3, pp. 462-463; 'Ali 'Izz al-Din Ibn al-Athīr, *Usad al-Ghābah,* vol. 3, p. 137-141; Ibn Kathīr, *al-Bidāyah*, vol. 7, p. 229, 251.

consolidation and the extension of his bai'ah over the nation, followed by the institution of the prosecution case by the inheritors of the killed (caliph) and its resolution according to the law.

The 'ulamā of the Ummah agree on this point that the imam can defer the application of qasās if he thinks it may lead to uprising and division.

A similar situation surrounded the case of Ṭalḥah and al-Zubayr. The two had not excluded 'Ali from the caliphate nor were they critical of his Islam, though they thought 'Uthmān's killers should be dealt first. 'Ali stuck to his view. And he was right."

While explaining the āyah from *al-Hujurāt*: 9, that is: *fa qātilū al-lati tabghī hattā tafī'a ilā amri Allah*, Qāḍi Abū Bakr says:

"In the then prevalent circumstances, 'Ali abided by this *āyah*. He fought against those who sought to impose their views on the imam and were making demands for which they had no right. For them the right course was to have accepted 'Ali's argument and gone to the court for their vengeance demand against the killers. If despite their having followed this course, 'Ali had failed to punish the accused, people themselves would have removed him from his office, saving them thus from the armed struggle."[21]

5. The fourth phase

With some 2,000 rebels still in Madīnah, Ṭalḥah and al-Zubayr along with some other Ṣaḥābah called on 'Ali. After exchanging pleasantries, they urged him to take action against the killers as their oath pledge to him, they said, was contingent on the enforcement of ḥadd.

"Brothers! I am aware of what you said," Ali responded. "But how can I apprehend those who have overpowered us. Do you see any opening for realizing your desire?"

21 Abū Bakr ibn al-'Arabi, *Aḥkām al-Qur'ān* (Cairo, 1958) vol. 4, pp. 1706-1707.

They said no.

'Ali added: "By Allah! I think the same way. Let the conditions improve so that people (shaken by the events) return to normalcy and the restitution of the rights is facilitated." [22]

After their meeting, the two elders went to Makkah to see Sayyidah 'Ā'ishah. The three agreed that in order to seek vengeance for 'Uthmān's blood they should raise an army from Basrah and Kūfah where Ṭalḥah and al-Zubayr had a large following. Together they left for Basrah.

From Banū Umayyah, Sa'īd ibn al-Āṣ and Marwān ibn al-Ḥakam joined the group. At Marrul-Zahrā, Sa'id suggested to his group that if they wanted vengeance for 'Uthmān's blood, they should kill those who were with them (he was referring to Ṭalḥah and al-Zubayr). As he said, Banū 'Umayyah believed that 'Uthmān's killers were not only the outside miscreants but also his Madinan critics who objected to his policies, or those who were present in Madīnah but did nothing to prevent his death. Marwān however opposed them: "No we will make Ṭalḥah, al-Zubayr and 'Ali fought each other. The defeated will die its death, while the victor will be weak enough to fight us."[23]

Thus, divided against themselves the caravan reached al-Baṣrah where they succeeded in mobilizing thousands of their followers.

The news of their convergence in Baṣrah made 'Ali change his plan of going to Syria against Mu'āwiyah: He decided to checkmate the new alliance. But a large number of the Ṣaḥābah and their followers who considered inter-Muslim feud disastrous for the Ummah, refused to go along with him. [24]

---

22 Al-Ṭabari, *Tārikh*, vol. 3, p. 458; ibn al-Athīr, *al-Kāmil,* vol. 3, p. 100, Ibn Kathīr, *al-Bidāyah*, vol. 7, p. 227-228.

23 Ibn Sa'd, *al-Ṭabaqāt*, vol. 5, pp. 34-35; Ibn Khaldūn, *Takmilah,* vol. 2, p. 155.

24 Ibn Kathīr, *al-Bidāyah*, vol. 7, p. 233.

The result was obvious: the same rebel group that had killed 'Uthmān and which 'Ali wanted to get rid of became his mainstay; they filled the ranks of his small army. This fact by itself resulted in his undoing. He lost his standing and the mischief spread further.

Eventually, the worst happened. At the outskirts of al-Baṣrah the forces led by Sayyidah 'Ā'isha and 'Ali came face to face. A large number of sincere people tried mediation in order to avoid the fight between the two. And at one point they even succeeded. But the hostile vested interests were also at work. The killers of 'Uthmān who formed the battle line on 'Ali's side knew well that reconciliation between the opposing camps would result in their eventual elimination while the conspirators in the 'Ā'ishah army were intent on the clash between the two in order to weaken them for the benefit of the third party. Thus before the mediation effort could have born results they instigated an undeclared war that swept away the peace effort into a bad patch in history. The battle of Jamal took place over the heads of the peace seekers on both sides.[25]

In fact, 'Ali took the peace initiative. Before the battle of Jamal, he sent his emissary to Ṭalḥah and al-Zubayr for a talk. They came to his camp. 'Ali reminded them of the Prophet's saying on the subject and exhorted them to stay away from war. Affected by his speech, al-Zubayr left the battle scene while Ṭalḥah shifted himself from the vanguard formation to the back of the troops.[26] But unfortunately al-Zubayr was killed by a trailing assassin 'Amr ibn Jarmūz, while according to some reports, Ṭalḥah was killed by Marwān ibn al-Ḥakam.[27]

The war thus erupted exacted a toll of 10,000 people from both sides, making it the second misfortune after 'Uthmān's shahādah

---

25 Ibid. pp. 237-239.

26 Al-Ṭabari, *Tārikh*, vol. 3, p. 415; Ibn al-Athīr, *al-Kāmil*, vol. 3, pp. 122-123; Ibn Kathīr, *al-Bidayah,* vol. 7, pp. 240-241, 247; Ibn 'Abd al-Barr, *al-Isti'āb*, vol. 1, p. 207; Ibn Khaldūn, *Takmilah*, vol. 2, p. 162.

27 Ibn Sa'd, *al-Tabaqāt*, vol. 3, p. 223; also Ibn al-Athīr, *al-Kāmil*, vol. 3, pp. 124, vol. 5, p. 38; Ibn Kathīr, *al-Bidāyah*, vol. 7, pp. 240-241, 247; Ibn 'Abd al-Barr, *al-Isti'āb*, vol. 1, pp. 207-208. Says Ibn 'Abd al-Barr, there is no dispute to the effect that Marwān killed Ṭalḥah, although the former was in his army. Ibn Kathīr has also subscribed to this well-known report. See *al-Bidāyah*, vol. 7, p. 247.

(martyrdom) that fell to the lot of Islamic history. It brought the Ummah a step closer to mulukīyah (monarchial absolutism).

The post-Jamal situation made the national scene fractious with deeper divisions. The Iraqis who constituted the bulk of the 'Ā'ishah force and got killed in 5,000 numbers at the hands of 'Ali could not have been expected to give support to 'Ali as the Syrian gave theirs to Mu'āwiyah.

In the Ṣiffīn battle and the events afterwards the unity found in the Mu'āwiyah camp and the discord on the 'Ali side owed much to the Jamal incident. Its avoidance, despite the problems created by 'Uthmān's death, could have averted the advent of the mulukīyah. Marwān saw the ineluctable dynamics in the battle of Jamal going in the monarchists favour. To make sure that the battle does take place, he accompanied Ṭalḥah and al-Zubayr to Baṣrah. Unfortunately, his expectations fructified in the loss for the Muslim Ummah.

'Ali's attitude throughout this period was reminiscent of the pious caliphs. Never for a moment did he deviate from the Sharī'ah. He forbade his army to pursue the fleeing troops or to kill the injured and enter the opponents' houses. After overpowering them, he himself led the funerals of the killed from both sides and gave them an equal burial. He refused to distribute the belongings of the opponents as war booty. Instead, he gathered all the goods into a pile in al-Baṣrah's central masjid, asking people to take back their belongings.

Rumours were spread by certain miscreants that he desired massacre of the Baṣrah people and enslaving their women. He promptly refuted it:

> "People should least fear it from a man of my conduct, for this kind of treatment is given to nonbelievers and not the Muslims."

While entering Baṣrah, he was greeted by abuses and taunts from women flung at him from every house. His orders to the troops were:

> "Beware! Do not violate anyone's privacy; avoid hurting women even when they abuse your elders and the pious ones. We were told not to hurt them when they were still non-believers. How we can now put our hands on them when they are believers." [28]

To 'Ā'ishah who inspired the coalition against him for justice to 'Uthman's blood, he was particularly respectful and never caused her a moment of discomfort. He bade her to Mādinah under special security umbrella. [29]

With al-Zubayr's sword tucked in his hand, his assassin came in the hope for reward but in return he gave him the news of hellfire. Recognizing al-Zubayr's sword he exclaimed, "How many a time this sword came to the Prophet's defense."[30]

When Ṭalḥah's son came, he greeted him with respect and made him sit beside him. He returned his father's property to him and said: "I hope that on the Judgement Day between your father and me the same thing will transpire that Allah the Exalted has said in the Qur'ān: 'We will take rancour from their hearts and they will sit like brothers beside each other on the elevated seats'."[31]

6. The fifth phase

After 'Uthmān's shahādah (18 Dhul Ḥajjah, 35 A.H.), Nu'mān ibn Bashir carried his bloodstained shirt and his wife Nā'ilah's amputated fingers to Mu'āwiyah in Damascus. Making use of the relics, Mu'āwiyah hung them in a public square to provoke the Syrians.[32] Obviously, he wanted revenge for 'Uthmān through unjustified

---

28 Al-Ṭabari, *Tārikh*, vol. 3; pp. 506, 510, 542; Ibn al-Athīr, *al-Kāmil*, vol. 3, pp. 122, 131-132; Ibn Kathīr, *al-Bidāyah*, vol. 7, pp. 244-245; Ibn Khaldūn, *Takmilah,* vol. 2, pp. 164-165.

29 Ibn Kathīr, *al-Bidāyah*, vol. 7, p. 248; al-Ṭabari, *Tārikh*, vol. 3, p. 547.

30 Ibn al-Athīr, *al-Kāmil*, vol. 3; Ibn Kathīr, *al-Bidāyah*, vol. 7, p. 249; Ibn Khaldūn, *Takmilah*, vol. 2, p. 162.

31 Ibn Sa'd, *al-Ṭabaqāt*, vol. 3, pp. 224-225.

32 Ibn al-Athīr, *al-Kāmil*, vol. 3, p. 98, Ibn Kathīr, *al-Bidāyah,* vol. 7, p. 227; Ibn Khaldūn, *Takmilah,* vol. 2, p. 152.

means. People were already infuriated by his untimely, unnatural, death. To provoke them further made no sense.

On the other hand, immediately after resuming caliphate, 'Ali removed Mu'āwiyah from the Syrian governorship (Muḥarram 36 A.H.) and substituted him by Sahl ibn Ḥunayf. The Syrian troops intercepted him close to Tabūk and asked him to go back: "If you have come from 'Uthmān, you are welcome. And if you have been sent by someone else, then go back."[33] This was a clear signal to the effect that the Syrian province was unwilling to submit itself to Madīnah.

In the following month 'Ali sent another person to Mu'āwiyah with a letter but he made no response.

The forebodings were ominous. The Syrian governor was giving negative signals by his firm stand against the killers of 'Uthman and not listening to Madīnah excuse for more time until the situation improves for taking 'Uthmān's killers to justice.

Almost sixteenth years of continuous governorship of a strategic province and his good governance gave Mu'āwiyah a loyal following. Historians' narration of Mu'āwiyah's removal by 'Ali gives one the impression as if he had little sense in him. True, 'Ali set aside Mughīrah ibn Shu'bah's advice not to provoke Mu'āwiyah but if he had not dismissed the latter, it would have been a grave error. Mu'āwiyah's refusal to accept his dismissal exposed his intentions.

Not seeing change in Mu'āwiyah's attitude, 'Ali started preparing for taming Syria. Situation was not yet out of his reach and he could have brought Syria to come back into the caliphal orbit. The Arabian Peninsula, Iraq and Egypt were under his control. And Syria alone did not have the resources and the will to resist the caliphate. Besides, the Islamic World would not have encouraged it nor the Syrians would have stood by Mu'āwiyah for long. But unfortunately the new alliance between Ṭalḥah, al-Zubayr and Sayyidah 'Ā'ishah, already mentioned, caused chinks in 'Ali's effort to mount attack on

---

33 Ibn al-Athīr, *al-Kāmil*, vol. 3, p. 103, Ibn Kathīr, *al-Bidāyah*, vol. 7, p. 228; Ibn Khaldūn, *Takmilah,* vol. 2, p. 152.

Syria. The emergent situation forced him to turn towards Baṣrah in Rabī‘ al-Thāni, 36 A.H.[34]

Having finished with Jamal (Jamādi al-Thāni, 36 A.H.), ‘Ali refocused himself on Syria. Jarīr ibn ‘Abdullah al-Bajalī was deputed to persuade Mu‘āwiyah to come under the caliphal umbrella and avoid causing schism in the Ummah. Mu‘āwiyah dilly-dallied the answer. His mind was already set on defiance. ‘Amr ibn al-‘Āṣ’ advice made him firm. Both thought the Jamal incident had deprived ‘Ali of a united army. Iraq, his stronghold, was wayward while Syria was solidly behind Mu‘āwiyah.[35] Meanwhile, availing his stay in Syria, Jarīr met several influential people to convince them that ‘Ali had no hand in ‘Uthmān’s killing. Upset by Jarīr’s successful moves, Mu‘āwiyah asked someone to prime a couple of witnesses for testimony before the Syrians as to ‘Ali’s involvement in ‘Uthmān’s death. The man brought five witnesses to the effect.[36]

Eventually the two protagonists met at Ṣiffīn – a place close to the west bank of the Euphrates. Mu‘āwiyah had already made sure that the river’s water was under his control. With no choice left, ‘Ali fought his way to the river to break the siege and asked his troops to let the opponents have the water as well.[37]

In Dhi al-Ḥajjah before the hostilities started off, ‘Ali sent a delegation to Mu‘āwiyah for final persuasion but his response was not encouraging.

When in Muḥarram 37 A.H. hostilities were disrupted, ‘Ali sent another delegation led by ‘Adiy ibn Ḥātim to Mu‘āwiyah to persuade him to accept ‘Ali’s caliphate as other than him people have given their consent to his leadership. Mu‘āwiyah’s repeated his previous stand though with a spin added to it. “He should deliver ‘Uthmān’s assassins to us so that we kill them. We will then abide by your suggestion and will merge ourselves with the jamā ‘at (community).”

---

34 Ibn al-Athīr, *al-Kāmil,* vol. 3, p. 113.
35 Al-Ṭabari, *Tārikh,* vol. 3, p. 561; Ibn al-Athīr, *al-Kāmil,* vol. 7, p. 253.
36 Ibn 'Abd al-Barr, *al-Isti'āb,* vol. 2, p. 589.
37 Al-Ṭabari, *Tarikh,* vol. 3, pp. 568-569; Ibn Khaldūn, *Takmilah,* vol. 2, p. 170.

Mu'āwiyah followed with another delegation led by Ḥabīb ibn Maslamah al-Fihri, with a new proposal. "If you claim you are a nonparty in 'Uthmān's death, then those who have indulged in his murder should be delivered to us. We will kill them, followed by your resignation from the caliphate so that the new caliph is inducted by mutual consultation of the Muslims."[38]

In Ṣaffar, 37 A.H., the battle entered the decisive phase. But even in a conflict of that magnitude, 'Ali abided by the Sharī'ah demand and asked his troops not to violate it:

> Beware! Do not start the war by yourself unless they attack you. And when you defeat them, avoid killing the one who flees; do not lay your hand on the injured nor should you expose anybody's person, or mutilate the killed. Nor should you enter a house, snatch their belongings, or retaliate even when women abuse you.[39]

On the following day of 'Ammār's death (Ṣaffar 10), when the Mu'āwiyah army was about to flee, 'Amr ibn al-Āṣ suggested that their troops should mount the Qur'ān on their spears and shout: *Hādhā ḥaka.mun baynanā wa baynakum* – this is the judge between us."

Rationalizing his suggestion, 'Amr said, "This will cause split in 'Ali's camp. Some will say it should be accepted and some will insist on refusing it. In consequence, we will stay together, and they will be disunited. If they agreed [to proposal] we will have a lease on time."[40]

This obviously was a game plan. Making the Qur'ān as

---

38 Al-Ṭabari, *Tārikh,* vol. 4, pp. 3-4; Ibn al-Athīr, *al-Kāmil,* vol. 3, pp. 147-148; Ibn Kathīr, *al-Bidāyah,* vol. 7, pp. 257-258; Ibn Khaldūn, *Takmilah,* vol. 2, p. 149.

39 Al-Ṭabari, *Tarikh,* vol. 4, p. 6, Ibn al-Athīr, *al-Kāmil,* vol. 3, p. 149.

40 Al-Ṭabari, *Tārikh,* vol. 4, p. 34; Ibn Sa'd, *al-Ṭabaqāt,* vol. 4, p. 255; Ibn al-Athīr, *al-Kāmil,* vol. 3, p. 160; Ibn Kathīr, *al-Bidāyah,* vol. 7, p. 272; Ibn Khaldūn, *Takmilah,* vol. 2, p. 174.

arbiter was not their objective. Accordingly, the Mu'āwiyah army raised the Qur'ān on their spears and the result came out as was scripted by 'Amr. 'Ali tried persuading the Iraqi faction in his army not to be seduced by the opponents' trap and let the war go to its desired end, but they did not listen to his pleas.

Thus left with no alternative, he was forced to make the mediation agreement with Mu'āwiyah as suggested by him. But when the time for appointing the mediators came, he faced the same dilemma. While Mu'āwiyah had no problem with his nominee, 'Amr ibn al-'Āṣ, 'Ali's choice for 'Abdullah ibn 'Abbās, met opposition from the Iraqi segment who objected to him for his being 'Ali's cousin. They wanted to have a neutral person. With consensus tilting in favour of Abu Musa al-Ash'ari he had him go. 'Ali rightly felt that Abū Mūsā did not have in him the material needed for the occasion.[41]

7. The sixth phase

Last chance as it was to save the caliphate from receding into monarchial absolutism, it was vital that the two arbiters had given their verdict in accordance with the terms of the agreement. The chronicles profiled the agreement as under:

> Both arbiters must act in the light of what they find in the Book of Allah. And what they do not find in Allah's Book they should act in accordance with the just, comprehensive, non-controversial Sunnah.[42]

But when in Daūmat al-Jandal the two arbiters sat for resolving the issue, they never looked into it from the Sharī'ah perspective. The Qur'ān had this injunction that if the fight between two Muslim groups breaks out, the rebel group should be forced to correct its aberrant attitude.[43]

---

41 Al- Ṭabari, *Tārikh,* vol. 4, pp. 34-36; Ibn al-Athīr, *al-Kāmil,* vol. 3, pp. 161-162; Ibn Kathīr, *al-Bidāyah,* vol. 7, pp. 275-276; Ibn Khaldūn, *Takmilah,* vol. 2, p. 175.

42 Al-Ṭabari, *Tārikh,* vol. 4, p. 38; Ibn Kathīr, *al-Bidāyh*, vol. 7, p. 276; Ibn Khaldūn, *Takmilah,* vol. 2, p. 175.

43 Al-Hujurāt: 9. The Āyah says "But, if one of them transgresses against the other, then fight the group that transgresses until it reverts to Allah's command."

'Ammār's death had identified the rebel group in the light of the prophetic saying. The corpus of hadith also contained instruction on obeying the duly inducted amīr. The methodology for blood revenge was also available in the Sharī'ah to determine if the blood revenge issue had been raised rightly or wrongly. The agreement on mediation did not ask the two arbiters to adjudicate the caliphal issue.

But when they met together, 'Amr ibn al-'Āṣ asked Abū Mūsā al-Ash'ari if he had a solution to the problem?

> He said: "In my view we should remove the two (contenders) and leave the caliphal issue to the Muslims to decide through consultation."

'Amr agreed: "You have come up with the right solution."

Thereafter the two walked to the audience, consisting of four hundred people from each side, with some neutral individuals among them. 'Amr asked Abū Mūsa to recount the agreed decision to them.

Sensing trouble, 'Abdullah ibn 'Abbās intervened with Abū Mūsā and suggested that agreed decisions should be announced by 'Amr.

"I am afraid you have been trapped," he said.

"I have no such fear. Our decision is unanimous," replied Abū Mūsā.

Then he rose to speak. "I and my friend ('Amr) have agreed to a point that we remove 'Ali and Mu'āwiyah allowing people to choose their own amīr. I, therefore, dismiss 'Ali and Mu'āwiyah. You can now take the matter in your own hands and decide for yourselves the amīr you want.

Thereafter 'Amr spoke: "You have heard what he has said. He has removed his principal and I too like him seek his principal's removal and retain my principal for he is wali to 'Uthmān ibn 'Affān, the claimant to his blood, by far his most deserving successor."

That this sent Abū Mūsā into repulsion should not be surprising. Latching on to him he said: *Mā laka lā wa faka Allah, ghad rata wa fajrata* – what have you done? May Allah deprive you of the ability (taūfīq) to do good – you played deception (on me) and violated the agreement."

Equally disturbed Sa'd ibn abi Waqqāṣ vented his sadness on Abū Mūsā:

> "Woe to you Abū Mūsā. You turned out to be a very weak (person) before 'Amr's vile deceits."
> "What should I do now? This man agreed with me on a point and then broke it," exclaimed Abū Mūsā.
>
> "If Abū Mūsā had died before (the agreement) it would have been better for him," observed 'Abd al-Raḥmān ibn abī Bakr.

Mired in grief, 'Abdullah ibn 'Umar exclaimed, "Look at the calamity that this Ummah has fallen into. Its future was confided into the hands of two such individuals – one cared less about what he was doing and the other was weak."[44]

In fact, none of the audiences had any doubt about the agreement that Abū Mūsā had spelled out in his speech. They also knew that 'Amr's conduct was repugnant to the agreed formula.

The rest is history. 'Amr went to Mu'āwiyah and gave him the glad tiding of the caliphate. And Abū Mūsā overtook by shame and not having the courage to eye 'Ali left for Makkah.[45]

While explaining 'Amr's role in the incident Ibn Kathīr says that "he did not consider it wise to leave people without the imam, for he thought the then prevailing discord among the people might push them into a long strife. Thus, for expediency sake he retained

44 Al-Ṭabari, *Tārīkh,* vol. 4, p. 51; Ibn Sa'd, *al-Ṭabaqāt*, vol. 4, pp. 256-257; Ibn al-Athīr, *al-Kāmil,* vol. 3, p. 168; ibn Kathīr, *al-Bidāyah,* vol. 7, p. 283; Ibn Khaldūn, *Takmilah*, vol. 2, p. 178.

45 Ibn Kathīr, *al-Bidāyah,* vol. 7, p. 283; Ibn Khaldūn, *Takmilah,* vol. 2, p. 178

Mu'āwiyah – and ijtihād (one's reasoned judgment) could be right as well as wrong."[46]

Ibn Kathīr is of course entitled to his opinion but any fair-minded person who reads the whole proceeding from the raising of the Qur'ān to the agreed formula and the way 'Amr acted will find it hard to accept it was "ijtihād".

Undoubtedly, the Prophet's Ṣaḥābah enjoy an exalted status with us and by all means they are worthy of our unqualified respect. We also think that it will be great injustice and an act of barbarity if someone, because of their certain judgmental error, forgets their otherwise unblemished record of services to the cause of Islam and adopt irreverent attitude to them.

But it will be equally unfair if we club together the errors of great men in history into ijtihād. Would it be then possible for us to stop the coming generations from committing such ijtihādāt?

In fact, ijtihād (reasoned judgment) embodies an utmost effort to find the truth. Should an error take place in the process of finding the truth, it will still qualify for the reward from Allah. To act, however, intentionally in the wrong direction does not fall under ijtihād. In fact, in such matters both immoderation and indulging in excesses leading to a blanket condemnation of his whole person needs restrain.

Amr ibn al-'Āṣ is an elder of repute; it is equally true that in Islam's spread he played a great role. But on these two occasions, he made judgments which cannot be described anything but incorrect.

Setting aside the conflicting views on what the two mediators did, the whole proceedings in Daūmat al-Jandal were contrary to the agreement of mediation. The two assumed that they had the authority to dismiss 'Ali from his caliphal office despite the fact that he was constitutionally elected. Equally wrong was their assumption that Mu'āwiyah was claimant to the caliphate. The fact of the matter is that until that time he was only clamouring revenge for 'Uthmān's blood.

---

46 Ibn Kathīr, *al-Bidāyah,* vol. 7, p. 283.

That is why 'Ali rejected their decision. In his post-rejection speech, he said:

> "Listen, the two individuals that you made mediators have set aside the Qur'ānic ruling and have followed their own thoughts without Allah's guidance and have given verdict, which is not based on an explicit injunction or the past Sunnah. Their views varied and they did not reach the right decision."[47]

On reaching Kūfah, 'Ali started preparation for bringing Syria back to the fold of his caliphate. His speeches during this turbulent period reveal a disturbed mind that feared the imminent imposition of monarchy on the Ummah and how desperately he tried to save the rightly guided caliphate from man-made systems. In one of his talks, he says:

> "By Allah, if these people became your rulers, they will follow the ways of Kisrā and Heraclius."[48]

On another occasion he says:

> "Stand up to those who crave absolute powers so that they could prevail on Allah-created humans and turn them into their slaves."[49]

But the Iraqis had lost their resolve; the emergent Khawārij mischief was compounding the situation. Besides, Mu'āwiyah and 'Amr ibn al-'Āṣ further succeeded in wresting Egypt and North Africa from 'Ali's fold. The Islamic world was now practically fractured into two hostile camps. The split situation, however, ended with 'Ali's shahādah in Ramādān 40 A.H., followed by Hasan's reconciliatory attitude that cleared Mu'āwiyah's passage to absolute power.

---

47 Al-Ṭabari, *Tārikh,* vol. 4, p. 57.
48 Ibid, p. 58; Ibn al-Athīr, *al-Kāmil,* vol. 3, p. 171.
49 Ibid, p. 59; Ibid, p. 172.

With 'Ali gone and the new players in power, it soon became obvious even to neutral observers the high stakes that made him lose his life. This sense of deprivation found its echo in 'Abdullah ibn 'Umar's late-life lamentation: "I have no regrets other than the fact that I did not support 'Ali."[50]

Ibrāhīm al-Nakh'i says that Masrūq ibn Ajda' used to repent and say istighfār (seeking forgivness from Allah) on his inability to support 'Ali.[51]

Same were the feelings of 'Abdullah ibn 'Amr ibn al-'Āṣ, who had a lingering sense of shame on his favouring Mu'āwiyah over 'Ali.

During this tumultuous period, 'Ali's conduct by and large remained impeccable, reminiscent of a rightly guided caliph, with a caveat however which cannot be defended. After the Jamal battle, he changed his attitude towards 'Uthmān's killers. Until Jamal, he tolerated them because of the compulsive situation he found himself in and sought time to deal with them. When he sent Qa'qā' ibn 'Amr to Sayyidah 'Ā'ishah, Ṭalḥah and al-Zubayr, the former assured them saying: "'Ali has deferred action against the killers of 'Uthmān until he has power to punish them. Your pledge of support to 'Ali (at this moment) will make it easier to avenge 'Uthmān's blood."[52]

In a sitting just before the Jamal, Ṭalḥah ibn 'Ubayd Allah accused him of being responsible for 'Uthmān's death, which he countered by saying *"l'an Allah qatalah 'Uthmān* – Allah curse be on 'Uthmān's killers."[53]

But after then, the rebels steadily gained influence over him; so much so that he gave governorship to Mālik ibn Hārith al-Ashtar and Muḥammad ibn abī-Bakr the main culprits in killing 'Uthmān.

---

50 Ibn Sa'd, *al-Ṭabaqāt,* vol. 4, p. 187; Ibn 'Abd al-Barr, *al-Isti'āb,* vol. 1, pp. 30, 37.

51 Ibn 'Abd al-Barr, *al-Isti'ā,* vol. 1, p. 37.

52 Ibid, vol. 1, p. 371.

53 Ibn Kathīr, *al-Bidāyah,* vol. 7, p. 237.

This is the only aspect of his governance that constrains us to call it inappropriate.

Some critics also say that following 'Uthmān's practice 'Ali gave important posts to his relatives. They cite in this respect the names of 'Abdullah ibn 'Abbās, 'Ubaydullah ibn 'Abbās, Qutham ibn 'Abbās and so forth. But these critics forget that 'Ali gave offices at the time when those who were capable to wield them had withheld their support to him, and others had gone to the opposite side while the desertion in his own camp was high.

Forced thus, he had to rely on those whom he could trust. Certainly this situation has no parallel with the 'Uthmān's for he had a large pool of capable people that he could trust, with no compulsion to depend on his relatives.

8. The last phase

The power transfer to Mu'āwiyah was still an interim phase, but but the people who could read the normative change knew that the dynastic rule was now imminent. Thus when after his bai'ah (oath), Sa'd ibn abī Waqqāṣ met Mu'āwiyah, he greeted him:

> "As-salāmu 'alayk ayyuhal malik – greetings to you O king!"
>
> Mu'āwiyah felt the pinch and could not help say it:
> "What wrong would it have made if you had called me *amīr al-mu'minīn?*"
>
> Sa'd promptly corrected him:
> "By Allah, if I had the chance to have this government the way you had it, I would have refused it."[54]

Mu'āwiyah himself knew it. One time he himself acknowledged, "I am the first king (among the Muslims)."[55]

---

54 Ibid, p. 240.

55 Ibn al-Athīr, *al-Kāmil*, vol. 3, p. 405. Sa'd ibn abī Waqqāṣ' stance comes out pretty well in this episode. During the mischief era, his nephew Hāshim ibn 'Utbah ibn abī Waqqāṣ suggested him to stand up as a contender for the caliphate and he would find 100,000 swords in his support. He responded, "Of the 100,000 swords I only need one sword which may fall on the nonbeliever but not on a Muslim." See Ibn Kathīr, *al-Bidāyah*, vol. 8, p. 72.

With the assumption of power by Mu'āwiyah, the sole possibility of rebound to the real caliphate laid in his hands if only he had amended himself and left the issue of his succession to the Muslims. Or in case he wanted to avert post-death conflictive situation he could have called for the assembly of the wise and the pious to name someone suitable for the Muslim leadership. But unfortunately by naming his son Yazīd as his successor and coercing people to accept him, he foreclosed such a possibility.

That done, Mu'āwiyah wrote to Ziyād the governor of Baṣrah for his opinion on the matter. Ziyād sent for 'Ubayd ibn Ka'b al-Numyari, asking him to go to Mu'āwiyah and inform him that Yazīd had certain weakness in his character which called for caution, and that making any hasty decision about succession might become counter productive. 'Ubayd advised caution to Ziyād for he thought it might invite hostility from Mu'āwiyah. Instead, he suggested he would go to Yazīd and inform him that Amīr al-Mu'mīnīn has sought advice from Ziyād for his naming Yazīd as his successor, and he thought people would oppose him, for they did not like some of his ways. He should thus improve himself so that his succession was carried through. Ziyād liked 'Ubayd's modifier.

In Damascus, 'Ubayd first met Yazīd and advised him to improve his ways and later met Mu'āwiyah to restrain the move for succession.[56]

After Ziyād's death (53 A.H.), Mu'āwiyah began groundwork for Yazīd's succession. As a starter, he tried to persuade prominent individuals like 'Abdullah ibn 'Umar for his bai'ah to Yazīd. He refused to support him.

Ignoring objections, Mu'āwiyah turned to the Madīnah governor Marwān ibn al-Ḥakam to ask people their opinion on the succession issue. Marwān presented the proposal to the Madinese, who consented to the idea in general. But when Marwān spoke to the people in Masjid al-Nabawi, he faced a distraught audience.

"Amīr al-Mu'mīnīn," he said, "has spared no effort in finding a suitable person for you in naming his son Yazīd as his successor. That Allah has inspired him with this excellent choice. Nor is the successor idea an innovation. Abū Bakr and 'Umar had also nominated their successors."

56 Ibn al-Athīr, *al-Kāmil*, vol. 3, p. 249; Ibn Kathīr, *al-Bidāyah*, vol. 8, p. 79; For some aspects of this episode, see also Ibn Khaldūn, *Takmilah,* vol. 3, pp. 15-16.

Disturbed by the distortion, 'Abdul-Raḥmān ibn abī Bakr spoke out:

"You made a lie O Marwān and so has Mu'āwiyah. You do not have the well-being of Muḥammad's Ummah close to your heart. You want to turn (caliphate) into Caesarism – when a Caesar died his son took over. This is not the Sunnah of Abū Bakr and 'Umar. They never named their sons as their successors."

Taking courage from 'Abdul-Raḥmān ibn abī Bakr, al-Ḥusayn ibn 'Ali and others like 'Abdullah ibn 'Umar, 'Abdullah ibn al-Zubayr also refused to give their pledge to Yazīd.[57]

In the same period, Mu'āwiyah summoned delegations from different regions and sought their consent to Yazīd's succession.

In response, people made conciliatory speeches praising his nomination but Aḥnaf ibn Qays remained silent. Taking note of his silence, Mu'āwiyah asked: "Abū Baḥr, what do you say?" Forced thus he said:

"If we tell the truth we face your wrath. If we lie, we face Allah's wrath. Amīr al-Mu'mīnīn, you know everything about Yazīd – his nights and days, his private and public life, his ins and outs. If you really think he is good for Allah and this Ummah, then do not seek anybody's advice. And if you are convinced he is something else then while going to the hereafter do not relegate the world to him. As for we are concerned, our task is to follow what you say."[58]

After obtaining bai'ah (oath) from Iraq, Syria and other regions, Mu'āwiyah himself came to al-Ḥijāz for it was the heartland of Islam populated by eminent individuals who mattered and would have resisted the succession issue. At the outskirts of Madīnah, he

---

57 Al-Bukhāri has briefly sketched this event in his "*Tafsīr sūrah al-Aḥqāf*". Ibn Ḥajar has given its details in *Fatḥ al-Bari* on reports from Nasā'i, Isma'ili, Ibn al-Munzir, Abū Ya'lā, and Ibn abī Ḥātim. Ibn Kathīr has also borrowed some of its details on the authority of Ibn abī Ḥātim and Nasā'i in his *Tafsir al-Qur'ān al-'Azīm*. For further extrapolation of the subject see *al-Isti'āb*, vol. 2, p. 393; *al-Bidāyah*, vol. 8, p. 89; *al-Kāmil*, vol. 3, p. 250. Ibn al-Athīr writes: "According to some reports, 'Abd al Raḥmān ibn abī Bakr had died in 53 A.H. If this is correct, then he could not be present on this occasion." The authentic ḥadīth, however, contradicts it. Ibn Kathīr says Abd al -Raḥmān died in 58 A.H.

58 Ibn al-Athīr, *al-Kāmil*, vol. 3, pp. 250-251; Ibn Kathīr, *al-Bidāyah*, vol. 8, p. 80.

was met by al-Ḥusayn ibn 'Ali, 'Abdullah ibn al-Zubayr, 'Abdullah ibn 'Umar and 'Abdul-Raḥmān ibn Abī Bakr. But the matter did not materialize, and they left the city for Makkah making his task easy.

Finished with Madīnah, he went to Makkah and asked for audience with four of them. They met him outside Makkah. His attitude was of deference to them. He made them part of his entourage and together they entered the city. Later, in private he tried to persuade them to give their support to Yazīd's succession. 'Abdullah ibn al-Zubayr was the first to respond:

> "You may follow one of three options: Either you follow the Prophet (ṣal.lal.lahu 'alayhi wa-sallam) and name no one as your successor. People will themselves elect someone as their caliph, as they did by naming Abū Bakr or you go for the model that Abū Bakr followed when he nominated a person of 'Umar's caliber, who was not his relative or you follow the way of 'Umar who proposed a six-member [electoral] *shūrā,* which did not have anyone from his sons."

Mu'āwiyah asked the rest about the issue. They said they agreed with Ibn al-Zubayr. Mu'āwiyah flushed with anger.

With the last knell driven in the coffin of the caliphate, the dynastic rule entrenched itself. So lasting was this change that thereafter Muslims never had the blessed caliphate again.

We have no dispute with Amīr Mu'āwiyah's merits, his status of being a Ṣaḥabi also deserves our respect and so are his services in bringing the divided world of Islam under one flag and extending its domain far and wide. Anyone who abuses him does wrong. He has made, however, certain decisions, which changed the caliphate into monarchy.

Chapter Five

The Difference between the Caliphate and Monarchy

We have so far discussed in detail how the caliphate passed through different phases to jel into monarchial rule. From this discourse, it becomes obvious that the Muslims' loss of the rightly guided caliphate was not an accidental event that suddenly happened. Some causative factors were at play in its pulverization. It was also obvious that at each phase there were openings when they could have averted the fall. But unfortunate as it was for the Muslim Ummah and in fact the humanity at large, the causative factors proved stronger than everything else, and none of the openings could be made use of in making the turn around.

We will now discuss the qualitative difference between the caliphate and monarchial absolutism. What was the nature of change that it formulated on the collective life of the Muslim people?

1. The procedural change in the caliph's induction

The first primary change occurred in the constitutional mode of the caliph's induction. The rightly guided caliphate made sure that no person sought for the caliphal office other than through people's consent, the final arbiters of his suitability. In other words, bai'ah (the allegiance pledge) should not be the consequence of a person being in power but the cause of it – something obtained freely without his effort or conspiracy.

In the rightly guided caliphate, all the four caliphs came into power through this constitutional mechanism. None manipulated the situation; rather, they were impelled into the caliphal office. One can cite 'Ali's case – of his desire to be the caliph. But the most one can say is that he considered himself more qualified for the caliphate than others. History, however, is bereft of any such evidence that he ever tried to obtain it. To think himself suitable for the job is thus not violative of the constitutional mechanism. In fact, all the four caliphs abided by this Shar'ī principle: people confered caliphate on them, not that they forcibly obtained it.

The mulūkīyah (monarchy) had its beginning by the change in the electoral mechanism. Amīr Mu'āwiyah's coming into power did not encapsulate the principle of consensual caliphate. He sought it by force without people's mandate and when he got it, he extracted post-caliphal oath of allegiance. Denying him oath at that point in time would not have caused his ouster. Rather, it would have led to disorder and further bloodshed, which none would have preferred over peace and order. That explains why after Ḥasan's abdication (Rabi' al-Awwal, 41 A.H.) the Ṣaḥābah, tābi'un and the pious of the Ummah agreed on his allegiance oath, for they saw in it the end to disorder and conflicts.

Mu'āwiyah himself understood it. In the beginning of his caliphate while addressing the Madinans, he said:

اَمَّا بَعد، فَاِنِّى وَاللّٰهِ مَا وَلِيتُ اَمْرَكُمْ حِينَ وَلِيتُه وَاَنَا اَعْلمُ اَنَّكُمْ لَا تسرون بِوِلَايَتِى وَلَا تُحِبُّونَهَا وَاِنِّى لعالمٌ بِمَا فى نُفُوسِكُمْ مِّنْ ذَالِك وَلٰكِنِّى خالسْتُكُمْ بِسَيْفِى هٰذَا مُخالسةً... وَاِنْ لَّمْ تَجِدُونِى اَقْوَمُ بِحَقِّكم كله فَارضُوا مِنى بِبَعْضِهِ.

"By Allah, while taking hold of your government I was not unaware of the fact that you were displeased over my succession to power. In this respect, I know well what stirs in your hearts. But I have taken (the government) by the force of this sword. Now if you think that I am not delivering your right to you, then content yourselves with the little you have from me."[1]

Obviously, this heralded the era of despotism and monarchial rule in which the rulers freed themselves from the caliphal constraint and where power transfer was dynastic and not through people's

1 Ibn Kathīr, *al-Bidāyah*, vol. 8, p. 132.

consent. Bai'ah became peripheral – neither for the origination of power nor the causal factor in the removal from office. In the process, people lost their assertive will, for they knew they were inconsequential in the power play. And where they dared they were taught lesson.

Would the government obtained through power become legitimate once it entrenches itself? Such a discussion is meaningless for it is not the real issue. The issue that calls for consideration is whether Islam authorizes the path to caliphal office by force or through consent – the way the rightly guided caliphs were inducted into the seat of power, or the way Mu'āwiyah and his successors conducted themselves. Obviously, there are two ways to do a thing. One which is Islam-given; the other which is differently done and once it takes place, then Islam tells us to bear with it for otherwise the effort to change it might bring about a situation worse than before. The two cannot be equated. It would be extremely unjust to say that Islam considers them equally right. The first is not merely just but desired. The second is a compromise, tolerated but not desired.

2. The change in the rulers' lifestyle

The second change that became evident pertained to attitudinal changes. Kings in the guise of caliphs went after the ways of Caesar and Kisrā substituting the lifestyle of the Prophet ('alayhi as-salām) and the rightly guided caliphs. They started living in the opulence of the royal palaces; guarded by the security forces and intermediaries which distanced them from the people, making it almost impossible for the common men to reach them.

In consequence, they became dependent on the functionaries of the state about the plight of the people – a far cry from the way the rightly guided caliphs conducted themselves, who always preferred to stay linked with the people. They visited bazaars where people could see them, touch them and talked to them. They performed five-time Ṣalāh (prayers) in the masjid with people and in their Friday sermons would inform the congregation not only about their rights and obligations in Islam but also about the affairs of the state and its policies. They encouraged questions, redressed complaints and never got upset by their accountability. 'Ali followed the approach even when there were threats to his life in Kūfah.

The monarchial rule following the Caesar and Kisrā way, however, brought changes averse to Muslim temper.

3. Change in Bayt al-Māl

The third equally important change occurred in their attitude was towards bayt al-māl (public treasury). Islam held bayt al-māl as a trust given to the caliphs by Allah in behalf of the people whose use was not allowed to be personalized – neither anything added to it nor expended from it, without respect to the parameters set by the Sharī'ah. They were accountable no matter what they did to it. For his personal living, he could dip into it only to the extent of an average man's living and nothing else.

The monarchial rule changed its complexion as well as character of its dispensation. From trust, it turned into royal property. People who used to be its owners became its recipients as royal subjects. The way the royalty and the state functionaries lived was obscene, possible only because they usurped it.

When 'Umar ibn 'Abdul-'Aziz restored the rightly guided caliphate, he began the clean-up operation first with the ruling family. As a personal example, he surrendered his inherited property that generated 40,000 dinār worth of yearly income. This included income from Fadak, which after the Prophet's death had become part of the treasury in the caliphal setup. Abū Bakr even refused its deliverance to the Prophet's daughter. But when Marwān ibn al-Ḥakam assumed power, he appropriated Fadak as his personal property, later inherited by his sons.[2]

This being its dispensation, the incoming revenue also became questionable erasing the vital distinction between Ḥalāl (allowed) and Ḥarām (not allowed). In one of his decrees 'Umar ibn 'Abdul-'Aziz spelled out those wrong taxes that his predecessors extorted from the people.[3] Its reading reveals how ruthlessly they

2 Ibn al-Athīr, *al-Kāmil,* vol. 4, p. 164; Ibn Kathīr, *al-Bidāyah,* vol. 9, pp. 200,208.

3 Al-Ṭabari, *Tārikh*, vol. 5, p. 321; Ibn al-Athīr, *Usad*, vol. 5, p. 163.

violated the Sharī'ah injunctions on the revenue collection. The greatest injustice, however, was inflicted on the new Muslims who were subjected to jizyah (social security tax) on the pretext that their Islam was a simulation to save themselves from paying the tax. Gross as it was, they preferred taxes over the spread of Islam.

Ibn al-Athīr reports that his tax collectors had informed him that the dhimmīs were embracing Islam in large numbers settling in Basrah and Kūfah, which had caused decrease in revenues from jizyah and kharāj, Ḥajjāj ibn Yūsuf. Ḥajjāj responded by ordering their expulsion from the cities and the re-imposition of jizyah on them. Driven thus out, the new Muslims wept crying yā Muḥammadah! yā Muḥammadah! So helpless and pathetic a condition they were in that they found no recourse to the redress of their plight.

Touched by their plight, the 'ulamā and jurists rose in protest and while the new Muslims were being driven out of the cities they cried too.[4] When 'Umar ibn 'Abdul-'Aziz became the caliph, a delegation from Khurāsān came to see him, and complained against the governor that thousands of people who had embraced Islam have been re-subjected to jizyah (social security tax) by him. So great was the governor's prejudice, they said, that he had been loudly saying: "A person from my nation is dearer to me than hundred others."

Disturbed, 'Umar dismissed al-Jarrah ibn 'Abdullah al-Hākmi from governorship. In his dismissal decree he wrote: "Allah sent Muḥammad Rasūl Allah as a da'iy (caller to the truth) and not as a tax collector."[5]

4. The end of freedom

A still vital change involved loss of freedoms for the Muslims, especially in the exercise of *amr bil ma'rūf wa nahī 'an al-munkar* (social obligation to enjoin good and forbid evil), even though Islam had made its discharge binding on the Muslims. For sure, an Islamic society and state could only have preserved their ethos if the Ummah's conscience had maintained its spark and its tongue free – if they

4 Ibn al-Athīr, *al-Kāmil*, vol. 4, p. 79.

5 Al-Ṭabari, *Tārikh*, vol. 5, p. 314; Ibn al-Athīr, *al-Kāmil*, vol. 4, p. 158; Ibn Kathīr, *al-Bidāyah*, vol. 9, p. 188.

could bring to task the highest office of the land and say what they thought was right.

The rightly guided caliphate made sure that the freedom value is not only preserved but also encouraged in the people. Those who disagreed with them they honoured them; they responded to their detractors' criticism in a rightful, sincere way. But in the era of monarchy their tongues were silenced and conscience muffled. The mouth could now only be opened for praise or else silent. And if the stirrings in one's conscience were strong enough to resist and inclined towards expressing it, then be ready for incarceration, lashes and even death. That is why those who refused to abide by the despotic rule were subjected to the worst kind of punishments so much so that the whole Ummah got scared of them.

The new policy of governmental intolerance started in Amīr Mu'āwiyah's reign when Hujr ibn 'Adiy was executed in 51 A.H. He was a pious Ṣaḥābi – a front runner in acts of goodness, a man of high calibre among the pious of the Ummah. Seeing 'Ali abused in official pronouncements, he deeply felt the hurt like rest of the Muslims, who bore it in silence. One day he could not take it further and in response condemned Mu'āwiyah, while praising 'Ali.

As long as Mughīrah ibn Shu'bah held al-Baṣrah's governorship he ignored him. But with the administrative merge of Baṣrah with Kūfah and Ziyād its sole governor, Hujr's vulnerability increased. Ziyād used to abuse 'Ali and in return he would defend him. In one of the jumu'ah prayers when Ziyād prolonged it, he objected to it, which the former did not like. And eventually he nabbed him along with his twelve companions. To build up the case against him, he forced a large number of people to testify that "they formed a group which abuses the caliph openly and invites people to fight Amīr al-Mū'minīn. Their claim is that the caliphate justifiably belonged to 'Ali's progeny and none else. They cooked rebellion in the city and drove the city administrator out. They support Abū Turāb ('Ali) and send their salutation to him and abuse his opponents."

Among the witnesses Qāḍī Shurayh's name was also included but in a separate letter to Mu'āwiyah he absolved himself: "I have heard that among the testimony against Hujr ibn 'Adiy, my witnessing is also included. My real witnessing is that he establishes Ṣalāh (prayer), gives Zakāh (poor-due), frequently performs 'Umrah and Ḥajj, calls for goodness and forbids others from wrong. His blood and property are Ḥarām. You have the discretion to kill him or forgive him."

In this way, Hujr and his companions were sent to Mu'āwiyah who ordered for their execution. Before their death, the executioners asked them to repent: "We have been told that if you declare your separation from 'Ali and curse him you will be set free; otherwise, you will be killed."

None of them agreed. Hujr however added: "I cannot verbalize something that might annoy my Provider and Master!"

This tragic incident shocked every righteous person. 'Ā'ishah and 'Abdullah ibn 'Umar were saddened beyond words. She had already written a letter to Mu'āwiyah urging him to spare Hujr. Later on when he came to see her, she reprimanded him: "O Mu'āwiyah, you did not fear Allah while killing Hujr."

Mu'āwiyah's governor in Khurāsān Rabi' ibn Ziyād al-Ḥārithī was so overwhelmed by grief on Hujr's execution that on hearing the news he cried out: "O Allah, if in your knowledge there is any remnant of goodness left in me, then raise me from this world."

Hujr's death was not an isolated act; it became the state policy to use force in suppressing dissent. Marwān ibn al-Ḥakam while he was Madīnah's governor kicked Miswar ibn Makhramah because he objected to something he had uttered by characterizing it as bad.[6]

This policy of repression eventually made Muslims low spirited and compromising. Those who dared to speak out began to decrease among them. Sycophancy and selling conscience fetched higher values in the marketplace while truthfulness and integrity lost its price. Those with calibre, honest and conscientious felt alienated from governmental setup and people lost interest in the nation's affairs. They ended up as spectators to the incoming and outgoing

6 Ibn 'Abd al-Barr, *al-Isti'āb,* vol. 1, p. 353.

administration. The moral state of society declined to unbelievable low level of degradation. An instance speaks of it. 'Ali ibn Ḥusayn (Imām Zayn al- 'Ābidīn) recounts an event that involved him. He says that after the tragedy of Karbalah a person stole him to his house and treated him very well. Every time the man saw him he cried, giving him the impression as if he was the only one in the world who really cared. At that very moment, a public crier announced 'Ubayd Allah ibn Ziyād's 300-dirham bounty on his head. As he heard it, he came to him, his eyes brimming with tears, and began to tie his hands to his neck. Then, while still crying, he took him to Ibn Ziyād and obtained his reward.[7]

5. The end of the judicial freedom

Among the principles of governance, the judiciary's independence from the administration was crucial to its just functioning. Even though in the rightly guided caliphate the appointment of the qāḍī was done by the caliphs but once inducted, they operated free from any pressure other than Allah's fear and the compulsions of their conscience. None could dare interfere in the proceedings of the courts. The qāḍī could summon the caliph and give decision against him. But when dynastic despotism replaced the caliphate, the judiciary also suffered. The rulers claimed judicial immunity not only for themselves but also for their functionaries including princes, governors and other state dignitaries, making it difficult to obtain justice against them. This by itself was enough of a reason for capable upright 'ulamā to decline royal offers of judicial occupancy. And he who accepted would invite cynicism from the people. So great was the administrative encroachment on the judicial terrain that even governors got the powers to install and remove qāḍī.[8]

6. The end of the shūrā-based government

Still another important aspect of the Islamic state was its shūrā-based polity. It ran its affairs with consultation, especially of people who were knowledgeable, pious, honest, and whom people believed were capable of giving sound advice. In the rightly guided caliphate, the

---

7 Ibn S'ad, *al-Ṭabaqāt,* vol. 5, p. 212.

8 Jalāl al-Din al-Suyūti, *Husan al-Mahādirah* (Cairo: al-Matb'ah al-Sharafiyah, 1327 A.H.) vol. 2, p. 88.

best among the Ummah were their advisors; they were fearless and could give their opinion in a forthright manner. Their presence as consultants to the government made it sure that it would run on the right track. People recognized them as *ahl al-hall wa al-'aqd.* But monarchial rule changed this aspect as well. In place of shūrā, arbitrary personal decisions formed the pattern of policy-making. Knowledgeable truth seekers distended themselves from the kings and the kings distanced themselves from such people. Now their consultative circle included governors, their courtiers and the nobles among the royal family.

With a change of this magnitude vacuum was created. The non-presence of an authorized institution that could match its talent with the evolving larger civilization and make timely decisions that could have played its role in developing the Islamic laws became a problematic.

The royal council could make good or bad decisions concerning administration, internal or external matters and general policy issues, but it lacked competence to develop law. Even if they had tried doing so, people's collective conscience would not have swallowed it. They knew their position well and the people also recognized them as wrong doers. In other words, they lacked moral and legislative competence. To fill this vacuum, the 'ulamā and jurists issued religious edicts or interpreted the text in their teaching circles. Same went with the quḍā who in making court decisions used either their ijtihād or some scholarly opinion. This helped though in the growth of law but it did create a kind of a legal anarchy in the state. For almost a century, there was no codified law that the courts could have followed and gave uniformed decisions.

7. The rise of racial and nationalistic biases

The advent of the monarchial governance also saw the resurfacing of the old jāhilī social, ethnic and tribalistic biases, which Islam had so assiduously dissolved to create one Ummah with equal rights for everyone. The Umayyad government from the beginning was a partisan setup: it was less Islamic and more Arab in which there was no common equation between the Arab Muslims and the non-Arab

Muslims. So much so that in violation of the Sharī'ah, it imposed jizyah on the new Muslims. This not only scuttled the chances for the Islamic spread but also gave non-Arabs the feelings that the Islamic conquests have made them subordinate to the Arabs and that even if they accepted Islam, they would not be equal to them.

This further aggravated the matter. Even in Ṣalāh, judicial occupancy and administrative appointments consideration was given to a person's Arab origin. In Kūfah, Ḥajjāj ibn Yūsuf (perhaps to ensure proper pronunciation) ordered that none other than an Arab should be made the imam of the Ṣalāh.[9] When they arrested Sa'id ibn Jubayr and brought him to Ḥajjāj he reminded his favour to him that it was he who made him imām, a non-Arab.[10]

The rise of the Sh'ūbiyyah ('Ajami nationalism) and the spread of the 'Abbāsid message against the Umayyads in Khurāsān owed much to such non-Islamic attitudes. The 'Abbāsid made use of their hatred against the Arabs, and the non-Arabs supported them hoping that the revolution thus engineered would help them break the Arab hold in the Islamic domain.

The Umayyad narrow-mindedness was not peculiar to non-Arabs alone; once they ignited parochial and ethnic prejudices, the fire spread among the Arabs as well, and split them along the tribalistic line. The old feuds between 'Adnāni and Qahtāni, Yamani and Mudari, Azd and Tamīm, Kalb and Qays resurfaced again. The administration itself used one tribe against another and their governors openly favoured their own tribes at the expense of other identities and interests. Because of these disastrous policies, the inter feuds between Yamani and Mudari aggravated to such an extent that by making them fight against each other Abu Muslim Khurāsāni succeeded in overthrowing the Umayyad dynasty. Ibn Kathīr says that when the 'Abbāsid's forces assaulted Damascus the capital was rife with Yamani-Mudari prejudicial warfare. Even masājid (mosques) were not spared. In the central masjid two imams used to

9 Ibn 'Abdi Rabbih, *al-'Iqd*, vol. 2, p. 233.

10 Ibn Khallikān, *Wafayāt al-'Ayām* (Cairo: Maktabah al-Nahdah al-Misriyah, 1948) vol. 2, p. 115.

lead separate prayers and made separate khutbah (pre-Ṣalāh speech). None from these groups was willing to make Ṣalāh with others.[11]

8. Marginalization of law

The greatest calamity that befell Muslims in the monarchial era was the breach from the Sharī'ah rule, though the very purpose of the Islamic state was its uniform application over all aspects of life, without discrimination to any class of people – enemy or friend, Muslim or non-Muslim, a law-abiding citizen or a rebel. The Sharī'ah insists on observing its parameters.

The rightly guided caliphs without exception followed the Sharī'ah. For example, 'Uthmān and 'Ali even under most distressing circumstances did not overstep the Shar'ī parameters, for the four caliphs knew their limits: they were not monarchial absolutists.

But with the advent of monarchy the kings became selective with the Sharī'ah; in many cases subjecting it to their personal considerations. True, they retained majority of the Islamic laws, the courts also made decisions in their light and the daily run of the affairs conducted accordingly, but they never subordinated their politics to them. In this respect, they cared less for the limits of Ḥalāl (allowed) and Ḥarām (disallowed).

Imām al-Zuhrī says that during the Prophet and the rightly guided caliphs' era the kāfir (nonbeliever) could inherit from neither a Muslim nor a Muslim from a kāfir. Mu'āwiyah allowed Muslims to inherit from a non-Muslim relative but denied inheritance to a kāfir (nonbeliever) from a Muslim. 'Umar ibn 'Abdul-'Aziz restored the sunnah by retracting the violation. Hishām ibn 'Abd al-Malik, however, brought it back.[12]

Ibn Kathīr says that even in diyah (blood-money) matters, which allowed equal diyah to both Muslim and contractual non-Muslims, Mu'āwiyah altered the Sunnah by making it half for the

11 Ibn Kathīr, *al-Bidāyah,* vol. 10, p. 45.
12 Ibid, vol. 8, p. 139, vol. 9, p. 232.

non-Muslim while the other half he appropriated to himself.[13] Yet another bad practice was introduced by him to continue criticizing the 'Ali for not taking action against the killers of caliph 'Uthman but also ordered his governors to follow the practice from the pulpits in the masājid.

'Umar ibn 'Abdul-'Azīz, when he came into power, stop the practice of criticising 'Ali by the following Qur'ānic āyah (*al-Nahl:* 90) in the Friday khutbah:

Innal.lah ya' muru bil 'adl. wal. ihsān wa 'itā zil qurbā wa yanhā...

Even in distributing war spoils, there was a departure from the clear injunctions of the Book of Allah and the Prophet's Sunnah, which allows one-fifth share to treasury and the remainder four shares to the combatants involved in the war. The new policy laid down that from the war spoils gold and silver should be sifted for the ruler and the rest distributed according to the Sharī'ah.[14]

All this arbitrary use of power was the manifestation of a new governmental mindset that the governors and the military commanders were now free to enforce their writ the way they wanted. Expediency overruled the Sharī'ah.

9. Yazīd's reign

Yazīd's succession carried this practice of ignoring the Sharī'ah in political matters further, with serious consequences for the Muslim Ummah. Three events in this period had cataclysmic repercussions on the world of Islam.

The first event relates to al-Ḥusayn's *shahādah* (martyrdom). True, he was going to Iraq in response to the people's request to unseat Yazīd. And the Yazīd government perceived it as an act of open rebellion. We would ignore this question whether al-Ḥusayn's rising

13 Ibn Kathīr, *al-Bidāyah,* vol. 8, p. 139. His words are *wa-kāna Mu'āwiyah awal min qasr ha ila al-nasaf wa ākhaza al-nasaf li nafsihi.*

14 Ibn Sa'd, *al-Ṭabaqāt,* vol. 7, pp. 28-29; al-Ṭabari, *Tārikh,* vol. 4, p. 187; Ibn 'Abd al-Barr, *al-Isti'āb,* vol. 1, p. 118; Ibn al-Athīr, *al-Kāmil,* vol. 3, p. 233; Ibn Kathīr, *al-Bidāyah,* vol. 8, p. 29.

against Yazīd was Islamically right or not.[15] Although we do not find a single opinion among the Ṣaḥābah and later Muslims (tābiʿūn) that his rising was unjustified and that he was out to do a prohibitory act. Among the Ṣaḥābah who tried to stop him were of the view that they considered it unwise. But even when we accept the governmental view as correct, the fact was that he had no army with him.

All that he had was his family members, thirty-two riders and forty footmen. Nobody in his sanity would describe it as army. As against him, 'Umar ibn Sa'd ibn abī Waqqāṣ led an army of 4,000 soldiers. There was no need to engage this small group and kill them. They could have encircled and captured them. Al-Ḥusayn himself said that he would like to go back to Madīnah or that he might be allowed to go towards a certain border or that he should be taken to Yazīd. But his proposals were turned down. They wanted to take him to Ibn Ziyād the governor of al-Kūfah but he had his reservations. He knew the brutality committed by Ibn Ziyād with Muslim ibn 'Aqīl. Thus, they made him fight. Left alone, his companions all killed, they still attacked him. When he fell wounded on the ground, they slaughtered him, and his body trampled over by the horses.

Suppose for a moment that Yazīd's perception was correct and that Ḥusayn did rebel against him. Even then, was there no law in Islam to deal with rebellion? All the authentic fiqh books carry law on the subject. For example, in *Hidāyah Sharḥ Fatḥ al-Qadīr* (bāb al-bughāh) alone one can read it. Everything done in Karbalah was Ḥarām and extremely savage.

What Yazīd said and did in his court in Damascus is subject to conflicting reports. But we will set aside all those reports and take the following one as true that he had teary eyes when he saw Husayn's and his companion's heads and said: "I would have been content with your obedience without killing Ḥusayn. Allah's curse be on Ibn Ziyād. By Allah, if I were there, I would have forgiven Ḥusayn." He is also reported to have said: "By Allah, Ḥusayn if I were there facing you, I would have never killed you."[16]

---

15 I have given my view on this subject in my risālah, *Shahādat Ḥusayn*. Also, this issue will receive my comments in chapter 8 of this book.

16 Al-Ṭabari, *Tārikh,* vol. 4, p. 352; Ibn al-Athīr, *al-Kāmil,* vol. 3, pp. 298-299.

All said, what punishment did he give to his insane governor on this savage act? Ibn Kathīr says neither he punished Ibn Ziyād nor did he remove him, nor did he write a reprimand to him.[17]

The second calamitous event pertained to the battle of Harrah in 63 A.H., the last days of Yazīd. Briefly stated the people of Madīnah after having declared Yazīd as fāsiq (violator), fājir (sinner), and zālim (tyrannical) ousted his governor from the city and instead asked 'Abdullah ibn Hanzalah to lead them.

When Yazīd heard about it, he entrusted Muslim 'Uqbah al-Murri with 12,000 troops to vacate the city from the rebels' hold.

His instructions for the occasion were clear: Give them three days to submit; if they did not, then war against them; and when the rebellion was smashed free Madīnah to the troops for three days.

Imām al-Zuhrī says 700 prominent individuals and 10,000 common people were killed. Worse, the savage military (consisting of non-Muslims) entered homes and violated their privacy. Ibn al-Kathīr adds that women were also harassed and their privacy violated.[18]

Conceded that the Madinese revolt was unjustified, but did Islam justify such a treatment to a rebellious Muslim population or even to non-Muslims and hostile nonbelievers?

Hence, the situation was particularly disturbing. Madīnah was not just another city: it was the Prophet's city about which he had said, as reported in *al-Bukhari*, *Muslim*, and Aḥmad's *Musnad*, that one who did wrong to Madīnah, Allah would punish him.

He also said he who terrifies the people of Madīnah, Allah will terrify him. Upon him will be the curse of Allah, angels and the whole of humanity. At the Judgment Day, Allah will not accept anything in return for this sin.

---

17 Ibn Kathīr, *al-Bidāyah,* vol. 8, p. 203.

18 For details see al-Ṭabari, *Tārikh,* vol. 4, pp. 372-379; Ibn al-Athīr, *al-Kāmil,* vol. 3, pp. 312-313; Ibn Kathīr, *al-Bidāyah,* vol. 8, pp. 219-221.

A second group forbids it merely because it may not lead to cursing Yazīd's father or someone from among the Ṣaḥābah.[19]

The third incident relates to their attack on the Ka'bah as already stated by Ḥasan Baṣri. The same army that vandalized the Prophet's city and raped pious Muslim women was unleashed on Makkah to punish this time 'Abdullah ibn al-Zubayr. They brought catapults to stone the Ka'bah, demolishing one of its walls. Reports also exist saying that they fireballed the Ka'bah. But the fire, as some reports tell us, could have other causes as well. However, stoning the Ka'bah has consensus.[20]

---

19 The context to Imām Aḥmad Ibn Ḥanbal's quote, as cited by Ibn Kathīr in his *al-Bidāyah...*, vol. 8, p. 223, is as under:

> One time Imām Aḥmad's son 'Abdullah asked him: "What is the injunction behind sending curse on Yazīd." He replied: "Why should I not curse a person who has been cursed by Allah." Then in proof he recited the Qur'ānic verse, "Would you then if you were given the command work corruption in the land and sever your ties of kinship? Such are they whom Allah curses so that he defame them and made their eyes blind." (*Muḥammad*: 22-23) Afterward, he said what could be a greater mischief and breaching relations than Yazīd's. Aḥmad's word has been cited by Muḥmmad ibn 'Abd al-Rasūl al-Barjanji in *al-Aha'h fi Athrāt al-Sā'ah* and Ibn Ḥajar al-Haytami in *al-Sawā'q al-Muhariqah*. But Safārini and Ibn Taymiyah say more credible sources in- validate the idea that Imām Ahmad liked to curse Yazīd. Among the 'ulamā' of alh al-Sunnah, Ibn Jauzi, Qāḍī ibn Y'alā, Taftāzāni are convinced of cursing Yazīd. While Imām al-Ghazālī and Ibn Taymiyah disproved of cursing Yazīd. My own view is that a person who qualifies to be cursed can be cursed in a general way (for example, it can be said that the usurpers and victimizers be cursed) but a particular individual may not be cursed for if he is alive, it is possible that he may have the chance to repent. And if he has died, we have no knowledge in what state of imān he had his end. Thus, we should confine our criticism to their wrong and avoid cursing them. That will be better. This does not mean that Yazīd should be now praised and tagged as those who received Allah's pleasure and blessing.

One time someone addressed Yazīd as amīr al-mu'minīn in the presence of 'Umar ibn 'Abdul 'Aziz. The latter enraged said: "You call Yazīd as amīr al-mu'minīn!" He got him lashed twenty times. (Tahzib al-Tahzib, vol. 11, p. 361).

20 Al-Ṭabari, *Tārikh.*, vol. 4, p. 383; Ibn al-Athīr, *al-Kāmil,* vol. 3, p. 316; Ibn Kathīr, *al-Bidāyah*, vol. 8, p. 225; Ibn Ḥajar, *Tahzib*, vol. 11, p. 361.

These events obviously proved that the Umayyad dynasty gave priority to nothing but their hold on power. And from that they were willing to go as far as they could. In their calculus nothing was sacred.

10. The Banī Marwān era

The Banī Marwān era was marked by the deepening separation between dīn and politics. In fact, they could do anything to obtain their political goals. If it damaged the Sharī'ah, they gave a hoot to it.

Ironically, 'Abd al-Mālik ibn Marwān was an eminent faqīh (jurist). Before he stepped into power, he was ranked in knowledge with jurists of Sa'id ibn al-Musayyab, 'Urwah ibn al-Zabayr and Qabīsah ibn Dhuwayb's calibre. When on Yazīd's behest the Ka'bah was stoned, he lodged a strong protest. Power, however, changed him.

On reaching Damascus, the first thing he did was to depute Ḥajjāj ibn Yūsuf to Makkah to fight 'Abdullah ibn al-Zubayr who, with least regard to the occasion for Ḥajj, stoned the Ka'bah. This was a twofold offensive act, for it violated the Makkan as well as the Ḥajj sanctity. The Umayyads proved themselves even worst than the jāhilī Arabs who would avoid hostilities during the Ḥajj.

The catapult stoning, however, was interrupted on 'Abdullah ibn 'Umar's intervention for a while so that the pilgrims could perform the Ḥajj rituals. The pilgrims, however, could not go to Minā nor to 'Arafāt. As soon as the pilgrims performed Ṭawwāf (circumambulation), Ḥajjāj called for their expulsion from the sanctuary, and resumed flinging stones on the Ka'bah.[21]

Ḥajjāj was undoubtedly the harshest punishment that 'Abd al-Mālik and his son al-Walīd imposed on the people for twenty long years, with license to play with their lives and properties. His involvement in arranging diacritical symbols on the Qur'ānic words is his singular contribution that humanity will praise forever. The conquest of Sind (present-day Pakistan) is also among his achievements that brought Islam to South Asia. All said, even the whole good deeds of a person

21 Ibn al-Athīr, *al-Kāmil,* vol. 4, p. 23; Ibn Kathīr. *al-Bidāyah*, vol. 8, p. 329; Ibn Khaldūn, *Takmalah,* vol. 5, pp. 37-38.

cannot compensate for killing a Muslim without justifiable reason, not to talk of the savage act he perpetuated in his long rule.

Ironically, it was for this savage governor that 'Abd al-Malik willed to his sons:

> "Treat Ḥajjāj ibn Yūsuf well, for it is he who has paved the way for our rule, subjugated our enemies, and smashed those who rose against us."[22]

His will is symptomatic of the mindset with which those people ruled the Muslim World. Their only concern was their hold on power for which they were willing to go to any extent even while violating the Sharī'ah.

11. The blessed reign of 'Umar ibn 'Abdul-'Azīz

'Umar ibn 'Abdul-Azīz ruled only for two and a half years but it is the only relief in the 92-year Umayyad's dark rule. What brought a change in his life was an incident in the year 93 A.H., when he was the governor of Madīnah. In compliance with al-Walīd ibn 'Abd al-Malik's order, the young Khubayb ibn 'Abdullah ibn al-Zubayr was implanted with fifty lashes, followed by the pouring of cold water on his head in winter and making him stand on the Masjid al-Nabawi's door whole day long. Not bearing the rigours of the punishment Khubayb died.[23]

This was a blatant act of savagery in utter violation of the Sharī'ah, which 'Umar ibn 'Abdul-'Azīz had to carry out much against his disposition. But so saddened and penitent he felt that he resigned from the governorship. The subsequent days saw him withdrawn, soaked with Allah's fear.

In 99 A.H., he suddenly found himself in power because of Sulaymān ibn 'Abd al-Mālik's secret will. His succession was as much

22 Ibn al-Athīr, *al-Kāmil*, vol. 4, p. 103; Ibn Kāthir, *al-Bidāyah,* vol. 9, p. 67; Ibn Khaldūn, *Takmilah,* vol. 3, p. 58.

23 Al-Ṭabari, *Tārikh*, vol. 6, p. 26, Ibn Kathīr, *al-Bidāyah*, vol. 8, p. 258; also vol. 10, pp. 30-31; Ibn al-Athīr, *al-Kāmil*, vol. 4, p. 300.

a surprise for him as it was for his family. But his agenda was all laid out. He decided to make a u-turn toward the caliphate as fashioned by the Prophet's Sunnah and the rightly guided caliphs. His post-bai'ah speech bared it well:

> "They put me into the turmoil of the government, though I did not desire it nor did they consult me on the issue, nor did they seek consultation with the Muslims. I therefore free you from the yoke of your allegiance pledge to me, giving you the choice to make anyone you like as the custodian of your affairs."

The crowd responded with their approval for him. Thereafter he said:

> "In fact, there is no difference in this Ummah on (the issue of) their God, their Prophet and their religious book. Rather, it is about dinār and dirham. By Allah, I would not give a thing unrightfully to anyone nor would I hold someone's due right.
> O People, he who obeys Allah, his obedience is binding (on you). He who does not obey Allah, his obedience is not binding on you.
> [Thus] as long as I obey Allah, obey me and if I disobey Him, my obedience is not binding on you."[24]

[His induction to the caliphate was a sure indicator that he would not bear with the Umayyad practices]. His first act was to finish the royal trappings that his ancestors had acquired to show their kingly ways and made a return to the caliphal ways of the rightly guided caliphs. Next, he surrendered his estate that he had inherited from his parents including his wife's jewelry to treasury. Out of his 40,000-dinār annual income that he had from his estate, he retained only 400-dinār worth of property annual income to himself that rightfully belonged to him.[25]

After clearing himself before his Allah and the Ummah, he declared that anyone who had a claim against the royal family should come up with proofs of his ownership, and he would repatriate him.

24 Ibn Kāthir, *al-Bidāyah,* vol. 9, p. 87.
25 Ibid, pp. 212-213.

This obviously created anger and distress in the Umayyads. They made protests but he refused to budge from his stance. In desperation, they asked his paternal aunt Fātimah bint Marwān whom he held in great esteem, to stop him from degrading the royal family but he refused:

> "When the ruler's own relatives perpetuate injustice and he does not redress it, then how would he stop others from their excesses?"
> "Your clan threatens you with serious consequences," she cautioned him.
> "If I fear anything more than the fear of the Judgment Day, then I pray that I may not have peace from that thing [the threat]," he said. His answer was as firm as was his resolve.
>
> Frustrated, she returned to her clan.

So great was his sense of responsibility that after the burial of Sulaymān ibn 'Abd al-Malik when he returned, his face bore signs of distress and sadness. Asked what made him sad, he said:

> "There is not a single person in the Ummah of Muḥammad Rasūl Allāh spreading from East to West whose right I do not have to restitute without his asking for it."[26]

His wife witnesses that when she entered his room she saw him weeping on his prayer mat. She asked him the reason for his crying. He said, "I have taken upon myself the affairs of the Ummah of Muḥammad Rasūl Allāh. And when I think that somewhere there languishes a hungry person, a helpless patient, an aggrieved wronged without a reason, a helpless prisoner, an old man, or a poor with a family – in short, there are [a whole lot] of such people in every corner of the country, I know my Creator will ask me on the Judgment Day what did I do for them, while Muḥammad (ṣal.lal.lahu 'alayhi wa.sal.lam)

26 Ibn al-Athīr, *al-Kāmil,* vol. 4, p. 164, 'Ibn Kathīr, *al-Bidāyah,* vol. 9, p. 214.

will be the prosecutor against me. I fear that the case may not go against me. Thus, out of pity on myself I cry."[27]

To implement his agenda he appointed capable and honest officials in place of a heartless administration. He set aside all those wrong taxes that the Ummayds had levied on the people. He also removed jizyah on people who became Muslims. Besides, he did away with the practice of lashing people without legal justification, with clear instruction not to amputate anybody's hand or give him death penalty without informing the caliph.[28]

At the end of his reign, a Khārji group rebelled against him. Instead of retaliating against them, he wrote: "What is the use of shedding (one another's) blood? Why do you not come and have discussion with me. Should you be right I will give in. And if I am right, you will accept (my viewpoint). The group elder sent two persons to have discussion with him.

> Initiating the discussion, they said:
> "We agree that your ways are different than your family members'. You also consider their actions as atrocious. But what sense does make that even though you consider their actions as atrocious you still do not curse them."
>
> 'Umar ibn 'Abdul-'Azīz responded:
> "Is it not enough for their condemnation that I consider their acts as excesses? After this, why should it be important to curse them? How many times did you curse the Pharaoh?"

Every time they raised a question he answered them. At last one of them asked:

> "Can a just man bear with the fact that his successor is going to be an unjust person?"
> He said no.

27 Ibn al-Athīr, *al-Kāmil,* vol. 4, p. 164.
28 Ibid, p. 165.

> "Then, are you going to surrender the caliphate to (someone like) Yazīd ibn 'Abd al-Mālik when you know that he would not stay the course of justice?"
> "But my predecessor (Sulaymān ibn 'Abd al-Mālik) has already taken the bai'ah for his succession. What can I do now?" he said.
>
> "Do you think that the person who nominated Yazīd ibn 'Abd al-Mālik to succeed you had the right to do so and that his decision was justified?" they asked.

This made 'Umar speechless. When the sitting adjourned, his court heard him say again and again: "The Yazīd issue has killed me. I do not have answer to it. May Allah forgive me!" [29]

It was this incident that caused alarms to the Umayyads that he would not rest until he finished their dynastic rule, transforming it into shūrā-based caliphate. Thus terrified, they poisoned him after a short while. With his death, things regressed to their old habitat.

12. The 'Abbasids and their promise

The Umayyad government had a magnificent sprawl from Sindh (present-day Pakistan) to Spain. Apparently there was no reason to believe that it will go down one day. But based on power and not anchored in people's hearts, it was tottering inside. That is why within a century, the 'Abbasids uprooted it. And when it fell not a single eye wept for it.

The new claimant to the caliphate uprooted the Umayyads because they succeeded in assuring the common men that since they belonged to the Prophet's clan, they would work for them within the parameters of the Sharī'ah and establish the ḥudūd of Allah. In Rabi' al-Thāni when Abū al-'Abbās al-Saffāḥ received bai'ah (allegiance oath), he recounted the Umayyad's excesses followed by saying:

> "I hope that from the family that gave you goodness you will not have tyranny and injustice and from where you received felicity you will not have persecution."

29 Al-Ṭabari, *Tārikh,* vol. 5, pp. 314-315, 321; Ibn al-Athīr, *al-Kāmil,* vol. 4, pp. 156, 163.

After al-Saffāḥ, his uncle Dā'ūd ibn 'Ali assured the people:

> We are not out to garner wealth for ourselves or build palaces and stretch canals to them. What has brought us out is that the Umayyad denied our right and they persecuted the progeny of our uncle ('Ali's family) and followed bad ways among you by humiliating you; and usurping your bayt al-māl for unjustified spending. Now, we have this responsibility from Allah, His Messenger and al-'Abbās that we will conduct the affairs of the government according to the Book of Allah and the Sunnah of the Prophet.[30]

But no sooner did they receive power they proved by their deeds that it was all deception.

13. Their deeds

In Mūṣal, when rebellion broke out, al-Saffāḥ sent his brother Yaḥyā to quell it. As a starter, he announced that whoever would enter the central masjid would find peace. People in thousands thronged the place. Then he locked them in and killed them. About 11,000 people were killed on the spot. At night, he heard the wailing of the women left behind and he ordered them to be killed in the morning. For three days, Mūṣal was plunged into mass killing and arson. Neither women nor children nor the old were spared. Yaḥyā had 4,000 (non-Muslims) Zingis in his army who were allowed to rape women. Holding the halter of his horse a woman implored Yaḥyā to stop these atrocious acts. "You belong to the clan of Hāshim and the progeny of the uncle of Rasūl Allāh. You suffer from no shame that your Zingi soldiers are raping Arab-Muslim women." Stung by shame and remorse Yahyā lured his Zingi troops to assembly by offering pay increases and got them killed.[31]

---

30 Al-Ṭabari, *Tārikh,* vol. 5, p. 311; Ibn al-Athīr, *al-Kāmil,* vol. 4, pp. 155, 157; Ibn Khaldūn, *Takmilah,* vol. 3, pp. 162-163.

31 Ibn al-Athīr, *al-Kāmil,* vol. 4, pp. 333-334, 341; Ibn Kathīr, *al-Bidāyah,* vol. 10, p. 45; Ibn Khaldūn, *Takmilah,* vol. 3, pp. 132-133.

Al-Saffāḥ gave Yazīd ibn 'Umar ibn Hubayrah pledge of safety in his own handwriting and then got him killed.[32]

The famous Khurāsāni jurist Ibrāhīm ibn Maymūn al-Sā'igh spearheaded the 'Abbāsid call for change on their pledge to establish Hudūd Allah. His work won him the confidence of Abū Muslim Khurāsāni, becoming part of the latter's inner circle. But as the revolution consummated itself, their irreverential attitudes towards the Sharī'ah forced al-Sā'igh to press for its implementation as promised. In return Abū Muslim got him executed.[33]

In al-Manṣūr's reign even the 'Abbasid's claim that they had risen to seek revenge for the excesses done to Abu Ṭālib's clan proved to be shallow. Al-Manṣūr's search for Muḥammad ibn 'Abdullah al-Nafs al-Zakiyyah and his brother Ibrāhīm who were in hiding ended up in apprehending their whole family, for they would not reveal their whereabouts. Their properties were sold and they were moved from Madīnah to Iraq in chains. Al-Manṣūr tortured them in prison. Muḥammad ibn Ibrāhīm ibn al-Ḥasan was entombed in the wall alive. Ibrāhīm ibn 'Abdullah's father-in-law was stripped and lashed 150 times. Later, his severed head was paraded in Khurāsān as if it belonged to Nafs Zakiyyah.[34] After sometime when they succeeded in tracing Nafs Zakiyyah to Madīnah, they hacked off his head, showing it around different places. For three days, his beheaded body along with his companions' remained on the poles. Later, they threw their bodies in the Jewish grave yard near the Sala' mountain.[35]

The rapid succession of these events showed from the beginning that like the Umayyad's their politics was also divorced from religion, and that they felt no shame in exceeding the bounds of Allah. Their revolution changed only the rulers but not the system;

32 Ibn al-Athīr, *al-Kāmil,* vol. 4, pp. 338-340; Ibn Khaldūn, *Takmilah,* vol. 3, pp. 177.

33 Al-Tabari, *Tārikh*, vol. 6, pp. 107-109; Ibn al-Athīr, *al-Kāmil*, vol. 4, p. 338; Ibn Kathīr, *al-Bidāyah*, vol. 10, pp. 54-55; Ibn Khaldūn, *Takmilah,* vol. 3, p. 176.

34 Ibn Kathīr, *al-Bidāyah,* vol. 10, p. 68.

35 Al-Ṭabari, *Tārikh*, vol. 6, pp. 161,171-180; Ibn al-Athīr, *al-Kāmil*, vol. 4, pp. 370-375; Ibn Kāthir, *al-Bidāyah*, vol. 10, pp. 80, 82.

not one bad practice of the Umayyads they remedied nor did they restore the noble caliphate of the righteous. Instead, they formalized the monarchial absolutism into a permanent institution. The only difference that occurred was in the monarchical shapes, the Umayyads followed Caesar in Constantinople, the 'Abbasids mimicked Kisrā in Iran.

The shūrā also remained suspended and it formulated the same disastrous impact in running the state that the 'Umayyad had.

In usurping treasury they followed the Umayyad's practices, with least concerns for the inflow and outflow of funds. Bayt al-māl became the king's treasury which knew no accountability.

The judiciary also remained under the administrative and parochial pressure. In al-Mahdī's time a case involving his official and a trader came up for hearing before the Qāḍī 'Ubayd Allah ibn Ḥasan's court. The caliph wanted him to decide in the official's favour but he declined and thus was sacked.[36]

A similar case occurred in Hārūn al-Rashīd's time involving a person who had his wife Zubayda's favour. Qāḍī Hafs ibn Ghayāth, having decided against him, had to step down.[37]

14. The Shu'ūbiyah movement and the Zanādiqah

The racial, tribalistic and materialistic prejudices that the Umayyads ignited flared into a conflagration during the 'Abbāsid's time. In the first place, the 'Abbāsid uprising by itself was spirited by racial considerations of a clan's right to rule over the others. To ensure their success, they pitted Arab tribes against one another on the one hand and non-Arabs against the Arabs on the other.

The letter that Ibrāhīm ibn Muḥammad ibn 'Ali ibn 'Abdullah ibn Abbās, the leader of the 'Abbāsid movement, wrote to Abū Muslim Khurāsāni speaks of this policy exploiting differences among the different groups to pit the Yamani against the Mudari among the

---

36 Ibn Kathīr, *al-Bidāyah,* vol. 10, p. 90.

37 Al-Kathīb al-Baghdādi, *Tarikh al-Baghdād,* (Egypt: Matb'ah al-Sa'ādah, 1931) vol. 10, p. 309.

Arab. Second, if possible, make sure that not a single tongue that speaks Arabic.[38]

As a result, the reactive shu'ūbiyah, which simmered inside, caused by the Arab narrow mindedness in the Umayyad reign, blasted into a conflagration in the 'Abbāsid era. Worse, it was not only against the Arab prejudices but also went against Islam, raising an aggressive front of Zandaqah (atheism and secularism). Doubtless, historically the 'Ajamis carried seeds of racial superiority in them, considering Arabs inferior. In the early Islamic era when energized by Islam the desert Arabs trounced them, they felt humiliated. But the Islamic egalitarianism and sense of justice that they saw in the lives of the Ṣaḥābah (raḍi Allahu 'anhu) and tābi'ūn, 'ulamā, and fuqahā (jurists) balm their wounds. Charmed by their noble attitudes and the equal status they had gained for themselves in the new social setup, they began to melt in the Muslim Ummah. Had there been a similar administrative policy embracing the Islamic ideals, there would have been no separatist movement in the non-Arab Muslims. But first the Umayyads because of their Arab bias mistreated them and thus aroused in them a reactive bias and then the 'Abbāsid's tooling them for their political objectives gave them the chance to surface on the power scene and prevail on the sociopolitical apparatus.

The non-Arabs supported the 'Abbāsid cause for they hoped this would give them a perennial role in the new administration and thus enabling them to finish Arab domination. Their evaluation of the situation was correct and they got what they wanted.

Al-Jāhiz says that the 'Abbāsid government turned into a Khurāsāni government.[39] In al-Manṣūr's reign chief of the armed forces and governorship were by and large given to non-Arabs ending the Arab domination.[40] Al-Jihshayāri's list of al-Manṣūr's appointees

38 Tāsh Kubrāzādah, *Miftāh al-Sa'ādah* (Hyderabad: Dā'irah al-Ma'rāif, 1329 A.H.) vol. 2, p. 119.

39 Ibn al-Athīr, *al-Kāmil*, vol. 4, p. 295; Ibn Kathīr, *al-Bidāyah,* vol. 10, p. 28; Ibn Khaldūn, *Takmil'ah,* vol. 3, p. 103.

40 Al-Jāhiz, *al-Biyān wa al-Tabīīn,* (Egypt: Matb'ah al-Fatuh al Adbiyah, 1332 A.H.), vol. 3. p.181.

in his *Tarikh al-Wuzarā'* is mostly non-Arabs.[41] With political clout in their hands, they encouraged the shu'ūbiyah movement to its full potential, carrying in its fold the seeds of atheism and loose moral attitudes.

The shu'ūbiyah movement by itself started with discussions that the Arabs had no superiority over the non-Arabs but it soon turned into Arab hate. Ibn al-Nadīm's *al-Fihrist* details all the books written in condemnation of the Arabs and their tribes, including even the Quraysh.

The moderate Sh'ūbī did not go beyond it. But the extremists among them began to attack Islam itself.

The 'Ajami aristocracy, ministers, secretaries (kuttāb), and military commanders gave them secret support. Al-Jāhiz says: "A lot of people who entertain doubt about Islam got this disease through sh'ūbiyah. They were against Islam because the Arabs brought it."[42]

These people resurrected the faiths and ideas of Māni, Zoroaster, and Mazdak. They exalted the 'Ajami civilization and praised their statecraft. In the guise of poetry and literature they promoted loose manners and lewdness, making fun of religion and its ḥudud. They also seduced people to liquor and sins of the flesh, ridiculing pious living and lampooning people who reminded others of paradise and hellfire. Some fabricated ḥadīth to undermine Muslims' faith. Thus, when they apprehended Ibn abi al-'Aujā', a Zindīq, he admitted to have fabricated 4,000 ḥadīth altering Ḥalāl (allowed) and Ḥarām (disallowed). In al-Manṣūr's time the Kūfan governor Muḥammad ibn Sulaymān ibn 'Ali sentenced him to death.[43]

A person named Yūnus ibn abi-Farwah wrote a book condemning Islam and the Arabs; when presented with a copy, the Caesar of Rome awarded him.[44] Al-Jāhiz in his writings has detailed a

41 Al-Mas'ūdi, *Murūj al-Dhahab* (Egypt: Matb'ah al-Bihiyyah, 1346 A.H.) vol. 2, p. 515; Taqi al-Din Aḥmad ibn 'Ali ibn 'Abdul-Qādin ibn Muḥammad al-Maqrizi, *Kitāb al-Salūk* (Egypt: Dār al-Kutub al-Misriyah, 1934) vol. 1, p. 15.

42 Al-Jahshiyāri, *Tārikh al-Wuzurā'* (Viewer, 1926) pp. 139, 153, 155, 157.

43 Al-Jāhiz, *Kitāb al-Haywān* (Egypt: al-Matbāh al-Taqadam, 1906) vol. 7, p. 68.

44 Ibn Kāthir, *al-Bidāyah,* vol. 10, p. 113.

number of 'Ajami secretaries to the government who talked ill about the sequential layout of the Qur'ān and its alleged contradictions. They also refuted ḥadīth and created doubts about their authenticity. In praising the Ṣaḥābah (companions) their tongue twisted. When Qāḍī Shurayh, Ḥasan al-Baṣri and al-Sha'bi were exalted they hurled accusations on them. But they had all praise for Ardshayr Bābakān and Naushayrwān for their sagacity and state craft.[45]

Talking of the famous 'Ajamis of this era, Abū al-A'lā al-Ma'arri says they were all zindīq, including Di'bil, Bashshār ibn Burd, Abū Nūwās, Abū Muslim Khurāsāni, and so forth.[46]

This zandaqah (secularism and atheism) was not confined to mere perversion of beliefs but also to freedom from moral compulsions. Ibn 'Abdi Rabbihi says people knew well that liquor, fornication and corruption were the necessary companions of atheism.[47]

The Manṣūr reign (136-158 A.H./754-775 C.E.) saw this mischief blooming into a perfidious social and moral threat with potential to undermine Muslim society and state. His successor al-Mahdī perceived its threat potential. Making a digression from his clan's policies, he decided to crush this movement with a concomitant effort by the 'ulamā, which he prompted, to engage them in discussions and write books to counter their views.[48] Besides, he established a permanent department under 'Amr al-Kaluāzi, assigned with the task of exterminating the zanādiqah (atheists and secularists).[49] His instructions to his son al-Hādī speak of his concern:

> If ever this government fell into your hands, do not spare any effort in exterminating the Māni followers. They first invite people towards apparent goodness

45 Al-Sharif al-Murtadā, *Amāli al-Murtadā: ghurar al-fawā'id wa durar al-qalā'id* (Egypt: al-Matba'h al-Sa'ādah, 1907) vol. 1, pp. 90-100.

46 Al-Jāhiz, *Thalāth Rasā'il* (Cairo: al-Matb'ah al-Salāfiyah, 1344 A.H.) p. 42.

47 Abu A'lā al-Ma'ari, *Risā lah al-Ghufrān* (Egypt: Dar al-Ma'rāf 1950). p. 199.

48 Ibn 'Abd al-Barr, *al-'Iqd al-Farid*, vol. 2, p. 179.

49 Al-Mas'ūdi, *al-Tanūkhi,* vol. 2, p. 575,Taqi al-Din Aḥmad ibn 'Ali ibn 'Abdul-Qādin ibn Muḥammad al-Maqrizi, *Kitāb al-Salūk,* vol. 1, p. 15.

> such as staying away from lewdness, piety in worldly life and deeds for the hereafter, followed by exhorting them that eating meat is forbidden, taking bath (ghusal) is disallowed and so is killing animals. Later, they drive them to belief in two gods. And eventually, they declare marrying sisters and daughters as allowed together with taking bath with urine. Besides, they steal children so that they could be brought up in disbelief and perversion.[50]

Al-Mahdī's preceding statement shows that the 'Ajami zanādiqah (atheists) though had become apparently Muslims but in secret they were engaged in the revival of their old religions. Al-Mas'ūdi says the zanādiqah were spreading their ideas through translations from the Persian language, mostly within by Ibn abi al-'Aaujā' Ḥammād 'Ajrad, Yaḥyā ibn Ziyād, and Muti' ibn Iyās.[51]

15. The Ummah's reaction

In short, these were the changes that swamped the Muslim society by the transposition of the rightly guided caliphate with the monarchial absolutism. This also gives a fair idea of the consequences that the Ummah may face when an individual, clan or a group aspires for power and forcibly imposes it on the people. An individual may not even know the results that his ambition may crystallize nor may he have the intention to cause hurt to the Ummah; nevertheless, their natural outcome is bound to impact the sociopolitical and moral environment in due course of time.

All said, it will be wrong to deduce that the political vicissitudes led to the elimination of the Islamic system of life. Some people make a surface reading of history by concluding that Islam lasted for thirty years only. But the situation is contrary to their floppy surmise. In the following we will discuss briefly how the collective conscious of the Muslim Ummah responded to the distortion in its political system and saved Islam's collectivity.

---

50 Al-Ṭabari, *Tārikh*, vol. 6, pp. 389, 391, Ibn Kathīr, *al-Bidāyah,* vol. 10, p. 149.

51 Al-Ṭabari, *Tārikh,* vol. 6, pp. 433-434.

16. Split in leadership

We have already explained the merits of the rightly guided caliphate and how it can be described as the true successor to the Prophet (upon him be peace). The caliph was not only true to Islam but also a model guide. His work did not confine itself to running the state machinery and consigning troops to the battlefield. Rather, his was an extended role that saw to it that Allah's dīn in its fullness was established. His person invited in himself the sole central leadership who led the Muslim Ummah in the fullness of their faith – that is: dīn and values, morality and spirituality, law and Sharī'ah, culture and civilization, education and upbringing, da'wah and its spread. Like Islam which is wholesome, the caliphal leadership was also all-embracing in which Muslims had full trust.

The supervened monarchial absolutism was incapable of giving that kind of inclusive leadership nor were the Muslims inclined to give it the same moral status. The kingly misdeeds were so hideous that it emptied monarchy of any moral worth. Doubtless, they could bend people's necks and they did it by all means. They could also force millions of people by intimidation and material seduction to serve their wish, and that they did without any remorse. But whether they could find a place in their hearts as their religious leaders was far fetched. The new situation, therefore, splintered the Muslim leadership into two parts.

17. The political leadership

A vital part of leadership fell in the political realm appropriated by the kings. Sustained by ruthless power, people reluctantly accepted it. This leadership was after all not non-Muslim to have demanded total rejection by the Ummah. They believed in Islam and its laws. Nor did they deny the finality of the Qur'ān and the Prophet's Sunnah. Other than their politics which was free from the Islamic restraints they ran the state affairs according to the Sharī'ah. Perhaps this softened the people to accept their writ in so far as it assured peace in the state, secured the frontiers, sustained the jihād against enemies of Islam, established the Friday Ṣalah, maintained the societal structure, arranged for Ḥajj and en forced the Sharī'ah laws through the country. For these objectives if the Ṣaḥābah, tābi'ūn (second generation), and later people accepted their governance it was in this sense, and not because that they considered them as the rightful rulers or their governance as moral equal to the pious caliphate. Rather they were the de facto rulers to whom the masses surrendered.

18. Religious leadership

The second tier of leadership was headed by the Ṣaḥābah (companions), tābi'ūn (second generation), taba' tābi'ūn (third generation), fuqahā' (jurists), muḥaddith*ū*n (ḥadīth scholars) and the pious of the Ummah. The people accepted their leadership in the realm of their dīn without any reservation. Though not organized nor led by any titular head or any authoritative council to decide emergent matters, it presented a composite scene. They all worked in their individual capacity with no power to prevail other than moral. But since they were inspired by the same sources of the Qur'ān and the Sunnah, their mental mould was the same, though their temperaments and backgrounds were different. That is why even though they were scattered as atomized individuals they were in a position to provide the Ummah with a unified moral and intellectual leadership.

19. The linkage between the two leaderships

The two leaderships had little in common; their relationship was marked by hostility to indifference. Thus, whenever the political leadership sought to help religious leadership, it was either conditional or too small. At the same time, the religious leadership was not prepared to pay the price either of conscience or character. Added to this was the people's attitude, which looked at the 'ulamā-royalty liaison with disdain. Anyone who courted favour lost its place of respect in the Ummah's heart. Thus, indifference to royalty and fortitude against its wrath became the hallmark of the religious leadership. Commoners aside, even those who had sold themselves to kings were not willing to accept such 'ulamā who under kingly pressures would abject themselves before power and still be the emblem of the Ummah's Islamic aspiration.

Thus, from the middle of the first century after Hijrah the two had parted their ways,[52] each playing its role in its own orbit.

---

52 Al-Mas'ūdi, *Murrūj*, vol. 2, p. 515.

Whatever the 'ulamā did in the realms of tafsīr (exegesis), ḥadīth (Prophetic tradition), fiqh (law), usūl (jurisprudence) and other religious sciences they did it by themselves free from state patronage – in fact, many a time inspite of the state opposition to their work.

Also, the 'ulamā role in the field of the Muslim moral rehabilitation and restructuring their mindset was free from any governmental influences. The Islamic spread, which was phenomenal, took place because of their efforts. The kings of course secured for them territories, which gave Islam access to millions of peoples. But influencing their minds and hearts was left to the pious of the Ummah who because of their ennobling characters enhanced Islam's appeal to the masses.[53]

These are serious charges. True, a Ṣaḥābī can make judgemental errors. However, one must not forget that contrary to what al-Baṣri says about Mu'āwiyah's doomed hereafter, the Prophet had prayed for his exalted status. In al-Bukhārī's ghazwah al-Bahr's ḥadīth he has also been given the glad tiding of Paradise. It was because of his exalted status, that the caliph 'Umar ibn 'Abdul-'Azīz punished those who talked ill of Mu'āwiyah.

53 In the third-century hijrah when the 'Abbāsid began to have their fall, the religious leadership was still in the hands of the 'ulamā, fuqahā', and upright individuals but the political leadership splintered into two groups, eventually going into the hands of kings and feudal lord, who became defacto rulers while the 'Abbāsid caliphs were reduced to mere custodians of a heritage who held neither religious leadership nor political. They bore a cosmetic religious holiness that they had acquired because of the caliphate, which enabled them to crown sultāns (kings) and in return the kings delivered khutabah and issued currency in their names.

Chapter Six

The Rise of Religious Differences and their Causes

The downfall of the rightly guided caliphate carried in its swath religious differences, which in the absence of the caliphate gelled themselves into permanent sectarian schism and discord. To add to the calamity, monarchial absolutism (mulūkīyah) had no institution to resolve such differences.

In its incipience, this mischief did not appear to be ominous. It was just an irruption boiled over owing to some administrative and political shortcomings at the time of the caliph 'Uthmān.

At its back, the irruption had no ideology or philosophical outlook. But when 'Uthmān's life came to a sudden end, followed by civil war and bloody conflicts involving 'Ali and Mu'āwiyah in the battles at Jamal, Ṣiffīn, the subsequent arbitration episode (taḥkīm) and Nahrwān, certain questions began to plague the minds causing intense discussions. For example, people wanted to know who had the truth in those wars. If a party in dispute is viewed as right, then on what bases? Who is grounded in untruth and what makes him false (bāṭil)? And if someone maintains silence or is neutral in the conflict between the parties, then what justification has he? In response to such questions some definitive thoughts emerged which, though political in their origin, later got themselves situated in a theological context, with doctrinal underpinnings. That this paved way for these political groups to gradually descend into the mould of religious sects is thus not far from the truth.

It was possible to bring these group around into the mainstream Islam but the schismatic bloodshed, which accompanied political and theological differences and its continued spill over in the Umayyad's and 'Abbasid's dynastic rule, turned them into hardheaded splits, marked by intense partisan feelings. This posed a serious threat to the Muslim unity: inter-factional disputatious polemics became common raising new political, theological, and philosophical issues while splitting further each sect into small sub-sects. The Iraqi capital Kūfah was the largest theatre of conflicts as it was here in Iraq that the battles of Jamal, Ṣiffīn, and Nahrwān took place; it was here that the tragic death of al-Ḥusayn ibn 'Ali occurred; and it was here again that the Umayyads and 'Abbasids used excessive force to crush their opponents.

In this calamitous period of conflicts and schisms, the myriad of sects that emerged had their origin in four main schools of thought – Shi'ah, Khawārij, Murjiah, and Mu'tazilah. We will describe them here briefly.

1. The Shi'ah

In the beginning 'Ali's supporters were called Shi'ān-i 'Ali (supporters of 'Ali). Later, the nomenclature was changed to a simpler description of the Shi'ah only.

After the Prophet's death, some people of Banū Hāshim along with some companions (Ṣaḥābah) considered 'Ali as worthy of the caliphate and excelled over others especially 'Uthmān. Also, there were some people who by virtue of 'Ali's blood relationship with the Prophet preferred him to the caliphate than others. But these thoughts had not yet consolidated themselves into a creed or a sect. Such people were also not opposed to the caliph in power and even accepted the earlier three caliphs.

Their coalescence into a party with specific ideas occurred subsequent to the battle of Jamal, Ṣiffīn, and Nahrwān. Ḥusayn's martyrdom brought consolidation to their ranks adding fuel to their simmering passions. Besides, the Umayyad's use of brutal force caused hatred among the Muslims; the persecution of 'Ali's family members and their allies by the Umayyad and 'Abbasid created a sympathy wave in the masses for them. That in return gave an exaggerated impetus to the Shi'i call (da'wāh), with Kūfah becoming the seat of their power. Their chief concepts were as under:

- The phrase imāmah (imamate), which they used for the

Khilāfah, as they said, was not for the Ummah to decide. It is the prerogative of the Prophet to appoint the imām. In other words, it is not an electoral office decided by the Ummah.[1]

- The imām should be innocent, free from minor and major sins. Besides, he is infallible and anything he says is binding on others.[2]

- 'Ali was nominated by the Prophet and he was imām because of the clear edict in his favour.[3]

- The imām will appoint his successor, for the Ummah has no say in this matter.[4]

- The Shi'i sub-sects agreed among themselves that the progeny of 'Ali held exclusive right to the imāmah.[5]

After this all-inclusive agreement on the concept of imāmah, the Shi'i splintered among themselves on its certain aspects. For example, the moderates believed that 'Ali was superior in his makeup over others. Anyone who fights him and carries grudge against him is the enemy of Allah. He will always stay in Hellfire and he will share the fate of the nonbelievers (kāfirūn) and hypocrites (munāfiqūn). They also said that if 'Ali had refused to acknowledge the caliphate of Abū Bakr, 'Umar, and 'Uthmān and had not given his pledge to them and prayed Ṣalāh after them, they would have considered them as the dwellers of Hell.

---

1 Ibn Khaldūn, *al-Muqaddimah* (Egypt: Matb'ah Mustaphā Muhammad) p. 196; al-Shahristāni, *Kitāb al-Fasal fi Milal wa al-Hawā wa al-Nihal* (London) vol. 1, pp. 108-109.

2 Ibn Khaldūn, *al-Muqaddimah*, (Egypt: Mustaphā Muhammad, n.d.) p. 196; al-Shahristāni, *Kitāb...*, vol. 1, p. 109.

3 Al-Shahristāni, *Kitāb*, vol. 1, p. 108, Ibn Khaldūn, *al-Muqaddimah*, pp. 196-197.

4 Ibn Khaldūn, *al-Muqaddimah*, p. 197; al-Ash'arī, *Maqalāt al-Islamiīn* (Cairo: Maktab'ah al-Nahdah al-Misiriyah) first edition, vol. 1, p. 197; al-Shahristāni, *Kitāb...*, vol. 1, p. 109.

5 Al-Shahristāni, *Kitāb*, vol. 1, p. 108.

Other than the prophetic office, they reckoned nothing different between the Prophet and 'Ali.[6]

The extremists among the Shi'is, on the other hand, considered 'Ali's predecessor in caliphate as usurpers. Those who put them in the caliphal office were the wrongdoers for they disregarded the Prophet's alleged will on succession. The harder among them also charged the first three caliphs and those who supported them with disbelief.

The softest stance among them was that of the Zaidiyyah who followed Zaid ibn 'Ali ibn Ḥusayn (d.122 A.H./740 C.E.). They considered 'Ali as superior to others but it was also part of their belief that in the presence of the superior the lesser in stature could be the imām. Besides, they held that there was no clear-cut prophetic injunction in 'Ali's favour. That is why they accepted Abū Bakr's and 'Umar's caliphate as legitimate. Nevertheless, they held that when it comes to the imāmah, he should be from the stock of Sayyidah Fātimah provided he rises against the kings as claimant to the imāmah.[7]

2. Khawārij

The Khawārij were quite the opposite of the Shi'is and formed the next major group in prominence. They emerged when 'Ali and Mu'āwiyah agreed to resolve their differences through arbitration (taḥkīm). Before, they stood behind 'Ali. Nevertheless, arbitration alienated them from him saying that by agreeing to human arbitration in preference to Allah he had turned apostate. The subsequent period saw them exceeding the bounds in pursuit of their ideas. Inclined as they were towards violence in waging war against those who held different views than their's including unjust governments, they caused a great deal of protracted bloodshed. For a long time they stayed distended from the mainstream. Eventually, the 'Abbasids ended their power spread. Their largest power base remained Iraq where in the region of al-Batā'ih, between Baṣrah and Kūfah, they had a string of campsites. Summarized their beliefs are as under:

---

6 Ibn abi al-Ḥadīd, *Sharh Nahj,* vol. 4, p. 520.

7 Al-Ash'arī, *Maqālāt,* vol. 1, p. 129; Ibn Khaldūn, *al-Muqaddimah*, pp. 197-198; al-Shahristāni, *Kitāb,* vol. 1, pp. 115-117.

- They considered Abū Bakr's and 'Umar's caliphate as just but of 'Uthman, they thought he deviated from the path of justice and truth at the last leg of his rule and thus qualified himself to be killed or removed. Even 'Ali, in their perception, whom they supported first, committed a capital sin when he agreed to human arbitration. Besides, both arbitrators ('Amr ibn al-'Āṣ and Abū Mūsā al-Ash'arī) and those who proferred their names as well as those who were involved in the Jamal battle, like Ṭalḥah, al-Zubayr, and Sayyidah 'Ā'ishah, committed a capital sin.

- To them sin was disbelief (kufr) and anyone who indulged in major sin and did not repent was a nonbeliever (kāfir). That is why they not only declared them nonbelievers but also cursed them in public. [In their vituperative and kāfir-calling mindset], they did not spare the common Muslims either, for not only their lives were soiled with sins but they also took the above named as their leaders and derived the Shar'ī injunctions from their reported ḥadīth.

- About the caliphate, they held it could only come into being through free electoral process.

- They disagreed with the notion that only the Qurayshites qualified themselves to be the rulers. Any righteous Muslim who had the consent of other Muslims could become the caliph.

- They thought that as long as the caliph delivered justice and stayed the right path his obedience was binding on society; but if he deviated, he could be removed and even killed.

- Among the primary sources of Islam, they believed in the Qur'ān but in matters of ḥadīth and ijmā'(consensus), their thinking was different than that of the mainstream Muslims.

A large group among them (known as al-Najdāt) considered state unnecessary. The Muslims, they advocated, should themselves collectively follow Islam in their lives. If, however, they felt the need for the caliphate they might do so.

Their largest group known as Āzāriqah viewed everyone else as polytheist (mushrik). The Khawārij, they said, must not respond to the call for Ṣalāh made by someone other than them, nor must they eat the flesh of an animal slaughtered by a non-Khawārij or marry others or inherit from people other than themselves. To kill their women and children and to deprive them of their belongings were justified in their sight. They also considered their own group members, who withheld themselves from such a jihād, as nonbeliever (kāfir). Cheating their opponents in their view was allowed (Ḥalāl). So perverse they were in their extremism that non-Muslims were safer at their hands than the Muslims were.

The softest among them in their posture were Ibādiyah who though called common Muslims as nonbelievers but refrained from describing them as polytheists (mushrikūn). To them, they were non-mū'min, whose testimony they accepted, married among them, and considered inheritance from both ends as valid. They also avoided calling their territories as dār al-ḥarb (the land of fight) or dār al-kūfr (the land of disbelief) for they considered them as dār al-tawḥīd. The power centres were, however, exception, which they condemned as usual. They did not like attacking Muslims unannounced and preferred declared war against them.[8]

3. Murjiah

From the extreme contradictory views of the Shi'is and Khawārij, a third group arose known as Murjiah. They represented a cross section of the people who kept themselves away from 'Ali's dispute for they were either neutral or considered civil war as harmful to the Muslims, or they were confused about the party that carried the truth. They knew for a fact that Muslims spilling each other's blood was a grave evil but they were unwilling to criticize any of the contending parties. For them, it was for Allah to sift the truth from untruth on the

8 For details see 'Abd al-Qāhir al-Baghdādi, *al-Farqu Bayn al-Firaq* (Egypt: Matb'ah al-Ma'ārif) pp. 55, 61, 63-64, 67-68, 82-83, 99, 313-315. See also, al-Shahristāni, *Kitāb,* vol 1, pp. 87, 91-92, 100; al-Ash'ari, *Maqālāt,* vol. 1, pp. 156-157, 159, 189-190, al-Mas'ūdi, *Murūj*, vol. 2, p. 191.

Judgment Day. To that extent, their views were not different from the general mass of the Ummah. But when the Shi'is and the Khawārij began raising issues of belief (imān) and disbelief (kūfr) in support of their extreme views and an unending polemical fight started declaring others as nonbelievers, this neutral stratum of society also reacted by providing theological support to their posture:

- Faith (īmān), they said, is the effort to cognize the existence of Allah and His messenger and hold belief in them. Deeds are not part of it. Thus, a person stays a believer (mu'min) even when he discards obligatory part of Islam and indulges in capital sins.

- Salvation is tied to belief only. No violation of the Sharī'ah can hurt a person who can receive Allah's mercy provided he stays away from shirk and dies on his belief in the oneness of Allah (tawḥīd).[9]

A group of the Murjiah extended it into a doctrine that except shirk (polytheism) even the worst of the sins Allah would eventually forgive.[10] And some others extended it further by saying that if a person carries belief in his heart and declares his disbelief openly in dar al-Islam where he fears none, or embraces Judaism or Christianity or even worships an idol, he still will be a believer – Allah's friend and the dweller of Paradise.[11] The spread of these ideas encouraged people to indulge in all kinds of sins. The false assurance of Allah's forgiveness emboldened people to violate any norm they wanted and thus created a serious moral crisis in society.

Similar to this thinking was the concept that raising arms to force compliance of *amr bil mar'ūf* and *nahī 'an al-munkar* (stressing goodness and stopping wrong) was an impetus to disorder in society. People might condemn each other and that would be a legitimate act but to speak out against the wrong perpetuated by the government would be illegitimate.[12]

9 Al-Shahristāni, *Kitāb,* vol. 1, pp. 103-104; al-Ash'ari, *Maqālāt,* vol. 1, pp. 198, 120.

10 Al-Shahristāni, *Kitab,* vol. 1, p. 104.

11 Ibn Hazm, *al-Fasal fil al-Milal wa al-Hawā' wa al-Nihal* (Egypt: al-Matab'ah al-Adabiyah, 1317 A.H.) vol. 4, p. 204.

12 Al-Jassās, *Ahkām,* vol. 2, p. 40.

Abū Bakr al-Jassas is very bitter about it and says that by spreading such concepts they strengthened the hands of the oppressors and greatly weakened the Muslim will to resist deviationists and usurpers.

4. Mu'tazilah

In this turbulent period a fourth school of thought emerged which is remembered in Islamic history as i'tazāl (who separates or dissents). The first three groups were parented by pure political antecedents and later they invented for themselves a new theology to sustain their politics. Their growth was though apolitical but it succeeded in infusing into the political issues a few definitive concepts and joined the prevailing intense debate that went on in the Islamic world, especially Iraq. The founder of this new thought was Wāsil ibn 'Aṭā (d.130 A.H./748 C.E.) and 'Amr ibn 'Ubayd (d.144 A.H./761 C.E.) who agitated them first in Baṣrah. Summarized their ideas are as follows:

- To them the appointment of the imām (or the state) had a binding status in the Sharī'ah, though a few among them thought that there was no compulsion for having the imām. If the Ummah stays the course of justice, the imām has little relevance.[13]

- The majority of them believed that the imāmah was an elective office effectuated by their collective will.[14] Some of them added further conditionality to it. They held that the imāmah should reflect unanimity. In a discordant situation, the appointment of the imām was invalid.[15]

- They denied imāmah to any particular group. For them any righteous, capable Qurayshi, an Arab or a non-Arab was qualified to hold the office.[16] Some Mu'tazilah went further than that and maintained that a non-Arab was better for the imāmah than others were. It would be still better, they said, if

13 Al-Mas'ūdi, *Murūj,* vol. 2, p. 191.
14 Ibid.
15 Al-Shahristāni, *Kitāb,* vol. 1, p. 51.
16 Al-Mas'ūdi, *Murūj,* vol. 2, p. 191.

people made a freed slave as the imām, for if the imām had a following, then his removal from the office in the face of his oppressive policies would become difficult.[17] In other words, they were more concerned about his easy removal than the stability of the imāmah.

- They also held that offering Ṣalāh after a wicked imām was invalid.[18]

- Among their main concepts *amr bi a- ma'rūf wa nahī 'an al-munkar* had primacy. Rebelling against a government that has strayed from justice and truth was binding (wājib) in their perception, provided it could lead to a successful revolution.[19] That is why they participated in the rebellion against the Umayyad caliph al-Walīd ibn Yazīd (125-126 A.H./743-744 C.E.) so they could replace him with Yazīd ibn al-Walīd, for he subscribed to the Mu'tazilah school.[20]

- In the stormy conflict between the Khawārij and Murjiah on the constitutive nature of disbelief (kūfr) and belief (imān), their verdict was that a sinning Muslim was neither a nonbeliever nor a mū'min but somewhere in the middle.[21]

Besides these concepts, the Mu'tāzilah also gave their verdict on differences among the companions as well as on issues of the past caliphates. Wāṣil ibn 'Aṭā' held that between the contenders of the Jamal battle and Ṣiffin one of them was a violator (fāsiq), but he was not sure who committed fisq. Thus, Wāṣil would say that if 'Ali, Ṭalḥah, and al-Zubayr had to witness even for a sack of vegetable, he would not accept it, for they could be violators (fāsiqūn).

'Amr ibn 'Ubayd viewed both parties as fāsiq.[22] He was very harsh on 'Uthmān. So much so that a few among them did not spare

---

17 Al-Shahristāni, *Kitāb,* vol. 1, p. 63.
18 Al-Asha'ri, *Maqālāt,* vol. 2, p. 124.
19 Ibid, p. 125
20 Al-Mas'ūdi, *Murūj,* vol. 2, pp. 190, 1993; Jalāl al-Dīn al-Suyūti, *Tārikh al-Khulafā',* (Lahore: Government Press, 1870 A.H.) p. 255.
21 'Abd al-Qāhir al-Baghdādi, *al-Farqu,* pp. 94-55.
22 Ibid, pp. 100-101, al-Shahristāni, *Kitāb,* vol. 1, p. 34.

caliph 'Umar either.[23] Besides, many Mu'tāzilah considered ḥadīth and ijmā'(consensus) as invalid sources of the Islamic law.[24]

5. The mainstream Muslims

Among these conflicting extremities the mainstream Muslims stayed glued to those very incontrovertible concepts and principles that existed since the days of the rightly guided caliphate and which were embraced by the companions (Ṣaḥābah), later Muslims (tābi'ūn) and the general mass of the Muslim Ummah as true Islam.

Hardly eight-to-ten percent of the Muslim people were influenced by this schism; the rest stayed the course of the majority. On the beliefs of these emergent sects, different jurists and ḥadīth scholars though did express themselves through their edicts and attitudes on their certain aspects but none tried to formulate and expound the majority viewpoint on the contentious issues agitated by these schismatic groups in a methodical way before Abū Ḥanifah.

23 Ibid, pp. 133-134; Ibid, p. 40.
24 'Abd al-Qāhir al-Baghdādi, *al-Farqu,* pp. 138-139.

Chapter Seven

Abū Ḥanīfah's Accomplishment

We have already discussed how in the wake of monarchy Muslim leadership splintered into two kinds of leadership and its concomitant ill consequences. We have also talked about the distorted face of the political leadership, led by feudal aristocracy and royalty, and the religious leadership manned by the ʻulamā and the pious.

We would like to give now a brief profile of the religious leadership, the people who staffed it and the way they solved the burning problems of that turbulent era. For this purpose, we will take Imām Abū Ḥanīfah as a representative of that group and discuss his role as a jurist followed by his disciple Abū Yūsuf's work, who helped accomplish his unfinished agenda.

1. Brief life event

Abu Ḥanīfah's name was al-Nuʻmān ibn Thābit. According to authentic reports, he was born 80 A.H. (699 C.E.) in Kūfah. ʻAbd al-Malik ibn Marwān was then the Umayyad caliph while Ḥajjāj ibn Yūsuf was the Iraqi governor. He spent fifty-two years of his life under the Umayyads and eighteen years under the ʻAbbasids. When Ḥajjāj ibn Yūsuf died, he was fifteen years old. By the time ʻUmar ibn ʻAbdul-ʻAzīz came into power he was in the prime of his youth. He saw the turbulent years of Yazīd ibn al-Muhallab, Khālid ibn ʻAbdullah al-Qasriy, and Nasr ibn Sayyār's governorship of Iraq. He himself fell victim to the Umayyad governor Ibn Hubayrah's despotism. He saw the ʻAbbasid movement priming before his very eyes. Kūfah, his hometown, was the hub of its activities, and even when the ʻAbbasid movement succeeded, the city remained as the new rulers' seat of governance until Baghdad was built. He died in the reign of caliph al-Manṣūr in 150 A.H. (767 C.E.).

His family came from Kabul, present-day Afghanistan. Some people have recognized his grandfather's name as Zutā others as Zautā. The legend says his grandfather was a prisoner of war, brought to Kūfah. Later, he became Muslim and decided to stay in Kūfah under the patronage of Banī Taym Allah. He took to trade. There is sufficient evidence to suggest that he had cultivated friendly relation with 'Ali whom he would occasionally send gifts.[1] Abū Ḥanīfah's father followed the family tradition. Imām himself says his father had a bakery in Kūfah.[2]

Concerning his education, Abū Ḥanīfah himself says that in his younger years he studied the art of recitation, ḥadīth, grammar, literature, poetry and scholastics, which were in vogue at that time.[3] Later, he specialized in scholastics, and soon made his mark in it. Zufar ibn al-Hudhayl, his famous student, says that the Imām told him: "In the beginning I interested myself with scholastics and had reached a point that people began to talk of me."[4] In another report, he himself says:

> "I was a person who had mastered the contentious issues of scholastics theology. There was a time when I was mostly engrossed in debates and rhetoric. And since Baṣrah was the seat of contentious issues, I visited it over a twenty time. Sometime I would prolong my stay in the city for a period of six months to a year and would engage different groups of Khawārij, Ibādiyyah, Suffriyyah, and Hashwiyyah in arguments."[5]

One can presume that Abū Ḥanīfah must have mastered philosophy, logic and the conflicting issues of the then prevailing schools of thought for without such a grounding he could not

1 Ibn al-Bazzāz al-Kardari, *Manāqib al-Imām al-A'ẓam* (Hyderabad: Dāirah al-Ma'arif, 1321 A.H.) 1st Edition, vol. 1, pp. 65-66.

2 Al-Muwaffaq ibn Ahmed al-Makki, *Manāqib al-Imām al-A'ẓam,* (Hyderabad: Dā'irah al-Ma'ārif, 1321 A.H.) vol. 1, p. 162.

3 Ibid, pp. 57, 58.

4 Ibid, pp. 55, 59.

5 Ibid, p. 59.

have dared enter the field of scholastic theology. Later in his life, his contribution to the development of law and his fame as a distinguished legal mind owed much to his early education in logic and use of reason.

For a long time, he kept himself engaged in scholastic wrangling and polemical disputes until he found himself disgusted with it. Gradually, the usefulness and glamour of fiqh (Islamic law) lured him. Among the then existing schools, ahl al-Ḥadīth had no attraction for him. Kūfah was the metropolis of the Iraqi ahl al-Rāi'y (people of opinion) and thus he joined it. This school of thought originated with 'Ali ibn abi Tālib and 'Abdullah ibn Mas'ūd (d.32 A.H./652 C.E.). After them, their disciples Shurayḥ (d.78 A. H./697 C.E.), 'Alqamah (d.62 A.H./814 C.E.) and Masrūq (d.63 A.H./682 C.E.) created a niche for themselves in fiqh, known all over the Islamic world. They were followed by Ibrāhīm Nakh'ī (d.95 A.H.) and Ḥammād ibn abī Sulaymān (d.120 A.H.), whose tutelage Abū Hanifah sought and stayed with him for about eighteen years. But eager as he was to learn, he did not confine himself to his Kūfan teachers. He performed Ḥajj (pilgrimage) frequently in order to meet and exchange views with experts on fiqh and ḥadīth from all over the Islamic world.

In 120 A.H., when his teacher Ḥammād died, people belonging to his school of thought unanimously crowned him as his successor. There on that august seat for thirty years he performed the great task of expounding knowledge and giving verdicts on emergent issues that serve as the basis of the school named Ḥanafiyyah. Some people say he responded to sixty-thousand legal queries; other says eighty-three thousands, which were compiled in his life time under separate heads.[6] His students number seven to eight hundred who spread themselves across the Muslim world and became the source of knowledge and the centre of their affection and respect. Out of them at least fifty of his students became judges in the 'Abbasid reign; their madhhab (school of jurisprudence) became the law of a large

---

6 Ibid, p. 96, vol. 2, pp. 132-136.

part of the Islamic world. From the 'Abbasid to Saljūk empires and 'Uthmāniyah to the Mughal empires it remained their core law. Today, from China to Turkey, millions of Muslims follow it.

For his living, Abū Ḥanīfah pursued trade – his parental occupation. In Kūfah, he used to sell khazz (a particular kind of cloth). Gradually, he turned it into a big business, making the cloth in his own factory.[7] His house of business not only sold cloth in Kūfah but also in areas far off. Soon recognition came to him as a businessperson of moral integrity and rectitude. People's trust in him increased to an extent that they would deposit their cash with him turning his business house into a kind of a bank. At the time of his death, the deposits in trust with him amounted to 500 million dirham.[8] His vast experience in financial and business matters gave him a rare insight into the discipline that stood him out among his contemporaries and later-day law scholars. In the formulation of the usūl al-fiqh (jurisprudence), his business experience paid off. So great and known was his acumen in worldly affairs that in 145 A.H., when al-Manṣūr decided to build Baghdad, he asked Abū Ḥanīfah to execute the project, which he accomplished in four years.[9]

In his personal life he was the emblem of piety and trustworthiness. One time he sent his partner to sell cloth outside Kūfah. The part of the lot had a quality problem and he specifically instructed him to let the buyer know about it. Somehow, the man forgot it. Abū Ḥanīfah gave the entire amount of about 35,000 dirham in charity.[10] Historians have recounted numerous such incidents involving purchase transactions where inexperienced sellers would ask for a less amount and he would insist on giving them the real market price.[11] So greatly were his contemporaries impressed with his high sense of morality

---

7 Al-Yāfi'i, *Mirāt al-Jinān wa 'Ibrat al-Yaqzān fi Ma'rifāt mā Yu'tabar min Hawādith al-Zamān* (Hyderabd: Dā'irah al-Ma'ārif, 1337 A.H.) 1st Edition, vol. 1, p. 310.

8 Al-Makki, *Manāqib,* vol. 1, p. 220.

9 Al-Ṭabari, *Tārikh,* vol. 6, p. 238; Ibn Kathir, *al-Bidāyah,*vol. 10, p. 97.

10 Al-Khatib al-Baghdadi, *Tārikh al-Baghadād,* vol. 13, p. 358; Mullā 'Ali al-Qāri, *Dhayl al-Juwāhir al-Madiy'a,* (Hyderabad: Dā'irah al-Ma'ārif, 1322 A.H.) p. 488, first edition.

11 Al-Makki, *Manāqib,* vol. 1, pp. 219-220.

that they speak of him in the noblest possible terms. 'Abdullah ibn Mubārak, the dean of the ḥadīth scholars, says: "I have not seen a person of Abū Ḥanīfah's rectitude. What can be said of a person who was offered world and its possessions and he rejected them; who was lashed several times and he still refused to compromise; and whom high offices that people hanker after failed to seduce."[12]

Qāḍī ibn Shuberumah says: "The world leapt after him but he ran away from it; and the world ran way from us and we crazed after it."[13]

Ḥasan ibn Ziyād says: "By Allah! Abū Ḥanīfah never accepted a gift or endowment from the influentials."[14] Hārūn al-Rashīd once asked Abū Yūsuf about Abū Ḥanīfah, he said:

> "By Allah! He literally stayed away from the things Allah forbade. People were not his focus; often silent, people would find him lost in reflection and avoided unnecessary talk. If somebody asked him a question and if he knew its answer, he would respond. Amīr al-Mu'minīn, I know only this much that he would save his faith and self (nafs) from wrongdoing. Unmindful of the people, we often found him engaged with his own person and never talked ill of others."[15]

With money, he was generous to a fault and spent it, especially on people of knowledge and needy students. For this, he had earmarked a substantial amount of money from the fund generated by his business, which he dished out on a yearly basis. While helping them he would say: "Spend it on your needs and do not even feel indebted to anyone but Allah, for I did not give you a thing from my own pocket. This is Allah's beneficence given to me for your need.[16] A large number of his students depended on him, including the

12 Abu 'Abd Allah Al-Dhahabi, *Manāqib al-Imām abi Hanifah wa Sahibiyah*, (Egypt: Dār al-Kutab al-Arabi, 1366 A.H.) p. 115.

13 Al-Rāghib al-Isfahāni, *Mahādrāt al-Abdā'* (Egypt: Matb'ah al-Hilāl, 1902) p. 206.

14 Al-Dhahabi, *Manāqib...*, p. 26.

15 Ibid, p. 9.

16 Al-Baghdādi, *Tārikh,* vol. 13, p. 260; al-Makki, *Manāqib*, vol. 1, p. 262.

renowned Abū Yūsuf. He provided a safety net to his family for they were poor and wanted their son to discontinue his education and work for living.[17]

Such was the person who addressed himself to the important issues that arose in the first half of the second-century Hijrah following the dissolution of the rightly guided caliphate.

2. Abu Ḥanīfah's views

Here, we will take first those issues which the Imām responded to in the written from.

He himself never wrote a book. Thus, one has to go to other credible sources for the nature of his work. There were, however, some issues like the one raised by the Khawārij, Murji'ah and Mu'tazilah to which, contrary to his practice, he himself made a written response. In consequence, we have from him a brief but very pertinent creedal formulation of the mainstream Muslim Ummah (ahl al-Sunnah wa al-Jamā'ah). It is thus natural that we give priority to his writings on the subject.

We have already stated the composition of the schismatic difference that arose at the juncture of 'Ali's caliphate and the beginning of the Umayyad dynastic rule. We have also talked about the four sects that emerged because of those differences and their extreme views on some of the issues which they articulated in theological formulations making them as their article of faith. These views which were contrary to the complexion of the Muslim society, the Islamic state, the sources of the Islamic law, and the Ummah's past collective decisions called for a systematic treatment so that their negative impact could be invalidated. It was not that the mainstream Muslim had no opinion on such issues. Far from it, the opinion was well determined, as the common people firmly stuck to it and the great jurists often expressed it by their word and deeds. What Abū Ḥanīfah did was to reduce it in writing in an un-blurred way.

17 Ibn Khallikan, *Wafayāt al-A'ayān* (Egypt: Maktabah al-Nahfitah al-Misriyah, 1948) vol. 5, pp. 23, 422; al-Makki, *Manāqib*, vol. 2, p. 212.

2.1. The exposition of the mainstream creed

Abū Ḥanīfah's book *al-Fiqh al-Akbar*[18] deals with the position of the rightly guided caliphs. The book became important when against the backdrop of the emergent heresy and the various sects that rose from it began to question their legitimacy such as whether their caliphal status was valid or not? An adjunct to this question was who among them was superior. Yet another question asked was whether after assuming the caliphal office they remained Muslims? These questions by their nature did not simply state a historical opinion on some individuals in the past but in fact led to a single most important question: was the electoral process used for the election of these caliphs legitimate? Thus said, was it a justified constitutional mode of electing head of the Islamic state? Besides, once the caliphate's legal status is diluted, the question that still roll the mind will be whether their consensual decisions can be counted as part of the Islamic law. Also, what status the decisions of that particular caliph will have? Can we consider their decisions as legal precedents?

Further, the legality or illegality of their caliphate, the presence or non-presence of their belief (imān) as well as the superiority of one over the other obviously led to this ultimate question: should present-day Muslims have confidence in the Islamic society fashioned under the direct supervision of the Prophet ('alayhi as-salām)? Should they have trust in its credibility to absorb the nuances of his teachings and later transmit them to future generations with responsibility and rectitude? Also, should the Muslim Ummah feel itself bonded to its collective decisions?

Second, what status the Ṣaḥābah (companions) should be accorded in view of a group's opposition that considered almost all of them as usurpers, deviant, and worst kāfir (nonbeliever)? This was also not a question of historical import but had serious implications.

18 Before the term 'ilm al-kalām gained currency the word fiqh was used for 'aqā'id, usūl al-dīn and law. The distinction, however, was made in the sense that 'aqāid and usūl al-dīn were lumped under "al-fiqh al-Akbar". Imām Abū Ḥanīfah used this name for his *Risālah*. Lately, scholars have questioned the authenticity of some of its parts as later-day interpolation. However, the parts we are discussing are undoubtedly authentic, for the other sources like Abū Ḥanīfah's *al-Wasiyyah*, Abu Muti'h al-Balkhi's *al-Fiqh al-Absat*, and *'Aqidah al-Tahāwiyah,* in which al-Tahāwi has narrated from Abū Ḥanīfah and his disciples. Abū Yūsuf and Muḥammad ibn Ḥasan al-Shaybānī gives support to the contents of his *al-Fiqh al-Akbar*.

The Ṣaḥābah were the transmitters of the Prophetic practices. Can we accord those practices the status of a source of the Islamic law?

Equally important was the third question relating to belief – what constituted it? What separated belief from disbelief and the effects of sin and its consequences? On these questions Khawārij, Mu'tazilah, and Murjiah had strong debates. These questions were also not theological but had the potential to influence the composition of the Muslim society in a profound way. For no matter what answer was given, it had a legal implication affecting the collective rights of the Muslim people. Besides, it posed a serious problem to the authority of the Islamic state: how could a government manned by a sinful group manage the religious and political affairs of the state like establishing Ṣalāh (prayer), setting up justice courts, and waging jihād? Abū Ḥanīfah's attempt to formulate the mainstream position on these issues was as under.

2.2. The rightly guided caliphate

"After Rasūl Allāh (ṣal.lal.lahu 'alayhi wa sallam) the best among the people is Abū Bakr Siddique, followed by 'Umar ibn al-Khattāb, 'Uthmān ibn 'Affān and 'Ali ibn abī Tālib. They were all on the truth and stayed with the truth."[19]

In *'Aqidah al-Tahwiyah,* it is further expounded:
"After Rasūl Allah (sal.lal.lahu 'alayhi wa-sallam), we exalt Abū Bakr Siddique over the entire Ummah and affirm the first Khilāfah for him, followed by 'Umar ibn al-Khaṭṭāb, 'Uthmān ibn 'Affān and 'Ali ibn abī Ṭālib. And they are the rightly-guided khulāfā' and leaders of the pious."[20]

It may be of interest to note that Imām Abū Ḥanīfah in his person was inclined towards 'Ali over 'Uthmān.[21] At the same time, he believed that between the two none could be exalted over the other.[22] But since the Ummah had given its choice for 'Uthmān, he submitted

19 Al-Qāri, *Sharḥ al-Fiqh*, (Delhi: Tab'ah Mujtābai, 1348 A.H.) pp. 74-87; al-Maghnisāwi, *Sharh...,* (Hyderabad: Da'irah al-Ma'ārif, 1321 A.H.) pp. 25-26.

20 Ibn abi al-'Izz al-Hanafi, *Sharh al-Tahāwiya* (Egypt: Dār al-Ma'ārif, 1373 A. H.) pp. 403-416.

21 Al-Karadari, *Manāqib*, vol. 2, p. 72.

22 Ibn 'Abd al-Barr, *al-Intiqā'* (Cairo: al-Maktabah al-Qudsi, 1370 A.H.), p. 163; al-Sarakhasi, *Sharḥ...,* pp. 157-158. Imām Mālik and Yaḥyā ibn Sa'id al-Qattān held the same view; Ibn 'Abd al-Barr, *al-Isti'āb*, vol. 2, p. 467.

to it by going along with the collective belief that the sequence of superiority would be determined by the caliphal sequence.

2.3. The Ṣaḥābah

"We remember," he says, "Ṣaḥābah with nothing but reverence."[23]

> *'Aqidah al-Tahāwiyah* further explicates it:
> "We love all the Ṣaḥābah of Rasūl Allah (ṣal.lal.lahu 'alayhi wa-sallam); we neither exaggerate in our love for a particular Ṣaḥābī nor do we abuse or curse any of them.
> We dislike those who harbour ill for them and who recall their names with hatred. We call them to our memory with nothing but goodness and reverence."[24]

Abū Ḥanīfah do express himself on the factional feuds among the Ṣaḥābah but even then he is circumspect. He thinks 'Ali had the truth as opposed to others who fought against him.[25] He however stops here and avoids condemning the other party.

2.4. Belief defined

"Belief", he says, "is the name of affirmation and witnessing."[26] In *al-Wasiyyah*, the Imām explains it: "Belief is the affirmative pronouncement by one's mouth while the heart witnesses it." Adding to this, he says: "Neither affirmation alone is belief nor is ma'rifah belief. Further he says: "Deeds are separate from belief and belief is separate from deeds. The rationale is that sometimes a believer's belief fails to translate into deeds but his belief does not leave him ... For example, it can be said that Zakāh (poor-due) is not obligatory on a beggar but one cannot say that belief is not binding on him."[27]

---

23 Al- Qāri, *Sharḥ,* p. 87; al-Maghnisāwi, *Sharḥ,* p. 26.

24 Ibn abi al-'Izz, *Sharḥ*, p. 398.

25 Al-Makki, *Manāqib,* vol. 2, pp. 83-84; al-Kardani, *Manāqib*, vol. 2, pp. 71-72. Imām Abū Ḥanīfah was not the sole holder of this opinion. In fact, the whole ahl al-Sunnah had reached consensus on it as reported by Ibn Hajar in his *al-Isābah.* See vol. 2, p. 502.

26 Al-Qāri, *Sharḥ,* p. 33.

27 Mulla Husayn, *al-Jauharah al-Munifah fi Sharh Wasiyah al-Imām abī Ḥanīfah* (Hyderabad: Dā'irah al-Ma'ārif, 1321 A.H.) pp. 3, 6, 7.

Thus, he repudiates the Khawārij concept that one's deeds are constitutive of a person's belief and sin is for sure the equivalent of the absence of belief.

2.5. The difference between sin and a nonbeliever

"We cannot declare," he says, "a Muslim a nonbeliever no matter how great a sin he commits unless he thinks it was all right to do it. (By this) we do not invalidate his īmān (belief). Rather we consider him a real believer, for to us a believer may be a fāsiq (violator), but not a kāfir.[28]

In *al-Wasiyyah*, the Imām puts this subject in the following vein:

> "The sinners of the Ummah of Muḥammad (upon him be peace) are all believers, not kāfir."[29]

There is a further explanation to it in *'Aqīdah al-Tahāwiyah*: "A person does not expel himself from faith unless he repudiates that very thing whose affirmation in the first place brought him into the pale of faith.[30]

This creed and its social consequences are brought into sharp focus by the discussion he had with the Khawārij. A large group of them came to see him. They began saying suppose there were two funerals at the gate of the masjid – one pertained to a drinker who died while drinking; the other related to a woman who became pregnant owning to fornication and then out of shame committed suicide.

The Imām asked: "Which religion did they belong? Were they Jews?"

They said no.
"Were they Christian?" he asked.
They said no.
"Were they Magians?"
They said no again.

---

28 Al-Qāri, *Sharḥ,* pp. 86, 89, al- Maghnisāwi, *Sharḥ,* pp. 27-28.
29 Mullā Husayn, *al-Jauharah,* p. 6.
30 Ibn abi al-'Izz, *Sharḥ*, p. 265.

"Then to which nation do you belong?" he asked.

"The nation that witnesses Islam by pronouncing Kalimah (creedal pronouncement)," they said.

"Tell me, was this witnessing one third or one fourth or one fifth of their faith?" the Imām asked.

"The faith they professed had no one third or one fourth," they said.

"In your perception how much of the pronounced Kalimah will be constitutive of a person's faith?" he asked.

"The whole faith," they said.

"When you are yourselves declaring the dead as believers, then what is the point in asking me?"

"We want to know if the deceased were the dwellers of Paradise or Hellfire."

> "If at all you want to know, I will repeat what Allah's prophet Ibrāhīm said about the sinners worst than them.
> Allah, he who follows me is mine, and he who disobeys me, then (for him) you are the Forgiving the Merciful.[31]
> And, I would say the same that another prophet of Allah ('Isā) said about people who were even worst than the deceased were.
> If you punished them, they are your created beings; and if you forgive them you are the Mighty and the Wise.[32]
> Yet another prophet of Allah, Nūḥ said:
> To hold these people answerable falls within Allah's domain if only you had understood; and I am not of those who repel the believers."[33]

His response made the Khawārij admit their wrong stand.[34]

2.6. The end of the sinful believer

"We do not say that the sinful state is not harmful to the believer. Nor do we say that he will not be sent

31 *Ibrahīm*: 36.

32 *Al-Mā'idah*: 118.

33 *Al-Shu'arā*: 113-114.

34 Al-Makki, *Manāqib,* vol. 1, pp. 124-125.

to Hell and nor do we say that he will stay in Hellfire forever, if he is a fāsiq (violator)."[35]

"And we do not say like the Murji'ah that our good deeds will be per force accepted and our sins forgiven."[36]
Adding to it, *'Aqīdah al-Tahāwiyah* says:
"We do not rule on anyone among the ahl al-Qiblah as to his being the dweller of Paradise or Hell. Nor do we brand them for their disbelief, apostasy or hypocrisy unless there is evidence to its actual occurrence. We leave the matter of their intention to Allah alone."[37]

2.7. The consequences of the 'aqīdah (creed)

The Imām thus formulates a balanced 'aqīdah (creed) in the face of the Shi'i and Khawārij and Mu'tazilah and Murjiah extremism which saves the Muslim society from conflict and polemics on the one hand and an unfettered immorality and the encouragement to do wrongs on the other.

When one considers the turbulence of his times, his exercise in steering the society away from extremism turns out to be a great accomplishment. He demonstrated to these schismatic sects that the Ummah rejects their extreme views torn from the Islamic grid and affirms its belief in the early Islamic society shaped by the Prophet ('alayhi as-salām) and the collective decision it made as well as those it elected as caliphs and considers their decisions constitutionally valid. It also affirmed its faith in the whole corpus of the Sharī'ah, transmitted by the Ṣaḥābah to the Ummah in history, generation after generation.

For sure this 'aqīdah was not the invention of Imām Abū Ḥanīfah; it had a prior existence as the mainstream Muslim Ummah subscribed to it during the past one hundred fifty years. What Abū Ḥanīfah did was to reduce it in writing helping Muslims know their position in the face of the conflicting diehard views of the marginalized sects.

35 Al-Qāri, *Sharḥ*, p. 92; al-Maghnisāwi, *Sharḥ*, p. 28.
36 Al-Qāri, *Sharḥ*, p. 93; al-Maghnisāwi, *Sharḥ*, p. 29.
37 Ibn abi al-'Izz, *Sharḥ*, pp. 312-313.

3. The codification of the Islamic laws

Abū Ḥanīfah's greatest accomplishment, however, was his striving to fill in the horrible vacuum that surfaced after the demise of the rightly guided caliphate and the subsequent cessation of the shūrā institution. We have already talked about its serious repercussions elsewhere.

During the century that followed the demise of the rightly-guided caliphate, the reflective section of the Muslim society felt a great loss in the freezing of the creative lawmaking that spanned thirty years of legal activism, the hallmark of the early caliphate. Added to it was the ever-growing expansion of the political frontiers of the Islamic state from Sindh (present-day Pakistan) to Spain in Europe. The Muslim society had become polyglot with several ethnic identities. The growth of civilization also problematized trade, commerce, industry and agriculture along with constitutional, civil and criminal related aspects that called for Islamic redress. On the international front this great Islamic state had relations with almost every nation that mattered creating war and peace, diplomatic and commercial relations, land and sea travel-related problems. For the Muslims who had their own worldview and life concepts, it was imperative that they find answers to the emergent problems. In short, caught between the challenges of a new era and the absence of a constitutional entity primarily caused by monarchial absolutism that could have undertaken the exercise of lawmaking, the Muslim scholars and the fuqahā' had to respond to the challenge.

This loss was felt by all, from the caliph downward to governors, state functionaries and judges, for it was not worth the salt of everyone to make laws in emergent situations at the spur of the moment through personal ijtihād (independent thought). And even if it had created law, it would have given rise to a whole plethora of contradictory and conflicting laws which instead of solving the problem would have compounded the situation. Only a state could have set up a lawmaking institution but the Umayyad and the 'Abbasid caliphs knew for a fact that they suffered from a credibility problem which no amount of effort on their part would have solved it or made the masses to accept it as part of the Islamic laws. They also knew that they did not have the moral face to deal with the jurists who did not want to associate themselves with a government they considered as usurpers. In fact, Ibn al-Maqaffa' at one point did suggest to al-Manṣūr in his *al-Risālah al-Ṣaḥābah* to a broad-based council of eminent scholars to offer solutions to the new problems followed by its presentation to the caliph, who would give his own decision on each issue and that could be the law.

Tantalizing as the proposal was, al-Manṣūr however knew his worth. His decision could not have had the sanctity and the moral force of Abū Bakr and 'Umar-made laws. And even if he had ventured to do so, his laws would not have last beyond his life. Rather he knew well that not a single citizen would follow his laws in spirits, as none would consider them Islamic laws.

Under these circumstances, Abū Ḥanīfah thought of chartering a new path for his self by setting up a private lawmaking body; free from the governmental influences.

For sure, his idea was innovative as well as daring, which only a person of his mental ability and character could have thought of – a person who believed in himself and his potential to cash in on his credibility with the Muslim masses. He knew that if he ever undertook such an unusual exercise of lawmaking, people would embrace it even in the absence of any political sanction behind it for the simple reason that they believed in his Islamic scholarship, his rectitude and above all his sincerity to his faith. And seeing people accepting such laws, empires would adopt them as well. Abū Ḥanīfah was not a claimant to oracular knowledge. But he believed in himself. He also knew the ability of his coworkers, and the temperament of the Muslim people and the way things were moving. He ventured to do the impossible. Later developments validated his deep insight. Within a short span of fifty years, his visualized scenario materialized – his law became the law of the land.

The members of his legislative body were drawn from his own students whom he had trained in the theories of lawmaking, research methodology, and analogical reasoning. Besides, they had the benefit of receiving education in the Qur'ān, Ḥadīth, fiqh, and other auxiliary disciplines like lexicography, grammar, literature, history and siyar from the great scholars of their time. These students were themselves specialists in different disciplines. Some were experts in analogical reasoning; some were the repositories of ḥadīth and the judgments of the Ṣaḥābah and the caliphs while others were grounded in exegeses, grammar, and maghāzī. Once Abū Ḥanīfah himself described their excellence:

> "These are thirty-six people. Among them twenty-eight have the ability to perform as qāḍī (judge); six have the ability to give edict (fatwā); and two among them are competent enough to train qāḍīs and muftīs."[38]

According to al-Muwaffaq ibn Aḥmad al-Makki (d.568 A.H./1172 C.E.), Abū Ḥanīfah's prominent biographer, the methodology followed by this lawmaking body was astoundingly elaborate and painstakingly perfect:

> Abū Ḥanīfah formulated his school of thought (madhhab) after consultation with his graduate students. The passion that he had for Islam and the highly intense relationship that he had with Allah, His Messenger, and the Muslim Ummah made him not to undertake this exercise in his individual capacity. He would bring up every issue before them and expose its aspects to them in order to have their response and then cap it with his opinion. Sometimes an issue would take a month long discussion and even more. Eventually when the convergence of views would surface, Abū Yūsuf would write it down in *Kitāb al-Uṣūl*.[39]

Ibn al-Bazzāz al-Kardari the author of *al-Fatāwā al-Bazzāziyah* (d.827 A.H./1224 C.E.) says:

> "His students would make a detailed exposition of a problem from all [possible] angles of discipline, while the Imām would listen to their views with rapt attention.At the end, when the Imām would give his concluding observations silence would prevail as if he alone was present in the meeting."[40]

38 Al-Makki, *Manāqib,* vol. 2, p. 246.

39 Ibid, p. 133.

40 Al-Kardari, *Manāqib*, vol. 2, p. 108.

'Abdullah ibn Mubārak says that once for three days continuously they debated an issue. On the third day in the evening when he heard the shouts of Allāhu Akbar (God is Great), he came to know that the discussion had been formalized.[41]

In these sittings, the scribes would write down the Imām's views and subsequently read to him. Of the process his student Abū 'Abdullah says:

> "I used to read the Imām's views to him. While recording the proceedings of these sittings Abū Yūsuf would also write down his own views (on a problem). Thus while reading out to the Imām I would confine myself to his wordings. One day, I forgot to do so and read out the other view as well. The Imām asked whose opinion was the other one."[42]

We also knew from al-Makki's statement that they classified the proceedings of these sittings and catalogued into books and chapters during the Imām's lifetime.

Abū Ḥanīfah was the first person who codified the science of this Sharī'ah. Nobody else did this work before. Abū Ḥanīfah catalogued it into books and chapters under separate heads.[43]

As we said elsewhere, al-Makki reveals that this lawmaking body ruled on 83,000 legal problems. They did not only discuss problems that people faced but also anticipated problems that could emerge in the future and offered solution by lawmaking. These projected problems related to almost every sphere of law. International law[44] (for which the term used was al-Siyar), constitutional law, civil

---

41 Al-Makki, *Manāqib*, vol. 2, p. 54.

42 Al-Kardari, *Manāqib*, vol. 2, p. 109.

43 Al-Makki, *Manāqib*, vol. 2, p. 136.

44 Present-day people labour under the misimpression that international law is a modern instrument and that the first man who founded this new discipline is Hugo Grotius (1583-1645 C.E.). But anyone who has read Imām Abū Ḥanīfah's disciple Muḥammad ibn Ḥasan al-Shaybānī (749-805 C.E.) *al-Siyār* knows that 900 years before Grotius this discipline was structured and compiled by Abū Ḥanīfah covering almost every aspect of international law. Lately, a group of academics has acknowledged this fact. The Germany's al-Shaybānī Society of International Law reaffirms it.

and criminal law, evidence law, procedural code, mercantile law, marriage, divorce, inheritance, 'ibādāt (worships) – all these laws which this lawmaking body generated by its discussions are found in books later compiled by Abū Yūsuf and Muḥammad ibn Ḥasan al-Shaybānī.

The codification of law had its effect. The jurists, the mujtahidūn (people qualified to independent thought), and the muftīs who were doing their work in their personal capacity lost its worth before the person of Abū Ḥanīfah's knowledge and depth, who with a team of experts and their systemic approach distilled laws from the Qur'ān, Sunnah, and the decisions made in the past. Thus, the moment his work appeared the Muslim masses, state functionaries, and the courts to refer to it per force, for it was timely, people were waiting for it. The famous jurist Yaḥya ibn Ādam (d.203 A.H./818 C.E.) says that the views of the other jurists paled before Abū Ḥanīfah's work. Its influence spread fast all over the nation; the caliphs, state officials and jurists began making their decisions based on it.[45] By the time the caliph al-Māmūn (d.218 A.H./833 C.E.) came into power it had become the established law of the land.

When a rival jurist to Abū Ḥanīfah counselled Prime Minister Faḍl ibn Sahl to abolish the Ḥanifi fiqh, he called for a meeting of the wise for the decision, who constrained him not to do so.

> "This will not work," came the united reply. "The whole country will turn against you."

In their view, the person who had suggested the idea was mentally retarded.

Ibn Sahl agreed and said he did not subscribe to the idea nor would the caliph.[46]

Thus, an important event in history took place – the law developed by a private legislative assembly became the law of nations and empires owing to the moral stature of its framers.

---

45 Al-Makki, *Manāqib,* vol. 2, p. 41.

46 Al-Makki, *Manāqib,* vol. 2, pp. 157-158; al-Kardari, *Manāqib,* vol. 2, pp. 106, 107.

Conjoined to this development, it inaugurated a new approach in lawmaking for the coming Muslim jurists who would follow Abū Ḥanīfah's method even though they were different in their ijtihādī methodology and its results.

Chapter Eight

The Caliphate and its Related Issues: Abū Ḥanīfah's Approach

As opposed to other jurists, Imām Abū Ḥanīfah's views in the realm of politics are relatively comprehensive covering almost every aspect of state and leadership. Here, we will talk about his thought.

1. Sovereignty

Whatever may be the concept of state, it revolves around the issue of sovereignty – that is, who is sovereign? Imām Abū Ḥanīfah's view on this vital area of inquiry was a reflection of Islam's incontrovertible stance on Allah's sovereignty for He is the Real Sovereign; that the Prophet as His deputy on this Earth is bonded to His will, and that the Sharī'ah given by them is the Supreme Law to be followed. Since Abū Ḥanīfah was a man of law, he articulated his views in legal jargon rather than of a political discourse:

> "Whenever I come across an injunction in the Book of Allah, I grasp it. And when I do not find it there, I resort to the Sunnah of Rasūl Allah and his precedents which are known among the credible people, received by them from equally trusted sources. When I fail to find an injunction in the Book of Allah or in the Prophet's Sunnah, I turn to the Ṣaḥābah (companions), and follow their word (i.e. ijmā'). And in the event of differences among them, I take the saying of a Ṣaḥābi that sounds preferable to me and leave the rest. But outside them, I do not go after other's views ... As for the other people's [objection to my ijtihād] if they have the right to ijtihād (independent thought) so do I have."[1]

---

1 Abu Bakr al-Khatīb al-Baghdādi, *Tārikh al-Baghdādi*, (Egypt: Matb'ah al-Sa'ādah, 1931), vol. 13, p. 368, al-Makki, *Manāqib al-Imām al-A'ẓam Abū Ḥanīfah*, vol. 1, p. 89; al-Dhahabi, *Manāqib*, p. 20.

> Says ibn Hazm:
> "All the companions of Abū Ḥanīfah agree on this point that his method accepted even a weak ḥadīth in preference to analogical reasoning (al-qiyās) and opinion (rā'iy)."[2]

Obviously, this shows that Abū Ḥanīfah considered the Qur'ān and Sunnah as the final authority in lawmaking. His belief ('aqidah) rested in declaring Allah and His messenger as the originator of legal sovereignty. According to him, qiyās and rā'iy had their role in lawmaking only when there was no clear-cut injunction from Allah and His messenger on a subject. His preference to the sayings of the Ṣaḥābah also had the same reason that he thought there was a possibility of a prophetic practice behind them. In case of a conflictive situation on issues among the Ṣaḥābah, he would opt for one of them after weighing their views. He would make sure that his *rā*'iy (opinion) should not be different from the cumulative practice of the Ṣaḥābah, for it carried the possibility of an unintentional violation of the Sunnah. He did of course use qiyās to find out which say of the Ṣaḥābah was close to the Sunnah. Ironically, he was accused in his lifetime of preferring qiyās over injunction, which he refuted often.

> "By Allah, he foisted a lie on me who said that I prefer qiyās over injunction (nass). How could qiyās (analogical reasoning) have validity in the presence of an injunction?"[3]

Caliph al-Manṣūr once wrote to him voicing the allegation against him of giving preference to qiyās over ḥadīth. He wrote back:

> "Amīr al-Mu'minīn, what has reached you is not true. I first act on the Book of Allah, followed by the Sunnah of Rasūl Allah (ṣal.lal.lahu 'alayhi wa sal.lam), followed by the decisions made by Abū Bakr, 'Umar, 'Uthmān and 'Ali (Allah be pleased with them), followed by the decisions of the rest of the Ṣaḥābah. However, where there is a disagreement among them, then I resort to qiyās."[4]

---

2 Al-Dhahabi, *Manāqib*, p. 21.

3 Abū al-Wahād ibn Aḥmad al-Sha'rāni, *Kitāb al-Mizān* (Egypt: al-Matba'h al-Azhariyah, 1925) third edition, vol. 1, p. 61.

4 Ibid, p. 62.

2. The right way to instituting caliphate

Imām Abū Ḥanīfah viewed forced occupation of the caliphal office and its subsequent validation through oath of allegiance under duress as a prohibitory act (Ḥarām). A genuine caliphate comes into being only when people qualified to give their opinion (ahl al-rā'iy) agree to its institution. He expressed this view at a time when mouthing it had a higher probability of losing one's head. Al-Manṣūr's hājib (chamberlain) Rabi' ibn Yūnus is on record to have said that the caliph called for Imām Mālik, Ibn abī Dhi'b, and Imām Abū Ḥanīfah and confronted them with the question: "What do you think of this government that Allah the Exalted has granted to me? Do you think I deserved it?"

Imām Mālik replied: "If you had not deserved it, Allah would not have given it to you."

> Ibn abī Dhi'b said:
> "Allah gives kingdom to anyone whom he likes. But the kingdom in the ākhirah (hereafter) is given to one who seeks it with Allah's beneficence. You will have His beneficence if you are obedient to Him; otherwise, your disobedience to Allah will distance His beneficence from you. The fact of the matter is that the caliphate is established by the confluence of the pious. He who forcibly occupies it, for him there is no taqwā (Allah-consciousness). ... You and your helpers are excluded from Allah's beneficence and are the deniers of truth. Now if you seek Allah's protection and through your good deeds strive to have His pleasure, then you will have this thing; otherwise, you are your own seeker."

Abū Ḥanīfah says when Ibn abi Dhi'b was giving his views, I and Imām Mālik grabbed our clothes for we thought he could be beheaded and our clothes might get stains from his spilled blood. Thereafter, al-Manṣūr turned towards Abū Ḥanīfah and asked for his views. He said:

> "He who seeks truth for salvation stays safe from Allah's rage. If you probe your conscience, you will know by yourself that you did not call us for Allah's sake but you wanted us to say something supportive of you so that the people may know about it. The fact of the matter is that you inducted yourself in the caliphal office in a situation that did not have behind it even a gathering of two individuals capable of giving formal legal opinion, while the caliphate comes into being as a consequence of the Muslims' confluence, with their consultation. Abū Bakr withheld making decisions for almost six months until he received the allegiance oath from the people of Yemen."

The conversation over the three left. Al-Manṣūr gave three sacks of dirham to Rabi' and asked him to go after them. If Mālik accepts dirham, give him the sack, he was told. But if Abū Ḥanīfah and Ibn abi Dhi'b accept the sacks, then chop their heads off.

Imām Mālik accepted the caliphal gift. When Rabi' arrived at Ibn abi Dhi'b's house, he refused to have it saying he did not consider this money even permissible for al-Manṣūr, how can he have it for himself. Abū Ḥanīfah's response was equally non-compromising. He would not touch it, he said, even if they had his head severed.[5]

3. The conditionalities for the caliphate

Until Abū Ḥanīfah's time, the essential qualifications of a caliph had not been discussed in details the way later scholars like al-Māwardi and Ibn Khaldūn spelled them out, for these were well-known and thus there was no need to give them a theoretic framework. For example, that a caliph has to be a Muslim, male, freed man, knowledgeable and of sound mind and body were by then well established. However, there were two aspects which were then current and called for a methodological clarification. One, whether an oppressor and a violator of the Sharī'ah could be a rightful caliph?

5 Al-Kardari, *Manāqib...*, vol. 2, pp. 15-16. In this report from al-Kardari, I am unable to empathize with his report that Abū Bakr withheld making decision for about six month until the *bai'ah* from the people of Yemen came.

Two, if it was essential for one's candidature for the caliphal office to be a Qurayshite?

3.1. The leadership of the oppressor and moral violator

There are two aspects to Imām's opinion on the subject. First, one has to look into the then prevailing environmental context. Extreme posturing on two festering strains of thought in general tore Iraq in particular and the Islamic world in general. On the one side, it said that the leadership of the oppressor and the morally corrupt was illegitimate and that nothing done under its stamp could be beneficial for the Muslim Ummah. On the other hand, it said that once an oppressor and a morally corrupt person obtained power, his imāmah and caliphate become de jure. Abū Ḥanīfah presented a balanced view between the two extremes.

> In *al-Fiqh al-Akbar*, he says:
> "Making Ṣalāh after any believer pious or impious is valid."[6]
>
> While explaining the Ḥanafiyyah position, al-Tahāwi says: "And Ḥajj and Jihād will continue under the rulers of the Muslim Ummah until the Judgment Day, their being good or bad notwithstanding. Nothing can invalidate or interrupt these worships – Ḥajj and Jihād."[7]

For Imām Abū Ḥanīfah, however, 'adalah (justice) was essential to the caliphate. No person with a tyrannical bent of mind and morally corrupt can become caliph or a qāḍī or jurist or a state functionary.

If he becomes one, his imāmah will be bāṭil (invalid) and people are not bound to obey him. Nevertheless, if after having secured imāmah by force, Muslims continue to live by the Sharī'ah in their collective existence, his governance will have legal validity and whatever decisions his appointed judges will make they will have a binding effect. The famous Ḥanafī scholar Abū Bakr al-Jassās in his

6 Al-Qāri, *Sharḥ,* p. 91.
7 Ibn abi al-'Izz, *Sharḥ,* p. 322.

Aḥkām al-Qur'ān has dealt with this aspect of the problem at length. He says:

> "It is not justified for an oppressor to be a prophet or his deputy or a qāḍī. Nor is it justified for an oppressor to be a state official, whose edict in matters of religion by virtue of his situation has a binding effect on the people, for example, a muftī or a witness or someone who narrates a ḥadīth from the Prophet. The verse *lā yanālu 'ahadi al-zālimīn*[8] suggests this aspect that people whose saying in matters of religion count, they must be pious and just. ... This verse proves that the imāmah of a morally corrupt is invalid (bāṭil) – he cannot be the caliph. And if a person imposes himself (on the people) despite the fact that he is corrupt, his obedience is not binding on them. A similar statement comes from the Prophet that in violation of Allah's command, there is no obedience. This verse also alludes to this aspect that no corrupt individual can be an office holder (a judge or a magistrate). And if he becomes one, his decrees will have no sanctity to be complied with. Nor can his testimony be acceptable, or his narration from the Prophet be counted. Nor will his edict, if he is a muftī, have any binding force."[9]

Explaining it further, al-Jassās says that this constitutes Abū Ḥanīfah's position on the subject. He discounts the allegation that Abū Ḥanīfah justified the imāmah of the corrupt.

Some people conjecture that Abū Ḥanīfah justified the imāmah and caliphate of a morally corrupt person. ... If this is not an intentional lie foisted on him, then it is a gross misimpression about him.

For Abū Ḥanīfah says and other Iraqi jurists, whose opinion matter, also hold the same view that if the qāḍī is just then even when he is appointed by an unjust ruler, his court rulings will become

8 "My promise is not for the violators" *al-Baqarah*: 124.

9 Al-Jassās, *Aḥkām,* vol. 1, p. 80.

operative. [This equally applies to] the prayers. If people perform prayer after these unjust rulers, it will still be valid, notwithstanding their moral corruption. This stand (on the issue) is perfectly sound. But any rationale developed thereof that Abū Ḥanīfah considered a morally corrupt individual as qualified to have imāmah will be wrong.[10] Both Imām al-Dhahabi and al-Muwaffaq al-Makki cite Abū Ḥanīfah on this point:

> "An imām who misuses public money (fay) or while issuing the command violates the dictates of justice, his imāmah will be bāṭil and his edict invalid."[11]

From these excerpts, it becomes evident that contrary to Khawārij and Muʿtazilah, Abū Ḥanīfah cognized the difference between de jure and de facto aspects of the problem. According to the Khawārij and Muʿtazilah, if an imām was not just and pious, then the affairs of the whole Muslim society and state go awry – neither Ḥajj could be performed nor would the Friday and other congregational Prayers be valid, nor would the courts or other social and political institutions function. Abū Ḥanīfah rectifies their error by saying that if the rightful (de jure) imām is not available, then even under the de facto ruler who himself is unjust and morally corrupt, the system as well as the Muslims' collective life will continue.

As opposed to extremism of the Khawārij and Muʿtazilah, the other extreme, as represented by the Murjiah and some jurists of the mainstream ahl al-Sunnah held that the imāmah of a morally corrupt is as good as that of a rightful ruler confusing the separation between de facto and de jure governance. Abū Ḥanīfah tried to rectify this extremism as well, for if he had not, Muslims would have accepted any bad governance perpetuated by unjust, morally corrupt rulers without even bothering to change it or be worried about its nature and consequence. Abū Ḥanīfah condemned this kind of thought and declared the imāmah of such a people as false.

---

10 Ibid, vol. 1, p. 80-81, al-Sarakhsi in his *al-Mabsūt* has stated the same view of Imām Abū Ḥanīfah. See vol. 10, p. 130.

11 Al-Dhahabi, *Manāqib,* p. 17; al-Makki, *Manāqib*, vol. 2, p. 100.

3.2. The conditionality of the caliph being the Qurayshite

Whether the caliph should necessarily be a Qurayshite was yet another issue that plagued the sociopolitical scene. Imām Abū Ḥanīfah favoured the Qurayshite entitlement to the caliphate[12] not because he thought it was a Shar'ī position but because he cognized the then prevailing ground reality. And he is not a loner in his view. In fact, the whole ahl al-Sunnah agrees on this point.[13] Ibn Khaldūn has expounded the issue with the same dexterity that he is known for. To him, the real power behind the Islamic state was the Arabs, and if they could agree to something, it was the Qurayshi-based caliphate. Any other entrant to this office would have caused schism and conflict, endangering the very institution and the system that sustained it.[14] The Prophet ('alayhi as-salām) knew its perils and that is why he instructed the Muslim people to have imām from the Quraysh.[15] Had it been grounded in the Sharī'ah and not expediency, 'Umar would not have expressed his deathbed desire to have named Sālim as his successor, freed slave of Huzayfah who had died by then.[16]

In fact, the Prophet while advising Muslims to keep the caliphate within the Quraysh had clearly said that this office would stay with them as long as they had certain specific qualities in them.[17] Obviously, one can easily conclude from this that in the absence of those specified qualities, the caliphate could go to others as well. This is the crux of the difference between Abū Ḥanīfah and ahl al-Sunnah and the Khawārij and Mu'tāzilah, who insisted on giving the caliphate to a non-Qurayshi. Rather, they thought that it could be better to give the caliphate to a non-Qurayshi. In their eyes, the real importance was of democracy, though it might have led to anarchy. On the contrary, ahl al-Sunnah wa al-Jamā'ah sought stability of the state in the participatory system of the caliphate.

---

12 Al-Mas'ūdi, *Murūj,* vol. 2, p. 192.

13 Al-Shahrastāni, *Kitāb al-Milal*, vol. 1, p. 106, 'Abd al Qāhir Baghdādi, a*l-Farqu*, p. 340.

14 Ibn Khaldūn, *al-Muqaddimah*, pp. 195-196.

15 Ibn Hajar, *Fatḥ,* vol. 13, pp. 13, pp. 93, 96-97, Ibn Ḥanbal, *al-Musnad,* vol. 3, pp. 129, 183, also vol. 4, p. 421; Abu Dā'ūd, *al-Musnad,* ḥadīth 926, 2133.

16 Al-Ṭabari, *Tārikh,* vol. 3, p. 192.

17 Ibn Hajar, *Fatḥ,* vol. 13, p. 95.

4. Bayt al-Māl

Among wrongs committed by the monarchial absolutism of his time, he was highly critical of their unbridled spending and their appropriation of the people's properties. To him, persecutory decrees and usurpation of the public treasury were enough to disqualify the imām and his imamate as we have stated elsewhere citing al-Dhahabi.

Abū Ḥanīfah also decried the caliph's acceptance of foreign gifts as his personal possession. He suggested their consignment to the public treasury, for it was because of his office as the caliph of the Muslim Ummah and the international status of respect thus acquired due to the collective power of the Muslim people that he received gifts. Nobody would have sent him gifts in his status of a commoner.[18] Abū Ḥanīfah was also critical of non-justifiable spending and endowments to the favourites. This accounts for his refusal to accept caliphal gifts.

When he was having conflict with the caliph al-Manṣūr, the latter bitterly asked him why he had refused to accept his gifts.

Abū Ḥanīfah's response was forthwith: "Amīr al-Mu'minīn, when did you give me something from your personal holding that I refused to accept it. If you had given me from your personal account, I would have certainly accepted it. [On the contrary], you doled out the Muslim money to me from the treasury on which I do not have a claim. I neither fight in [the people's] defence to qualify for a soldier's share nor am I from among their children to have a child's share nor am I from among the beggars to have a beggar's share."[19]

Again when al-Manṣūr got him lashed thirty times for his refusal to accept the office of the high qāḍī and in consequence his body was bloodied, the caliph's uncle Abdul-Ṣamad ibn 'Ali was greatly disturbed. Reprimanding al-Manṣūr, he said: "What have you done? You have drawn over your head 100,000 swords. He is the jurist of Iraq nay of the entire people of the East."

---

18 Aḥmad ibn al-Ṭayyib al-Sarakhsi, *Sharḥ al-Siyar al-Kabīr* (Egypt: Matb'ah Shirkatah Masahamah Misriyah, 1957) vol. 1, p. 98.

19 Al-Makki, *Manāqib,* vol. 1, p. 215.

Realizing his mistake, al-Manṣūr sent him the compensatory amount of 30,000 dirham, 1,000 dirham for each lash. But Abū Ḥanīfah refused to take the compensatory amount. Al-Manṣūr felt bad about it but other than suggesting that he should accept the amount and dispose it off in charity, he could do nothing. Abū Ḥanīfah stuck to his grove and nonchalantly said: "Does he have anything rightful in his possession?"[20]

When confined to his deathbed, he instructed his family not to bury him in that part of Baghdād which al-Manṣūr wrongfully appropriated to build the city. When al-Manṣūr heard about his will, he raged: "Ah Abū Ḥanīfah! Who can save me from your hold in life and death?"[21]

5. Separation of judiciary from the administration

About judiciary, he held the view that in dispensing justice it should not only be free from administrative interference and pressure but should have also the power to interdict even the caliph on violating people's rights. In his last days when Abū Ḥanīfah had the feeling that the government would not spare his life, he gathered his disciples around and spoke, among others, on the human rights issues.

> "Should the caliph involve himself in a crime that violates human rights then the next in stature to the caliph – the chief qādī – must enforce the edict on him."[22]

His refusal to accept office in the governmental hierarchy, during the Umayyad and 'Abbasid periods, especially in the judiciary, was primarily because he saw the court's lack of writ on the caliph and his functionaries. He also feared that they might use him as an instrument of oppression and forced to make wrong decision effectuated by the caliph and his family.

---

20 Ibid, pp. 215-216.
21 Ibid, vol. 2, p. 180.
22 Al-Makki, *Manāqib*, vol. 2, p. 100.

He was first forced to accept office in the Umayyad's reign by the Iraqi governor Yazīd ibn 'Umar ibn Hubayrah. These were the turbulent times of the 130 A.H. The Umayyads were fast losing their popularity with the masses and their discontent was finding expression in an underground movement determined to overthrow the Umayyad setup. Ibn Hubayrah wanted to refurbish the waning Umayyad's image by installing in public offices the big names of law and jurisprudence like Ibn abī Laylā, Dā'ūd ibn abī al-Hind, and ibn Shuburmah. To meet this end, he also offered Abū Ḥanīfah the pivotal role in the administration with absolute powers to oversee any governmental decree issued by the governor or money dispensed from the public treasury. The Imām as usual declined the offer. Ibn Hubayrah locked him up in state penitentiary and threatened to lash him. The other fuqahā' pleaded with Abū Ḥanīfah to follow their footstep by accepting the job offer and avoid calamity to his person. His answer was true to his character:

> "Even if he asks me to count for him the doors of the Wastt masjid, I will not do it. He desires that he will write death for someone and I should stamp it. By Allah, I will not join him in this responsibility."

Ibn Hubaryah offered him some other jobs as well but he refused to accept them. Eventually he asked him to serve as Kūfah's qāḍī swearing to lash him if he declined. But if Ibn Hubayrah was insistent, Abū Ḥanīfah was adamant. His response was provocative. "Getting lashed at his hand," he said, "was far easier than punishment in the life hereafter." Then swearing back, he said: "By Allah, I will never accept (his job offer). He may kill me."

Ibn Hubayrah got him lashed twenty or thirty times. Some reports say he continued to lash him ten times a day for ten to eleven days. But Abū Ḥanīfah did not budge an inch from his principled stand. Eventually someone told Ibn Hubayrah that Abū Ḥanīfah might die. Angered, he exclaimed in desperation if someone could advise Abū Ḥanīfah to ask for time to reconsider the matter. When informed of Ibn Hubayrah's suggestion, he said he should be allowed to consult his friends. Released, he went straight to Makkah and refused to return to Kūfah until the Umayyad's fall from power.[23] In the 'Abbasid era, al-Manṣūr was favourably inclined to induct him in the chief qāḍī office. But it did not materialize. When al-Nafs al-Zakiyyah and his brother Ibrāhīm rose against al-Manṣūr, he supported them openly which turned the latter against him. In al-Dhahabi's word, al-Manṣūr was so angry with him that he burned in rage without fire.[24] What compounded his problem was Abū Ḥanīfah's popularity with the masses. He knew the kind of hate the Umayyads invited against themselves by killing Ḥusayn and how easily their rule was terminated. He therefore planned to bind him with chains of gold and use him for his ends rather than kill him. His repeated offers for the highest judicial office of the state to Abū Ḥanīfah aimed at neutralizing him. But he dodged him.[25] When al-Manṣūr increased his pressure, he gave his reasons for declining the former's offer. In one of his sittings with him, he explained his stand in a very soft way:

> "For the judicial office you need someone strong enough to enforce laws on you, your princes and the military commanders. I do not find this strength in me. When you call me to come [your scare overwhelms me] and I regain myself only when I return home safely." [26]

On another occasion, they had a harsh exchange of words. Addressing the caliph, he said:

> "By Allah even if I accept this office with consent, I will not qualify to come up to your expectations not to talk of being forced to accept it. If I made a verdict against you and you threatened to drown me in the River Euphrates or to alter the given decision, I will prefer to drown myself rather than change the verdict. Besides, you have a large number of courtiers. They

---

23 Ibid, pp. 21, 24; Ibn Khallikān, *Wafayāt,* vol. 5, p. 41; Ibn 'Abd al-Barr, *al-Intiqā',* p. 171.

24 Al-Dhahabi, *Manāqib*, p. 30.

25 Al-Makki, *Manāqib,* vol. 2, pp. 72, 173, 178.

26 Ibid, vol. 1, p. 215.

need a qāḍī who take care of their interests as well."[27]

His open refusal convinced al-Manṣūr that he was not the kind who could have been lured into the golden cage. This time he resolved to brute force. He subjected him to lashing along with incarceration and denial of food. Later, he confined him to a house where he died. Some say he died a natural death others say he was poisoned.[28]

6. The right to free expression

Abū Ḥanīfah gave equal importance to free expression in an Islamic state for which the Qur'ān and the Sunnah use the expression of "*amr bil ma'rūf wa nahī 'an al-munkar*." Mere right to free expression could create problems for a society; it could also be contrary to morality, honesty and even humanity, which no law tolerates. But by restricting it to forbidding evil and spreading goodness, Islam declares it not only as the right way to express one's self but also an obligation.

Abū Ḥanīfah strongly espoused it for he had witnessed its seizure by the rulers of his times. Its continual denial confused people even about its obligatory nature. On the one hand, the Murjiah were emboldening people to sin, the Hashviyah believed that *amr bil ma'rūf wa nahī 'an al-munkar* against the government was a fitnah (mischief), while the Umayyad and 'Abbasid governments crushed the Muslim spirit to criticize the wrongdoings of the high ups and their usurpation of the Sharī'ah. Abū Ḥanīfah through his word and practice tried hard to resuscitate the Ummah in these aspects. Al-Jassās says that to the famous Khurāsāni jurist Ibrāhīm al-Sā'igh's inquiry, Abū Ḥanīfah said *amr bi al- ma'rūf* was an obligation that must be discharged, for the Prophet ('alayhi as-salām), as narrated by Ibn 'Abbās, has said "the best of the shuhadā' (martyrs) was Ḥamzah ibn 'Abdul-Muṭṭalib and second the person, who would rise up before a tyrannical ruler to stop him from doing wrong and in consequence killed."

27 Ibid, vol. 2, pp. 170; al-Baghdādi, *Tārikh,* vol. 13, p. 320.

28 Ibid, vol. 2, pp. 173-174, 182; Ibn Khallikān, *Wafayāt*, vol. 5, p. 46; al-Yāfi'i, *Mirāt al-Jinān*, p. 310.

So greatly Abū Ḥanīfah's word affected Ibrāhīm that on his return to Khurāsān, he tried to restrain Abū Muslim Khurāsāni (d. 136 A.H./763 C.E.) from savagery and in result, the latter got him killed.[29]

When Ibrāhīm ibn 'Abdullah, Nafs Zakiyyah's brother, rose in revolt (145 A.H./763 C.E.) against the 'Abbasid's usurpation of power, Abū Ḥanīfah openly supported him, even though al-Manṣūr was in Kūfah at that time. The city was cordoned off by the security forces because of Ibrāhīm's advance towards the city.

Abū Ḥanīfah's famous student Zufar ibn al-Huzayl says that the former was actively engaged in opposing al-Manṣūr. Fearful of their lives, Zufar approached him: "You will not stop unless we all have noose around our necks."[30]

In 148 A.H., the people of Mūṣal rose for the second time in revolt against the 'Abbasids. In the previous aborted rebellion, al-Manṣūr had spared their lives and properties on condition that they would avoid becoming part of any mischief against the state, and that should they fail to abide by it, they would liable themselves to be killed and their properties confiscated by him. Now that they revolted, al-Manṣūr called for a meeting of the eminent jurists, including Abū Ḥanīfah, and asked their opinion on the issue of the Mūṣal people violating their pledge to the caliph and whether it gave him the right to punish them making their lives and properties permissible for him.

Majority of the fuqahā' were of the opinion that since the people had a contract with al-Manṣūr he could kill them and appropriate their properties. Nevertheless, if he forgave them it would be befitting his exalted status.

During the conversation, Abū Ḥanīfah remained quiet. Taking note of his silence, al-Manṣūr turned towards him:

"Yā Sheikh, what is your say in this matter?"

"The people of Mūṣal made those things permissible for you

29 Al-Jassās, *Aḥkām,* al-Makki, *Manāqib,* vol. 1, p.81.

30 Al-Khatīb, *Tārikh,* vol. 13, p. 330; al-Makki, *Manāqib,* vol. 2, p. 171.

which were not theirs (that is their blood) and you made them to accept a condition that you had no right to force down their throats. Tell me, if a woman offers herself to someone without matrimony, would she become permissible (Ḥalāl) for that person? If a person tells someone to kill him, would his killing become permissible for that person?" He replied.

"No," al-Manṣūr said.

"Then, hold your hand from killing the people of Mūṣal. Their blood is not allowed to you!"

This upset al-Manṣūr so much that he dispersed the meeting. Then he talked to Abū Ḥanīfah in private. "What you said is true. But you should not issue verdicts that might compromise your imām's authority and encourage the rebels."[31]

He also used his right to expression against judicial decisions that he thought involved misapplication of law or violation of a procedure. To him, respect for the courts did not mean to let them make wrong decisions. For his criticism of the courts' wrong rulings, he was debarred once from expressing his opinion on legal matters.[32]

In his defence of free expression, he would go to the extent of allowing it even against a legitimate imamate and its just rule. He thought that to criticize it, to curse the ruler or to express one's intent even to kill him did not call for punishment unless he rises in arms against him or creates problems of law and order in the land. He builds his rationale on the incident related to caliph 'Ali when they apprehended five people on the charge of openly abusing him in Kūfah. One among them even threatened to kill Amīr al-Mū'minīn. 'Ali ordered their release. They told him that one of them declared to kill him.

"Should I get him killed because he says so?"

They were abusing him, they said.

"If you want you can also abuse them (in return)," said he.

31 Ibn al-Athīr, *al-Kāmil,* vol. 5, p. 25; al-Kardari, *Manāqib,* vol. 2, p. 17; al-Sarakhsi, *Kitāb,* vol. 10, p. 129.

32 Al-Kardari, *Manāqib,* vol. 1, pp. 160, 166; Ibn 'Abd al-Barr, *al-Intiqā',* p. 125, 153; al-Baghdādi, *Tarikh...,* vol. 13, p. 351.

Abū Ḥanīfah also derived his rationale from 'Ali's declaration against the Khawārij. "We will not stop you from coming to the masjid. Nor will we deprive you of your share in the conquered wealth unless you raise arms against us."[33]

7. Revolt against a tyrant government

An issue that plagued the minds in that era related to armed rebellion against a morally corrupt and tyrant ruler: whether it would be justified to rise against him? The mainstream Muslims ahl al-Sunnah themselves differed on the matter. A large chunk of alh al-Ḥadīth believed that only verbal condemnation of oppression should be enough but not rebellion, even though the ruling regime indulges in killing without justification, violates people's rights, and openly commits immorality.[34]

Imām Abū Ḥanīfah not only declared an oppressive regime as bātil (invalid) but also liable to be opposed and risen against provided such an effort could lead to the induction of a just and morally upright individual. Abū Bakr al-Jassās explains Abū Ḥanīfah's position on the issue:

> "His school of thought is known for its stand on armed uprising against the tyrants and victimizers. That is why al-Auzā'i had said we bore with everything Abū Ḥanīfah said until he came out with the sword (that is, he got convinced about armed uprising against the tyrants) and this was intolerable for us.
> Abū Ḥanīfah used to say that to exhort for goodness and forbid evil should be done through mouth in the beginning and later wājib (compulsory) with sword, if the regime showed no inclination to change itself."[35]

At another place, al-Jassās cites Abū Ḥanīfah on the authority of 'Abdullah ibn Mubārak. This was the time marked by Abū Muslim al-Khurāsāni's excesses against people. The Khurāsāni jurist Ibrāhīm al-Sā'igh came to see the Imām and talked with him on the subject

33 Al-Sarakhsi, *Kitāb,* vol. 10, p. 125.
34 Al-Asha'rī, *Maqālāt,* vol. 2, p. 125.
35 Al-Jassās *Aḥkām,* vol. 1, p. 81.

of *amr bi al-ma'rūf.* The Imām himself narrated it later to 'Abd Allah ibn Mubārak:

> "When we agreed that *amr bi a-ma'rūf wa nahī 'an al-munkar* obligatory, Ibrāhīm suddenly said 'extend your hand so that I pledge my support to you.' On hearing it, the world turned dark before me. (Ibn Mubārak says I asked him why?) He said he had invited me towards one of Allah's Ḥaqq (right) and I refused to accept it. At the end, I said if a single person stood for the (discharge of) obligation, they will kill him and nothing good will come out of it. However, if he gets support from the pious people along with a leader who could be trusted in upholding the word of Allah, then there is no excuse in not doing it.
>
> Afterward whenever Ibrāhīm came to me, he would insist on my taking up the challenge like the harsh moneylender. I would tell him a single person could not accomplish this task. Even prophets did not have the strength to do it unless charged to this task by the heavens. This obligation is unlike ordinary obligatories, which even a single individual can discharge. But by its nature, this task entailed losing one's life. I fear he would get himself killed by a fiat. And when killed, his death would discourage others as well from pursuing this course."[36]

7.1. Imām's conduct in the matter of uprising

For sure, the cited conversation between Abū Ḥanīfah and Ibrāhīm al-Sā'igh exposes the Imām's stand on this crucial issue. Nevertheless, we will fail to understand his whole position unless we know the way he conduced himself during the uprisings of his time.

7.2. Zayd ibn 'Ali's uprising

The first uprising was instigated by Zayd ibn 'Ali, whom the Shi'i sect Zaydiyah considers as their originator. A great scholar, a jurist and a pious of his time, he was the grandson of Ḥusayn ibn 'Ali ibn abī Ṭālib and the brother of Imām al-Bāqir. Even Abū Ḥanīfah benefited

36 Ibid, vol. 2, p. 39.

from Zayd's scholarship. In 120 A.H. (738 C.E.) when Hishām ibn 'Abd al-Mālik ousted Khālid ibn 'Abdullah al-Qasri from the governorship of Iraq, he summoned Zayd from Madīnah to witness against him. His visit stirred Kūfah for it was after a long time that an eminent member of the 'Ali clan had come to the city, the centre of 'Ali's followers. His presence electrified the crowd. Fed up with the Umayyad's draconian policies, they needed someone like him – pious, scholar and a jurist, scion of the 'Alawī family. They assured Zayd that 100,000 people in Kūfah would stand by him should he decide to lead them against the Umayyads. What gave credence to their enthusiasm was the personal pledge given to him by 15,000 people, asking him to enter their names in his register. Meanwhile, when preparations for the uprising were underway in secret, the Umayyad governor got wind of it. To counteract the government move, Zayd made a hasty uprising call in 122 A.H. (740 C.E.), before its scheduled time. But when the battle line was drawn, the Kūfan Shi'is deserted him with only 218 peoples standing beside him. During the battle, an arrow struck him and lost his life.[37]

In Zayd's uprising, Abū Ḥanīfah's sympathies were with him. He not only financially assisted him but asked people to join his effort.[38]

He likened his uprising to the Prophet Muḥammad's battle with the nonbelievers at Badr.[39] By which he meant that as the Prophet ('alayhi as-salām) was rightly on truth so was Zayd. But when Zayd's envoy came to him for support, he said: "If I had known that people will not desert him and will stand by him with conviction, I would have joined him and struggled along with him for he is the true imām. But I fear that these people would betray him as they betrayed his grandfather (Ḥusayn). I would though help him with money."[40]

This stand is consistent with his theoretical formulation against the oppressive regimes. He knew well the psychology of

37 Al-Ṭabari, *Tārikh,* vol. 5, pp. 482-505.
38 Al-Jassās, *Aḥkām*, vol. 1, p. 8.
39 Al-Makki, *Manāqib,* vol. 1, p. 260.
40 Ibid, vol. 1, p. 260.

the Shi'is in Kūfah. He was also familiar with their poor history of waywardness and betrayal since the time of caliph 'Ali. Dā'ūd ibn 'Ali (the grandson of 'Abdullah ibn 'Abbās) also had a negative view of the Kūfans and tried to persuade Zayd not to follow the collision course against the Umayyads.[41]

Further, Abū Ḥanīfah knew that the anti-Umayyad movement remained confined to Kūfah and had no following in other parts of the empire lending strength to Zayd's effort. Another reason that accounts for his not joining Zayd's uprising was his relatively unknown status among the masses at that time, which would not have played a decisive role in tilting the scale for Zayd. Until 120 A. H., Ḥammād had the exclusive leadership of the school of ahl al-rāi'y, and Abū Ḥanīfah was his student. By the time Zayd decided to rally support against the Umayyad, his takeover of this school was hardly a year and a half old. He had yet to be exalted to the rank of "the jurist of the East." Nor he had the influence he earned later for himself.

7.3. Al-Nafs al-Zakiyyah's uprising

The second uprising was led by Muḥammad ibn 'Abdullah (al-Nafs al-Zakiyyah) and his brother Ibrāhīm ibn 'Abdullah in 145 A.H. (763 C.E.). They came from the family of Ḥasan ibn 'Ali. By then Abū Ḥanīfah was in the prime of his influence.

The two brothers spearheaded the covert movement. Even al-Manṣūr gave his pledge of loyalty to al-Nafs al-Zakiyyah.[42] The movement went underground when the 'Abbasid came into power and continued spreading their message in Khurāsān, al-Jazīra, Ray, Tabaristān, Yemen and North Africa. Nafs Zakiyyah himself stayed in al-Ḥijāz; his brother Ibrāhīm shifted to Baṣrah in Iraq. According to Ibn al-Athīr, in Kūfah alone they had 100,000 people ready to come out in their support.[43] Al-Manṣūr was already aware of their covert movement and was scared of its spread as the 'Abbasid movement ran

41 Ibid, pp. 155-156.
42 Ibid, pp. 155-156.
43 Ibn al-Athīr, *al-Kāmil*, vol. 5, p. 18.

parallel to it and succeeded in establishing the 'Abbasid rule. Aware of its organization and strength, al-Manṣūr was bent on crushing it.

When in the month of Rajab 145 A.H., al-Nafs al-Zakiyyah rose in revolt from Madīnah, al-Manṣūr left the Baghdād construction site and reached Kūfah. Gripped by fear, he was not sure if the 'Abbasid rule would continue.

For him in the extirpation of the opposition movement was the survival of his rule. Many a time he would exclaim in desperation "By Allah! I do not know what to do?" News of the uprising were coming from Baṣrah, Persia, Ahwāz, Madā'in and Sawād. And it appeared as if the rebels' hands would reach him soon. For almost two months, he wore the same clothes and would not have a wink of sleep sitting on the prayer rug, asking for forgiveness and help from Allah.[44] He kept his horses ready for escape from Kūfah should the situation call for it.[45]

Abū Ḥanīfah's response to the uprising this time was different. Al-Manṣūr used to be in Kūfah in those days with curfew clamped all over the city, but it did not scare Abū Ḥanīfah into indifference. Instead, he openly supported the movement for restoring the caliphate. His disciples were apprehensive of the law agencies catching them for he instigated people to pledge their support to Ibrāhīm.[46]

He considered participation in the uprising as equal to fifty-to-seventy nonobligatory Ḥajj in its reward from Allah.[47] To a person named Abū Ishāq al-Fazāri he said his brother's support to Ibrāhīm was superior to his Jihād against the nonbelievers.[48] Abū Bakr al-Jassās, al-Muwaffaq al-Makki and Ibn al-Bazzāz al-Kardari, author of *Fatawā al-Bazzāziyah,* have recorded these statements of Abū Ḥanīfah. According to these juristic opinions, hauling up a Muslim

---

44 Al-Ṭabari, *Tarikh,* vol. 6, pp. 155-263.
45 Al-Yāfi'i, *Mirāt al-Jinān,* vol. 1, p. 299.
46 Al-Kardari, *Manāqib,* vol. 2, p. 72; al-Makki, *Manāqib,* vol. 2, p. 84.
47 Al-Kardari, *Manāqib*, vol. 2, p. 71; al-Makki, *Manāqib*, vol. 2, p. 83.
48 Al-Jassās, *Aḥkām,* vol. 1, p. 81.

society from an Islamically derailed governance is far superior to fighting the nonbelievers outside.

The most dangerous thing he did was to stop al-Manṣūr's military chief and his confident Ḥasan ibn Qahtubah from fighting Nafs Zakiyyah and Ibrāhīm. Ḥasan's father Qahtubah was a brilliant military-man who together with Abū Muslim's political acumen succeeded in laying down the 'Abbasid reign. He replaced his father after his death. Among his generals, al-Manṣūr had great trust in him. To al-Manṣūr's misfortune, he fell to Abū Ḥanīfah's scholarship and personal piety.

Once Ḥasan opened up to Abū Ḥanīfah saying that in view of his sins committed during his generalship under al-Manṣūr, was there still a chance for his forgiveness from Allah? The Imām gave him hope: "If you assure Allah that you really regretted your past misdeeds and that in the future if asked to kill an innocent Muslim, you will die instead and that you pledge to Allah you will not regress to your past misdeeds, then it will be your atonement."

Ḥasan pledged to the Imām that he would abide by it. Soon after when Nafs Zakiyyah and Ibrāhīm rose against the 'Abbasid, al-Manṣūr asked Ḥasan to war against them. He came to Imām Abū Ḥanīfah and told him about the new moving order.

Said the Imām, "The hour has come to show you have really repented. If you stayed put to your pledge, your repentance would stay as well. Otherwise, you will be held accountable before Allah for your past and what you will do now ..."

Ḥasan renewed his pledge and declared before the Imām that even if they killed him, he would not go on this campaign.

Thus, when he faced al-Manṣūr, he told him bluntly. "Amīr al-Mū'minīn, I will not go for this campaign. If what I did so far in your obedience was owing to Allah's will, then it is enough for me and if it was in violation of Allah's will, I will not go beyond it and indulge in more sins."

Enraged, al-Manṣūr ordered his arrest. Faced with the serious situation, Ḥasan's brother Ḥamīd interjected. "Since the last year his ways have been unusual. It appears his mind has gone hay wire, I will myself go on this campaign."

Later al-Manṣūr checked with his trusted circles of people to find out whom did Hasan go for advice. They told him he often went to Abū Ḥanīfah.[49]

Abū Ḥanīfah's conduct was consistent with his well-formulated thesis that if there were probabilities of a successful change towards the restoration of the caliphate, then an uprising against an oppressive regime was not only justified but also a compulsion (wājib). Interestingly enough, Abū Ḥanīfah was not a loner in his view. Imām Mālik had a similar view. Asked how could they join al-Nafs al-Zakiyyah's uprising when they have already pledged their loyalties to al-Manṣūr, Mālik's response was that their pledge to al-Manṣūr was extracted by force and thus any pledge by force or a divorce (ṭalāq) under duress is not valid (bāṭil).[50] It was because of his edict that a large number of people became part of Nafs Zakiyyah's effort to dislodge al-Manṣūr. Later, he had to pay for it. The 'Abbasid governor Ja'far ibn Sulaymān got him whipped, dislocating one of his arms from his shoulder.[51]

---

49 Al-Kardari, *Manāqib,* vol. 2, p. 22.

50 A person has claimed that 'Ali was not superior to other Ṣaḥābah and thus he did not have the kind of exaltedness that would have won him the people's approval for the Khilāfah. Such as assertion is out of place because the best deciders for the caliphal issue were the people who belonged to that era and not someone today. The people then made their choice. When 'Umar fell to the assassin's dagger, the shūrā asked 'Abdul-Raḥmān ibn 'Auf to pulse the people's choice for the caliphal office. Ibn Kathīr writes: 'Abdul-Raḥmān ibn 'Auf set out to seek people's opinion secretly and openly, severely and collectively of the chiefs and the influentials. He even asked the opinion of the veiled women, the students in the schools, and the outsiders coming to Madīnah. For three days and nights, he kept himself engaged in the task. ... Then he talked to 'Ali and 'Uthmān: I have solicited people's opinion about you. I did not find a person who considered anyone equal to you. ... Then, 'Abdul-Raḥmān ibn 'Auf spoke (in the prophet's masjid): "Brothers! I have sought your opinion both secretly and openly. I did not find you to prefer anyone over these two. Nor did you endorse 'Ali or 'Uthmān." *Al-Bidāyah*, vol. 7, p. 146.

51 Al-Ṭabari, *Tārikh,* vol. 6, p. 190; Ibn Khallikān, *Wafayāt* vol. 3, p. 285; Ibn Kathīr, *al-Bidāyah* , vol. 10, p. 84, Ibn Khaldūn, *al-Muqaddimah,* vol. 3, p. 191.

8. Abū Ḥanīfah is not unique in his view

Here it would be wrong to think that on the uprising issue Abū Ḥanīfah's views were unique among ahl al-Sunnah. The fact of the matter is that in the first Hijrah prominent elders held the same view that Abū Ḥanīfah expressed later through his words and deeds. In his post-allegiance speech, Abū Bakr said:

> "Obey me as long as I obey Allah and His Prophet. But if I disobey Allah and His Prophet, then you are not bound to follow me."[52]

> The second caliph 'Umar said:
> "He who gives his pledge to someone without consultation with the Muslims deceives himself as well as the one whom he gave his pledge and qualified his person to be killed."[53]

At the time of Ḥusayn's uprising against the established government of Yazīd a large number of the Prophet's companions were still alive and so were the whole group of the jurists belonging to the second generation. But we do not have on record of a single Ṣaḥābi or a tābi'i who described his uprising as Ḥarām.

Even those who tried to persuade Ḥusayn did it on grounds that the Kūfans were not reliable and that they might not come out in his support exposing him to serious consequences for his life. In other words, their opinion on the issue was similar to Abū Ḥanīfah's – that the uprising against an Islamically-derailed governance by itself

52 Ibn Hishām, *al-Sirah al-Nabawiyyah* (Egypt: Matb'ah Mustaphā al-Bābi, 1936) vol. 4, p. 311; Ibn Kathīr, *al-Bidāyah,* vol. 5, p. 248.

53 These are the words of al-Bukhārī's report (Kitāb al-Maharbiin, Bāb rajm al-hablabā min al-zinā'). In another report, 'Umar's words are that he who is given imārah without shūrā, he should not accept it for it is Ḥarām for him. See *Fatḥ al-Bari*, vol. 12, p. 125.
Imām Aḥmad has cited 'Umar's words that he who gives his allegiance oath (bai'ah) to someone without consultation with the Muslims his bai'ah will not be valid nor that of the person whom he gave his bai'ah. See Aḥmad's *al- Musnad*, vol. 1, ḥadīth 391.

was not wrong, though it would be pertinent to probe the matter from all aspects whether it would be possible to replace a distorted system with a pious one?

Imām Ḥusayn received a large mail from the Kūfans, which he misread as support to his cause. Swayed by their effusive emotions he thought he would be able to bring about a successful revolution. He left Madīnah in the face of opposition from well-wishing Ṣaḥābah, who tried to persuade him from going to Kūfah. Based on his father 'Ali and his brother Ḥasan's experiences with the Kūfans who betrayed them, their argument was that they were untrustworthy.

Thus, the difference between Ḥusayn and the Ṣaḥābah was of tactical nature and not of validity or invalidity of his desire to challenge the system.

Likewise, when during the oppressive reign of Ḥajjāj ibn Yūsuf, 'Abdul-Raḥmān ibn Ash'ath rebelled against the Umayyads, prominent fuqahā' (jurists) like Sa'īd ibn Jubayr, al-Sha'bi, Ibn abi Laylā and Abū al-Bakhtarī stood by him. Ibn Kathīr says a whole regiment of the qurrā' ('ulamā and fuqahā') was with him. Even those who lagged behind in supporting him did not question the validity of his uprising. The speeches made by such jurists before Ibn Ash'ath's army speak of their view. Ibn abi Laylā said:

> "O believers, he who witnesses oppression, sees people prompted to evil doing, and feels bad about it from his heart has acquitted himself and saved. And if he disapproves of it, he will be recompensed and his rank superior to the first one.
> But he who opposes such people by (the force of) his sword in order to elevate the word of Allah and to humiliate the word of the oppressors is the finder of the true path, his heart blazed by the light of conviction.
> So war against those who have violated the sanctity of Ḥalāl (allowed) and Ḥarām (disallowed) and

> innovated new ways in the Ummah, who are disregard truth (Ḥaqq) and give no respect to it, who follow tyranny (zulm) and do not consider it bad."
>
> Al-Sha'bi said:
> "Fight them and do not think that to fight them is a bad thing. By Allah, I do not know of another group on the face of this planet who is more tyrannical and unjust in its decision-making than these are. So let not complacency takes over you in the fight against them."
>
> Sa'id ibn Jubayr said:
> "Fight them for they are unjust in governance and rebellious in their attitudes towards religion; they humiliate the weak and waste their prayers."[54]

As against these fuqahā', those who refrained from giving support to Ibn Ash'ath did not consider the uprising as invalid but viewed it as ill-timed. Thus, when Ḥasan al-Baṣri was asked about the legitimacy of the rebellion, he said:

> By Allah! Allah did not impose Ḥajjāj on you without a reason. Rather, it is a punishment for you, which you should not oppose by sword but by patience, and implore forgiveness from Allah.[55]

This sums up the opinion of the first-century pious Muslims. Imām Abū Ḥanīfah grew up in this environment of righteous indignation and non-conformism with the ruling elite. The second opinion of avoiding armed rebellion if it had small chance to succeed, by the stance of the mainstream ahl al-Sunnah began inviting attention at the end of the second-century Hijrah. It started gaining ground not because it was based on some clear-cut injunctions that were hidden from the first-century elders or that Allah forbid they

---

54 Al-Ṭabari, *Tārikh,* vol. 5, p. 163.

55 Ibn Sa'd, *al-Ṭabaqāt,* vol. 7, p. 164; ibn Kathīr, *al-Bidāyah,* vol. 9, p. 135.

had adopted a stance contrary to the injunctions. In fact, they were two reasons for its becoming popular. First the power-crazed rulers had preempted all avenues to peaceful change, which convinced the practitioners of power to abandon it. Second, the consequences of the armed uprising without exception had not been pleasant: it inclined people to resignation.[56]

56 For an exposition of this issue, see my *Tafhimāt* (Lahore: Islamic Publications, 1996) vol. 3, pp. 300-320, and *Tafhim al-Qur'ān*, tafsīr Sūrah *al-Ḥujurāt*, footnote 17.

Chapter Nine

Imām Abū Yūsuf and his Work

Abū Ḥanīfah's self-imposed alienation from the centres of power caused tension between the Ḥanafiyyah and the 'Abbasids, which continued even after his death when his renowned disciple Zufar ibn al-Hudhayl (d.158 A.H./775 C.E.) spurned the 'Abbasid offer of the qāḍī position in the judicial hierarchy and then fearing possible retaliation went into hiding.[1] As a matching response, from al-Manṣūr to Hārūn al-Rashīd's early period, the 'Abbasid made sure to reduce the Ḥanafiyyah influence. Their adversarial relationship can be seen in the attitudes of al-Manṣūr and his successors who were inclined to plug the legal vacuum, created by the emergent new realities, by some other codified law. Both al-Manṣūr and al-Mahdī tried to launch Imām Mālik ibn Anas as a great jurist in their reigns.[2] In his 174 A.H. Ḥajj, Hārun al-Rashīd even expressed his desire to have Mālik's book *al-Muwattā'* as the law of the land.[3]

With developments like these, when everything was going against the Ḥanafiyyah school of thought, it threw up an exceptional man who by his legal acumen stamped out the legal anarchy of the 'Abbāsid empire, and gave a constitutional frame to the empire, making Ḥanafī jurisprudence the law of the land. This was the person of Abū Hanifah's great disciple – Imām Abū Yūsuf.

1. Life history

Born in 113 A.H. (731 C.E.) his real name was Ya'qūb. Though domiciled in Kūfah, he came from the Arab tribe of Bajilah and had a maternal link with the anṣār of Madīnah. After his early education,

---

1 Al-Kardari, *Manāqib,* vol. 2, p. 183; Tāsh Kibrizādah, *Miftāh al-Sa'ādah,* vol. 2, p. 114.

2 Ibn 'Abd al-Barr, *al-Intiqā'*, pp. 40-41.

3 Abu Nu'aym al-Isfahāni, *Hilyah al-Auliyā',* (Egypt: al-Matb'ah al-Sa'ādah, 1355 A.H.) vol. 6, p. 332; Kibrizādah, *Miftāh,* vol. 2, p. 87.

he opted for specialty in jurisprudence (fiqh) and joined the academic circle of 'Abdul-Raḥmān ibn abi-Laylā followed by Imām Abū Ḥanīfah's, which turned into a lifelong affiliation. His parents were extremely poor and had insufficient means to help him continue his education. When Abū Ḥanīfah came to know about his parents' poor financial status he not only sponsored Abū Yūsuf's education but also his family's needs. Abū Yūsuf himself says that he never had to ask for money from Imām Abū Ḥanīfah, who would periodically dish out the requisite amount of money to his family, taking away the worry load from his mind.[4]

From the beginning, Abū Ḥanīfah thought highly of his student. Thus, when Abū Yūsuf's father wanted to take him out of the school, the Imām stopped him, saying, "Abū Ishāq, this boy, if Allah willed, will become a great man."[5]

2. Academic excellence

Besides Abū Ḥanīfah, he acquired knowledge from some of the great men of learning of his time, obtaining from them excellence in ḥadīth, tafsīr, maghāzi, Arabic history, diction, literature and rational theology (kalām), especially in ḥadīth, which he knew well and committed to his memory. Scholars like Yaḥyā ibn Mu'īn, Aḥmad ibn Ḥanbal, and 'Ali ibn al-Madini rated him very high.[6] His contemporaries unanimously thought of him as peerless among Abū Ḥanīfah's students. Ṭalḥah ibn Muḥammad says he was the greatest among the jurists and none reached his calibre.[7] Dā'ūd ibn al-Rashīd says if Abū Ḥanīfah had produced only him as his student that would have sufficed for his pride.[8] Abū Ḥanīfah himself thought of him highly as a great scholar, who had acquired knowledge more than any body else.[9] Once he became seriously ill diminishing hope for his recovery. The Imām visited him and while coming out said: "If this young man died, he would leave behind no jurist (faqīh) greater than himself on this planet."[10]

---

4 Al-Makki, *Manāqib*, vol. 2, p. 212.
5 Ibid, p. 214.
6 Ibn Khallkān, *Wafayāt*, vol. 5, p. 422; Ibn 'Abd al-Barr, *al-Intiqa'*, p. 172.
7 Ibn Khallkān, *Wafayāt,* vol. 5, p. 424.
8 Al-Makki, *Manāqib,* vol. 2, p. 232.
9 Al-Kardari, *Manāqib,* vol. 2, p. 126.
10 Ibn Khallikān, *Wafayāt,* vol. 5, p. 424; al-Kardari, *Manāqib,* vol. 2, p. 126.

3. The compilation of the Ḥanafī fiqh

Like Imām Abū Ḥanīfah and in line with the Ḥanafī stance, he remained indifferent to power for almost sixteen years concentrating on the scholarly pursuits of his mentor. This showed itself in his effort to compile books topically on almost all aspects of the law that incorporated the decisions made by the legislative body (majlis) of Abū Ḥanīfah and his own.[11] When these books spread across the nation, they influenced not only academics in different sections of society but also the courts and official circles in the government hierarchy paving way for the Ḥanafī fiqh to prevail as there was no other legal corpus to have met the emergent needs of the 'Abbasid empire. Although Imām Mālik's *al-Mawattā'* soon made its appearance, it was neither comprehensive nor was its compilation systematic enough to have answered the needs of a sprawling state.[12] A spin off of Abū Yūsuf's work was that even before he could have saddled the government seat, the Ḥanafī fiqh had made its way into the people's mind, waiting for formal declaration to its being the law of the land.

4. Justice department

Perhaps Abū Yūsuf would have followed his mentor's isolation from the government if only his economic situation was not that strait. Abū Ḥanīfah's death deprived him of his financial support leaving him to his own wits. Soon he was penniless.

Pushed to adversity, he sold the roof beam of his wife's house to avert hunger. This enraged his mother-in-law, who barraged him with insults, forcing him to reconsider his attitudinal indifference to the government job. Forced thus in 166 A.H., he went to see the caliph al-Mahdī, who appointed him as qāḍī of the eastern Baghdād. He continued in this office even in al-Hādī's time. By the time Hārūn al-Rashīd came into power, the two had developed a relationship of

11 Ibn al-Nadīm, *al-Fihrist* (Egypt: al-Matb'ah al-Rahmāniyah, 1348 A. H.) Ibn al-Khallikān writes on the authority of Ṭalḥah ibn Muḥammad that Abū Yusūf was the first person who complied books on all primary aspect of *fiqh* according to the Ḥanafī school and thus spread Abu Ḥanīfah's thought across the Muslim world. See vol. 5, p. 424.

12 The compilation of the Mālikī school that could cater to the needs of an empire was later accomplished on the model of Imām Muḥammad's books.

trust and companionship, which slung him into the high seat of chief justice becoming its first occupant in the Muslim history.[13] It is of interest to note that the chief justice office not only related to law enforcement and its interpretation but also administrative in so far as he made appointment for the courts across the nation. In this sense, the ʿAbbasid chief justice was a far different entity than the present-day chief justice. He guided the state in its internal and external affairs, giving him a far greater stature than an ordinary chief justice had. He was more or less a minister for law.

Qāḍī Abū Yūsuf's elevation to this office formulated three important consequences for the development of the Hanafi law:

- One, he got a wider spread of influence giving him a chance to deal directly with the affairs of the greatest state of its time and thus apply the Ḥanafī law to real life situations, making it more functional as a system as compared to the limited circle of teaching and writing books.

- Two, since he had the power to appoint qāḍīs all over the nation, it obviously gave him the chance to draw upon the pool of Ḥanafī jurists, which in turn paved the way for the Ḥanafī law to become the law of the land.

- Three, because of his great moral and scholastic influence he bonded the Muslim state to a written constitution that had been run since the Umayyad times in the absolutist tradition of the kings without a constitutional template. Fortunately, this is still available with us under the name of *Kitāb al-Kharāj*.

5. His lofty character

Before we talk about his constitutional work, it is necessary to dispel a misunderstanding about him. His biographers have spun stories giving others the impression as if he was a sycophant and created legal pretenses for the kings to pursue their selfish interests, which, they imply, was the reason for his close relations with them. This is

---

13 Al-Makki, *Manāqib*, vol. 2, pp. 211-239; Ibn Khallikān, *Wafayāt*, vol. 5, p. 421.

not tenable, for a person can have access to the kings by tampering with the Sharī'ah but he would not have moral influence over them. Now if we look into those incidents involving him with the caliphs, ministers, and army chiefs mentioned in authentic histories, it becomes difficult to believe that a sycophant could have shown such courage and fortitude.

In al-Hādī's reign when he was just a qāḍī in eastern Baghdād he ruled against the caliph.[14]

A similar incident took place in Hārūn al-Rashīd's time when an old Christian sued the caliph disputing his ownership over a garden. Abū Yūsuf not only instituted the hearing before the caliph but also made him to take oath in countering the plaintiff's claim. Still until his death, he regretted his omission of not making the caliph stand beside the plaintiff [in the court].[15]

He declared Hārūn's prime minister 'Ali ibn 'Isā as untrustworthy on reason that he heard him say "anā 'abd al-khalīfah (I am the slave of the caliph)." If he was really a slave, he said, then his testimony was not acceptable and if he has lied to please [the caliph], he is not dependable.[16] The same kind of moral punishment he gave to one of the commanders of Hārūn.[17]

'Abd Allah ibn al-Mubārak says that Abū Yūsuf would go right up to the inner sanctum of the palace (where even the prime minister had to go on foot) and the caliph would himself greet him.[18]

Once Hārūn was asked how he had given such a high place of honour to Abū Yūsuf, he replied: "I tested him in every field of knowledge and found him perfect. Besides, he is trustworthy, a man of strong character. Show me a person equal to his merits."[19]

In 182 A.H., when he died Hārūn al-Radhīd walked with his funeral, led the prayer and buried him in his own family graveyard.

14 Al-Kardari, *Manāqib,* vol. 2, p. 128.
15 Al-Sarakhsi, *Kitāb,* vol. 16, p. 61; al-Makki, *Manāqib*, vol. 2, pp. 243-244.
16 Al-Makki, *Manāqib,* vol. 2, pp. 266-227.
17 Ibid, p. 240.
18 Ibid; al-Qāri, *Dhayl,* p. 526.
19 Al-Makki, *Manāqib,* vol. 2, p. 232.

He described his death as a collective grief for Muslims across the land.[20] His work *Kitāb al-Kharāj* is a monument to his greatness. The tone of its preface does not suggest of a sycophant.

6. *Kitāb al-Kharāj*

In Hārūn al-Rashīd, Qāḍī Abū Yūsuf had found a caliph who carried mixed traits in his person: he was a fierce soldier, a king who lived in opulence and still a God-fearing religious man. Abū al-Faraj al-Isfahānī makes a comprehensive statement on him in a single sentence: "While listening to a speech of exhortation and warning none could match his mellowed temperament – he would weep copiously; and in rage he would be singularly ruthless."[21] It redounds to Abū Yūsuf's credit that without inciting the weak aspects of Hārūn al-Rashīd's person he began influencing the religious man in him by his knowledge and piety until the hour came when the former himself asked him to write a book of constitution for the state so that it could run accordingly. *Kitāb al-Kharāj* was a response to the caliph's desire. As the Imām says in his preface to the book:

> "Amīr al-Mū'minīn has desired that I should write a comprehensive book on the collection of land revenue (kharāj), tithe ('ushr), charities (ṣadaqāt) and social security tax (Jizyah*)* and other related aspects, whose flow and distribution fall under his realm of authority. … He has questioned me on some of the issues involved and wanted me to answer them in details so that he could take action on them."

In his book, he has frequently referred to the questions formulated by Hārūn al-Rashīd suggesting as if it was a questionnaire sent to the ministry of law on some of the important issues relating to constitutional, legal, administrative and international aspects of the then prevailing situation so that it could serve as a permanent code of law for the state. The name of the book is seemingly deceptive as if revenue receipts are its only concern but its scope is wider as

20 Al-Kardari, *Manāqib*, vol. 2, p. 130.
21 Abū al-Faraj al-Asfahānī, *Kitāb al-Aghāni* (Egypt: Matb'ah al-Misriyah Bulāq, 1255 A.H.) vol. 3, p. 178.

it discusses almost every aspect of the state. Leaving aside other matters, we will focus on the subject of the nature of the state and how should it run.

6.1. Reversion to the pious caliphate

The first thing that strikes *Kitāb al-Kharāj*'s reader is Abū Yūsuf's sincerity: he sets himself to the task of deflecting the caliph from following the Romans and Persian practices of statecraft adopted by the Umayyads and 'Abbasids, and prod him to follow the pattern of the pious caliphate.

He never tells him to give up the practices of his predecessors, but at the same time, he never invokes the precedents set by the Umayyads or even the practices of Hārūn's ancestors. In every matter, he either builds his rationale from the Qur'ān and the Sunnah or he brings out the precedents relating to the era of Abu Bakr, 'Umar, 'Uthmān, and 'Ali. Among the later caliphs when he invokes their precedents, it is not from al-Manṣūr or al-Mahdī but from the 'Umayyad caliph 'Umar ibn 'Abdul-'Azīz. What it means is that in framing the 'Abbasid's constitution he ignores the whole era of almost 132 years from 'Ali ibn abī Ṭālib to Hārūn al-Rashīd. Written as a moral exhortation by a truthful jurist in his non-governmental capacity, it would have carried little significance. But when we see that it has been done by a chief justice and minister of law in his official capacity on a task assigned to him by the caliph, its significance increases.

6.2. The governance concept

In the beginning of his book, he presents the governance concept to the caliph as follows:

> "O Amīr al-Mu'minīn! Allah the Exalted, Who alone deserves laudation, has placed a heavy load on you. Its reward is of a great magnitude and so is its punishment: He has reposed the Ummah leadership in you [and because of that] you help build lives of a large number of people. He has made you their

> guardian by installing you as their head and through them He tests you. He has made you responsible to run their affairs. What is based on other than Allah's fear has little stay; Allah overturns it and makes him fall who thinks of it and helps it happens. All custodians will have to account for themselves before their Creator the way a shepherd is answerable to the herd master.... Do not walk the crooked path for your herd will follow it as well. ... Treat everyone in Allah's Sharī'ah as equal whether he is close to you or farther. ... You must not go tomorrow before Allah's tribunal as one involved in excesses, for the Master of the Judgement Day will decide peoples' fate on their deeds and not on their worldly status. ... Be fearful of neglecting your herd, for the Master of the herd will severely take you to task [for negligence]."[22]

Afterwards in the book, he keeps giving incremental reminders to Hārūn al-Rashīd that he was not the master of the Muslim lands but the vicegerent of the Real Master.[23]

If he becomes a just ruler, he will have the best of the ends. And if he turns into an unjust ruler, he will face the deadliest consequences.[24]

At one place, he tells him of 'Umar's saying: "Not a single person, who is a rightful claimant to a position, has the status to command obedience in violation of Allah's will."[25]

6.3. The Democratic Spirit

Abū Yūsuf favoured not only the caliph's answerability to Allah but also to the people. To support his viewpoint, he stacks up citations from the ḥadīth and the companions and shows that the Muslims have the right to question their rulers and the government functionaries,

22 Abu Yūsuf, *al-Kharāj*, pp. 3-5.
23 Ibid, p. 5.
24 Ibid, p. 8.
25 Ibid, p. 117.

and that in the freedom of accountability lies benefit for the ruled as well as the ruler.[26]

Amr bi al-ma'rūf wa nahī 'an al-munkar (ordering good and prohibiting evil) is the Muslims' right as well as their obligation. To close its doors means that the Ummah invites upon itself punishment from the above.[27]

The ruler should have the disposition to listen to truth. There is no harm greater than his irritable temper and lack of patience.[28]

Muslims have the right to question their rulers for the violation of their rights which the Sharī'ah allows them. Above all, they can question their rulers about the use of the revenues placed in trust with them.[29]

6.4. The obligations of the caliph

The caliph's obligations as he extrapolated them are as under:

- To establish the parameters set by Allah.
- To retrieve the rights of the people after due probe and then return them to the people.
- To revive the practices of the pious rulers (discarded by past brutal governments).[30]
- To stop oppression and to alleviate people's complaints after due process of investigation.[31]
- To command people to obey Allah's injunctions and to stop them from committing sin.
- To implement Allah's law on everyone, including one's self and others, without any consideration to whom it affects.[32]
- To obtain revenues with justice and spend them judiciously where called for.[33]

26 Ibid, p. 12.
27 Ibid, pp. 10-11
28 Ibid, p. 12
29 Ibid, p. 117
30 Ibid, p. 5
31 Ibid, p. 6
32 Ibid, p. 13
33 Ibid, p. 108

6.5. Obligations of the Muslim citizen

He also lists people's obligations concerning their rulers:

- Obey your rulers and avoid disobedience to them.
- Do not raise arms against them.
- Do not speak ill of them.
- Bear with their harshness.
- Do not deceive them.
- Do goodness to them with sincerity.
- Strive hard in preventing them from doing bad.
- And help them in their good works.[34]

6.6. Bayt al-Māl

Abū Yūsuf describes treasury (bayt al-māl) as trust that belongs to Allah and the people. He frequently reminds the caliph about what 'Umar said on the subject – for the caliph public treasury is akin to the orphan's property for his guardian. If he is a person of means, he should not, as the Qur'ān says, take a penny from the orphan's property and instead manage his property freely for Allah's sake. And if he is a person of lesser means, he should take rightfully a measured amount considered just by everyone.[35]

Abū Yūsuf also allude to the caliph 'Umar's conduct concerning public exchequer which he spent with extreme caution, more than one treats his own money. In this respect, he cites an incident of 'Umar sending a qāḍī, a wālī, and a revenue official to Kūfah. He allowed them to have one goat a day from bayt al-māl for their families. "Daily procurement of a goat," he cautioned, "from the [same] land for the government functionaries may soon cause its ruination."[36]

Abū Yūsuf also suggests the caliph to restrain state functionaries from using public property for personal use.[37]

---

34 Ibid, pp. 9-12
35 Ibid, pp. 36-117
36 Ibid, p. 36
37 Ibid, p. 186

6.7. Principles of collecting revenues

In imposing taxes, Abū Yūsuf lays down the following principles:

- Impose tax only on the surplus wealth of the people.
- Seek their consent on taxing them.
- Do not burden a person beyond his ability to bear.
- Take tax from the rich and spend it on the poor.[38]
- In assessing taxes and their rates make sure that the administration does not squeeze them to death.
- In obtaining taxes avoid oppressive means.[39]
- The government should not subject citizens to undue taxation, nor permit the landowners or officials to take anything from the people.[40]
- A dhimī (non-Muslim citizen) who embraces Islam must not be subjected to jizyah.[41]

Abū Yūsuf alludes to the practices of the rightly-guided caliphate as a model for emulation. For instance, he reminds Hārūn al-Rashīd of an incident involving caliph 'Ali when he asked his 'āmil (collector) in front of the people to be strict in collecting full kharāj from them. But later, he called for his 'āmil in private and told him not to beat them or make them stand in the sun. Nor should they be subjected, he cautioned, to hardship to the extent that they sell their clothes, materials or animals.[42]

He also cites caliph 'Umar's practice that he would cross-examine his revenue official to assure himself that in levying taxes they have not burdened them beyond their ability to pay. Whenever the state received revenues, he would call for people's representatives to testify that the taxes' collection from a Muslim or a non-Muslim was fair free from excesses against his person and property.[43]

38 Ibid, p. 14
39 Ibid, pp. 16, 37, 109, 114
40 Ibid, pp. 109, 132
41 Ibid, pp. 122, 132
42 Ibid, pp. 15-16
43 Ibid, pp. 37, 114

6.8. The rights of the non-Muslims

For the non-Muslim subjects (al-dhimma) of the Islamic state, Abū Yūsuf repeatedly cites three principles of caliph 'Umar:

- Contractual obligations made with them must be fulfilled.
- Defending the Islamic state is not their responsibility but Muslims'.
- They must not be burdened for Jizyah and other state revenues beyond what they can easily pay.[44]

He also adds that the poor, the blind, the aged, and the monks are exempt from paying jizyah and so are the workers in religious institutions, women, and children. There is no Zakāh on the dhimma properties and cattle. They must not be subjected to physical torture for obtaining jizyah from them.

Should they fail to pay their stipulated amount, they can only be imprisoned. It is Ḥarām (disallowed) to obtain from them more than their owed amount. Among the dhimma, those who are handicapped and unable to support themselves should be taken care of by the state.[45]

Abū Yūsuf cites historical instances to convince Hārūn al-Rashīd that it serves the state well if a policy of accommodation and generosity is adopted towards the dhimma. It was because of such largesse of spirit that in 'Umar's time the Syrian Christian preferred Muslims to their faith-mates Romans.[46]

6.9. The land laws

Concerning land revenues, Abū Yūsuf declares it illegal to install someone on the tiller's land with powers to collect whatever he can in addition to the government's share of the revenues. He describes it as extremely oppressive, which must not be resorted to for it can lead to a country's decimation.[47]

---

44 Ibid, pp. 14, 37, 125
45 Ibid, pp. 122-126
46 Ibid, p. 139
47 Ibid, p. 105

Likewise, he also declares as one of the prohibited acts to dispossess someone of his land and give it to other as state grant. He says: "An imām is not empowered to dispossess a Muslim or a dhimmī of his belongings unless the law sanctions it or gives him a known binding right." To him, snatching people's belongings and giving it to others as a grant amounts to highland robbery.[48]

About state grants, he says these should be given for cultivation or as reward to those who have served the community interests only when such lands are not under cultivation or owned by someone with none to claim their title. Such grants must remain confined to a certain reasonable limit. Further, if lands are not put to agricultural use within three years, the grants should be retracted.[49]

6.10. End to tyranny

Advising Hārūn al-Rashīd he cautions that to appoint cruel and corrupt people in the governmental setup or even use them elsewhere is Ḥarām (disallowed) for him. Whatever excesses they would indulge in, their consequences would have to be shared by him [on the Judgment Day].[50]

Repeatedly he says that the caliph should employ pious and Allah-fearing individuals as functionaries. People selected for administrative jobs must be screened for their ability as well as their morals. Once selected, their work should be monitored so that if they deviate and resort to repressive measures or indulge in wasting public money or corruption, the caliph should know in time and hold them to account.[51]

He also tells Hārūn to attend public grievances himself. Even if he spares a day in a month for easy access to people and solve their problems, the government functionaries would know that their misdeeds could reach the purview of the caliph and thus correct themselves.[52]

48 Ibid, pp. 58, 60, 66
49 Ibid, pp. 59-66
50 Ibid, p. 111
51 Ibid, pp. 106-107, 111, 132, 186
52 Ibid, pp. 106, 107, 111, 132, 186

6.11. Judiciary

Judiciary, Abū Yūsuf says, should be wedded to dispensing justice. He who is entitled to punishment and spared punishment and he who does not deserve punishment and punished are equally wrong in the sight of Islamic law and morality. In doubt, there is no punishment. To err in forgiveness is better than erring in punishment. In dispensing justice, consideration should not be given to one's status in society nor intervention in the process be allowed.[53]

6.12. Safeguarding personal freedom

Abū Yūsuf says that nobody should go to prison on mere allegation. The state must make sure that the accused receives just prosecution with supporting evidence or released. He advises the caliph that those incarcerated should also receive a thorough probe and released for wanting evidence. All governors should have standing instructions not to incarcerate anyone without a fair trial on mere allegation.[54]

He goes even further and suggests that an accused should not be punished. According to the Sharī'ah, a person's back is safe (from the stripes) unless the court calls for lashing him.[55]

6.13. Reforming the prisons

His suggestions for improving prison system include, among others, that an incarcerated person has the right to be fed and clothed by the government treasury. He severely criticizes the Umayyad and the 'Abbasid's way of taking the prisoner's out on the street to beg for food with chains around their hands and feet. Abū Yūsuf asks the caliph to stop this humiliating practice; the government, he stresses, should feed the prisoners and cloth them.

Equally shameful is the practice of burying an uncared for prisoner without a coffin and burial prayer. Their proper burial, he says, should be the state concern.

53 Ibid, pp. 111, 212
54 Ibid, pp. 176-175
55 Ibid, p. 151

Last, he suggests that the prisoners other than killers should not be manacled.[56]

7. The real value of Abū Yusūf's work

This is the summary of those constitutional proposals which Imām Abū Yūsuf as minister for law and head of judiciary submitted to an absolute ruler some twelve hundred years ago. When placed before the fundamental principles of the Islamic state and the practices of the rightfully-guided caliphs as well as the teaching of his teacher Imām Abū Ḥanīfah, his suggested measures pale before them. We do not find in his suggestions even a reflection of the electoral caliphate. There is also no allusion in them to shūrā-run government. Likewise, there is no concept in his suggestions of a ruler's loss of right to rule if he is an oppressor, and that the people have the justification to strive for his removal and bring about a better setup. In short, his suggestions fall behind the original ideal of an Islamic state. But that does not mean that his state concept is defined by his suggestions enunciated in his work *Kitāb al-Kharāj* or that he had no impulse to go beyond his suggestions. In fact, as a realist this was the maximum he could expect from the 'Abbasid. He did not want to go for an all-embracing concept of the Islamic state, which could be perfect as an idea but in the situation then prevailing, it had little chance of implementation. Instead, he wants to have a reform scheme that had the minimum essence of an Islamic state and at the same time realizable.

56 Ibid, p. 151

Bibliography

'Abd al-Qāhir al-Baghdādī, *al-Farqu Bayn al-Firāq* (Egypt: Matb'ah al-Ma'ārif).

'Abd al-Raḥmān ibn Muḥammad ibn Khaldūn: *Kitāb al-'Ibar wa diwān al-Mubtadā' wa al-khabar ... (Tārikh)* also known as *Takmīlah*; Ibn Khaldūn, *al-Muqaddimah* (Egypt: Matb'ah Mustaphā Muhammad).

'Abdullah ibn 'Abdul-Raḥmān, *Sunan al-Dārmi*, "Bab al-futiyā wa mā fih min al-shaddah."

'Abdullah ibn Muslim ibn Qutaybah, *al-Imāmah wa al-Siyāsah*; also, *'Uyūn al-Akhbār* (Egypt: Matb'ah Dār al-Kutab, 1928).

Abdus al-Jahshiyāri, *Tārikh al-Wuzurā'* (Viewer, 1926) also known as *Kitab al-Wuzara' wa al-Kuttab.*

Abu 'Abd Allah Al-Dhahabi, *Manāqib al-Imām abī Ḥanīfah wa Ṣaḥibiyah*, (Egypt: Dār al-Kutab al-Arabi, 1366 A.H.).

Abū 'Abdullah Muḥammad ibn Sa'd, *al-Ṭabaqāt al-Kubrā* (Beirut: Dār Sādr, 1957).

Abū 'Umar Yūsuf ibn 'Abdullah ibn Muḥammad ibn 'Abd al-Barr, *al-Isti'āb, fi M'arifat al-Aṣḥāb*, (Hyderabad: Dā'irah al-Ma'ārif, 1326 A.H.); also *al-Intiqā'* (Cairo: al-Maktabah al-Qudsi, 1370 A.H.).

Abu 'Uthmān 'Amr ibn Baḥr al-Jāhiz, *Kitāb al-Haywān* (Egypt: al-Matbāh al-Taqadam, 1906); also *Thalāth Rasā'il* (Cairo: al-Matb'ah al-Salāfiyah, 1344 A.H.).

Abu A'lā al-Ma'ari, *Risālah al-Ghufrān* (Egypt: Dar al-Ma'ārif, 1950).

Abū al-Faraj al-Asfahāni, *Kitāb al-Aghāni* (Egypt: Matb'ah al-Misriyah Bulāq, 1285 A.H.).

Abū al-Ḥasan 'Ali ibn Ḥusayn ibn 'Ali al-Mas'ūdi, *Murūj al-Dhahab* (Cairo: al-Matb'ah al-Bihiyyah, 1346 A.H.).

Abū al-Qāsim Maḥmūd ibn 'Umar al-Zamakhshari, *al-Kashshāf an Haqā'iq al-Tanzīl* (Cairo: al-Matb'āh al-Bihiyyah, 1343 A.H.).

Abū al-Wahhāb ibn Aḥmad al-Sha'rāni, *Kitāb al-Mizān* (Egypt: al-Matba'h al-Azhariyah, 1925).

Abū Bakr Aḥmad ibn Ḥusayn al-Bayhaqi, *al-Sunan al-Kubrā* (Hyderabad: Dā'irah al-Ma'ārif, 1355 A.H.).

Abu Bakr al-Jassās, *Aḥkām al-Qur'ān*, (Egypt: al-Matb'ah al-Bahiyyah, 1347 A.H.).

Abu Bakr al-Khaṭīb al-Baghdādī, *Tārikh al-Baghdādī*, (Egypt: Matb'ah al-Sa'ādah, 1931).

Abū Bakr Muḥammad ibn Aḥmad al-Sarakhsī, *al-Mabsūt*, (Cairo: Matb'ah al-Sa'ādah, 1324 A.H.); also, *Sharḥ al-Siyar al-Kabīr* (Egypt: Matb'ah Shirkatah Masahamah Misriyah, 1957).

Abū Bakr Muḥammad ibn Zakaria al-Rāzi, *Mafātih al-Ghayb* (Egypt: al-Matb'ah al-Sharafiyah, 1324 A.H.).

Abū Bakr ibn al-'Arabi, *Aḥkām al-Qur'ān* (Cairo, 1958).

Abū Dā'ud al-Tayālisi, *Musnad* (Hyderabad: Dā'irah al-Ma'ārif, 1321 A.H.)

Abū Faḍl Shihāb al-Dīn Aḥmad ibn 'Ali ibn Hajar al-Asqalāni, *al-Isābah fi Tamyīz al-Ṣaḥābah* (Cairo: Matb'ah Mustaphā Muhammad, 1939); *al-Duraru al-Kāminah* (Hyderabad: Dā'irah al-Ma'ārif, 1348

A.H.); also, *Fatḥ al-Bāri Sharḥ Ṣaḥīḥ al-Bukhārī* (Cairo: al-Matb'ah al-Khayriyah, 1325 A.H.).

Abu Ḥasan al-Ash'ari, *Maqalāt al-Islamiīn* (Cairo: Maktab'ah al-Nahdah al-Misiriyah).

Abū Ja'far Muḥammad ibn Jarīr al-Ṭabari, *al-Jāmi' al-Bayān fi Tāwīl al-Qur'ān* (Cairo: al-Matb'ah al Amiryah, 1324 A.H.); also, *Tārikh al-'Umūm wa al-Malūk*, (Cairo: al-Matb'ah al-Astaqāmah, 1935).

Abū Muḥammad 'Ali ibn Aḥmad ibn Sa'īd ibn Hazm, *al-Faṣal fil al-Milal wa al-Hawā' wa al-Nihal* (Egypt: al-Matab'ah al-Adabiyah, 1317 A.H.) vol. 4, p. 204.

Abū Nu'aym al-Isfahāni, *Hilyah al-Auliyā'*, (Egypt: al-Matb'ah al-Sa'ādah, 1355 A.H.).

Abū Qāsim Ḥusayn ibn Muḥammad al-Rāghab al-Asfahāni, *al-Mufrādāt fi gharīb al-Qur'ān* (Cairo: al-Matba'h al-Khayriyah 1322 A.H.); also, *Mahādrāt al-Abdā'* (Egypt: Matb'ah al-Hilāl, 1902).

Abū Yūsuf Ya'qūb ibn Ibrāhīm al-Anṣārī, *Kitāb al-Kharāj* (Egypt: al-Matb'ah al-Salafiyah, 1325 A.H.).

Abu'l 'Abbās Aḥmad ibn Khallikan, *Wafayat al-A'ayān wa Anba Abna al-Zamān* (Cairo: Maktabah al-Nahdah al-Misriyah, 1948).

Abu'l Al'ā Mawdūdi, *Tafhīmāt*, (Lahore: Islamic Publication, 1996).

Abu'l Muntaha Aḥmad ibn Muḥammad al-Maghnisāwi, *Sharḥ al-Fiqh al-Akbar* (Hyderabad: Da'irah al-Ma'ārif, 1321 A.H.).

Aḥmad ibn Muḥammad ibn Ḥanbal, *al-Musnad* (Cairo: Dār al-Ma'ārif, 1949).

Al-Kāmil ibn Humām, *Fatḥ al-Qadir* (Egypt: al-Matb'ah al-Amiryah, 1316 A.H.).

Al-Khatīb al-Tabrizi, *al-Mishkāt al-Masābiḥ.*

Al-Muwaffaq ibn Aḥmad al-Makki, *Manāqib al-Imām al-A'ẓam,* (Hyderabad: Dā'irah al-Ma'ārif, 1321 A.H.) vol. 1, p. 162.

Al-Shahristāni, *Kitāb al-Fasal fi Milal wa al-Hawā wa al-Nihal* (London).

Al-Sharīf al-Murtadā, *Amāli al-Murtadā: ghurar al-fawā'id wa durar al-qalā'id* (Egypt: al-Matb'ah al-Sa'ādah, 1907).

Al-Yāfi'i, *Mirāt al-Jinān wa 'Ibrat al-Yaqzān fi Ma'rifāt mā Yu'tabar min Hawādith al-Zamān* (Hyderabd: Dā'irah al-Ma'ārif, 1337 A.H.).

Anwar Shah Kashmiri, *Fayḍ al-Bārī* (Dābīl: Majlis 'Ilmi, 1938).

Burhān al-Dīn Abū al-Ḥasan 'Ali ibn Abū Bakr al-Marghināni, *al-Hidāyah* "Kitab Adab al-Qāḍī."

Fatāwā ibn Taymiyah (Egypt: Matb'ah Kurdistān al-'Almiyah 1322 A.H.).

'Ibn al-Qayyim al-Jauzī, *Sīrah 'Umar ibn al-Khaṭṭāb,*

'Imād al-Dīn Ismā'il ibn 'Umar ibn Kathīr, *Tafsīr al-Qur'ān al-'Aẓīm* (Egypt: Matb'ah Mustaphā Muhammad, 1937).

'Izz al-Dīn Abu al-Ḥassan 'Ali ibn Muḥammad al-Jazāri ibn al-Athīr, *al-Kāmil fi al-Tārikh* (Cairo: Idārah al-Taba'tah al-Muniriyah, 1356 A.H.); also *Usad al-Ghābah.*

Ibn 'Abī Rabbih, *al-'Iqd al-Farid* (Cairo: Lajanata al-Tālif wa al-Tarjumah, 1940).

Ibn abi al-'Izz al-Ḥanafī, *Sharḥ al-Tahāwiya* (Egypt: Dār al-Ma'ārif, 1373 A.H.).

Ibn abi al-ḤadḤd, *Sharḥ Nahj al-Balāghah* (Cairo: Dār al-Kutb al-Arabiyah, 1329 A.H.).=

Ibn al-Bazzāz al-Kardari, *Manāqib al-Imām al-A'ẓam* (Hyderabad: Dāirah al-Ma'ārif, 1321 A.H.).

Ibn al-Nadīm, *al-Fihrist* (Egypt: al-Matb'ah al-Rahmāniyah, 1348 A.H.).

Ibn Hajar al-Haytami in *al-Sawā'q al-Muhariqah.*

Imām Ibn Taymiyah, *Yazīd ibn Mu'āwiyah* (Karachi: Ibn Taymiyah Academy).

Jalāl al-Dīn al-Suyūti, *Ḥusan al-Mahādirah* (Cairo: al-Matb'ah al-Sharafiyah, 1327 A.H.); also, *Tārīkh al-Khulafā'*, (Lahore: Government Press, 1870 A.H.) p. 255.

Muḥammad 'Abdul-Malik ibn Hishām, *al-Sīrah al-Nabawiyyah* (Cairo: Matb'ah Mustaphā al-Bābi, 1936).

Muḥammad ibn Ismā'il al-Bukhārī, *al-Jām'i al-Ṣaḥīḥ*, "Kitāb al-Ḥudūd,"

Muḥammad ibn Shākir al-Kutabi, *Fawat al-Wafayāt* (Cairo: Matba'h al-Sa'ādah).

Muḥammad ibn 'Abd al-Rasūl al-Barjanji, *al-Ashrāt fi Athrāt al-Sā'ah.*

Mullā 'Ali al-Qāri, *Dhayl al-Juwāhir al-Madiy'a,* (Hyderabad: Dā'irah al-Ma'ārif, 1322 A.H.); also, *Sharḥ al-Fiqh al-Akbar*, (Delhi: Tab'ah Mujtaba'i).

Mullā Ḥusayn, *al-Jauharah al-Munifah fi Sharḥ Waṣiyah al-Imām abī Ḥanīfah* (Hyderabad: Dā'irah al-Ma'ārif, 1321 A.H.).

Sheikh 'Ali al-Muttaqī, *Kunz al-Ummāl* (Hyderabad: Da'irah al-Ma'ārif, 1955).

Taqi al-Dīn Aḥmad ibn 'Ali ibn 'Abd al-Qādir ibn Muḥammad al-Maqrizi, *Kitāb al-Salūk* (Egypt: Dār al-Kutub al-Misriyah, 1934).

Taqi al-Dīn Aḥmad ibn Taymiyah, *Minhaj al-Sunnah al-Nabawiyyah* (Egypt: Matb'ah Amiriyah, 1322 A.H.).

Tāsh Kubrizādah, *Miftāh al-Sa'ādah wa Mishbah al-*Siyādah (Hyderabad: Dā'irah al-Ma'ārif, 1329 A.H.).

Yāqūt al-Hamāwi, *Mu'jam al-Buldān,* (Beruit: Dār Sādir, 1987).

Index

N

O

P

V

W

Y

Z